Original Brand Manufacturing Business Model

Young Won Park · Geon-Cheol Shin ·
Kyung-Soo Lee

Original Brand Manufacturing Business Model

Springer

Young Won Park
The Graduate School of Humanities
and Social Sciences
Saitama University
Shinjuku-ku, Tokyo, Japan

Kyung-Soo Lee
COSMAX
Seongnam-si, Korea (Republic of)

Geon-Cheol Shin
aSSIST University
Seoul, Korea (Republic of)

Kyung Hee University
Seoul, Korea (Republic of)

ISBN 978-981-95-0252-3 ISBN 978-981-95-0253-0 (eBook)
https://doi.org/10.1007/978-981-95-0253-0

This Springer imprint is published by the registered company Springer Nature Singapore Pte Ltd.
The registered company address is: 152 Beach Road, #21-01/04 Gateway East, Singapore 189721, Singapore

Executive Summary

This book explores the transformation of global manufacturing through the lens of Original Brand Manufacturing (OBM), with a focus on how OBM enablers—firms that provide the platforms and infrastructure necessary for others to launch and scale their own brands—are reshaping the competitive landscape in the digital economy. As the traditional OEM/ODM models that characterized industrial growth in many Asian economies face diminishing returns, OBM has emerged as a pathway for firms to gain autonomy, brand equity, and long-term value creation. The OBM enabler plays a pivotal role in this shift, acting as both infrastructure and catalyst. By combining R&D, digitalization, regulatory knowledge, and sustainability frameworks, OBM enablers such as COSMAX empower a new generation of brand creators across industries and geographies.

Chapter 1 lays the foundation by framing OBM as a strategic progression from OEM and ODM. Unlike OEMs that manufacture to client specifications or ODMs that include product design, OBM firms own the brand, control product development, and engage directly with consumers. This ownership allows OBM firms to capture greater value while managing reputation, innovation, and supply chain standards. The chapter discusses the industrial upgrading pathways in East Asia, particularly in Korea, Taiwan, and Vietnam, where firms have used OEM/ODM experience as a steppingstone toward OBM capabilities. Importantly, it introduces COSMAX as a global case that embodies this transition—not merely as a firm that transformed itself, but as a platform enabling others to do so.

In Chapter 2, the role of digital transformation is explored in depth. The OBM model in the digital era demands a new set of competencies, including data-driven marketing, consumer personalization, and omnichannel engagement. The rise of digital-native indie brands and direct-to-consumer platforms has accelerated demand for flexible, fast-moving product development models. OBM enablers like COSMAX have responded by embedding AI, IoT, and cloud-based tools into their operations—providing clients with predictive analytics, formulation simulations, and market-testing platforms. These digital capabilities allow even small brands to launch products with speed and precision, supported by the infrastructure of an enabler that operates globally. COSMAX's integration of social listening, influencer analytics, and digital feedback loops makes it not only a manufacturer but a strategic partner in digital branding.

Chapter 3 addresses the importance of purpose-driven leadership in OBM. In contrast to OEMs, where firms are often invisible to end consumers, OBM firms must articulate a clear identity and social value proposition. This chapter examines how purpose management enables firms to align internal culture with external expectations, especially in sustainability and inclusivity. COSMAX's philosophy—anchored by founder Lee Kyung-soo's belief in service-driven leadership—illustrates how corporate purpose can serve as a compass for ESG commitments, long-term partnerships, and employee engagement. The firm's internal culture of proactive suggestion-making and its governance structures show that being an OBM enabler involves more than operational excellence—it requires visionary leadership and shared values.

Chapter 4 turns to R&D, highlighting how it functions not only as a technical capability but also as the core platform of OBM enablement. The COSMAX case illustrates how an enabler can provide R&D-as-a-service, supporting thousands of OBM clients with modular formulation systems, trend forecasting, regulatory compliance, and rapid prototyping. Its distributed research centers in Korea, the United States, and China allow for local adaptation while maintaining global consistency. COSMAX has pioneered innovations such as jelly-type cosmetics and microbe-based emulsions, offering breakthrough products to both multinational firms and startup brands. Through a design-led and sustainability-focused R&D approach, it transforms consumer insights into scalable product platforms. In this sense, COSMAX's R&D operation does not just serve clients—it amplifies their brand value and accelerates their market entry.

Chapter 5 focuses on marketing, branding, and consumer engagement, which are essential to OBM success. In a saturated marketplace, OBM firms must tell compelling brand stories that resonate with target audiences. Unlike OEMs, OBM firms cannot rely on cost or efficiency alone—they must differentiate through emotional connection, aesthetic appeal, and lifestyle alignment. OBM enablers help clients articulate their brand identity through collaborative development, packaging design, and digital storytelling tools. COSMAX supports this by integrating consumer trend data, ESG narratives, and product storytelling into its client services. Its deep understanding of regional market preferences—whether in K-beauty, J-beauty, or halal-certified Southeast Asian markets—allows brands to localize their strategies while maintaining global relevance.

In Chapter 6, the book examines how OBM production strategies must evolve to meet demands for speed, flexibility, and environmental accountability. OBM enablers play a central role in this transformation by offering smart manufacturing, traceability systems, and lean customization models. COSMAX's smart factories, real-time quality monitoring, and closed-loop logistics enable brands to scale without compromising compliance or sustainability. In addition, the ability to offer low-MOQ (minimum order quantity) production allows smaller OBM entrants to test products and adapt quickly—crucial in fast-moving consumer sectors. As production becomes more modular and responsive, OBM enablers become both innovation hubs and risk buffers for client brands.

Chapter 7 explores the evolving dynamics of supplier relationships in the OBM context. Because OBM firms are ultimately responsible for the full value chain—including ethical sourcing, labor practices, and environmental impact—they must elevate sustainability as a sourcing criterion. OBM enablers help firms do this by providing ESG-vetted supply chains, compliance monitoring, and supplier training. COSMAX, for instance, employs supplier scorecards, sustainability audits, and ESG co-education programs, thereby lifting the entire value network. In doing so, OBM enablers institutionalize responsible sourcing and offer assurance to consumers and regulators alike. This chapter shows that sustainability is not only a moral imperative but also a strategic necessity in OBM ecosystems.

Chapter 8 positions OBM firms at the forefront of the circular economy. As global regulations tighten and consumers demand transparency, OBM firms must design for reuse, recyclability, and minimal impact. The chapter highlights how circular innovation begins at the design stage, where 80% of environmental impact is determined. COSMAX's efforts in developing biodegradable packaging, refillable containers, and circular business models such as product-as-a-service illustrate how an enabler can embed circularity into client brands. Through its CCB (COSMAX Conscious Beauty) framework and plastic elimination roadmap, it enables OBM firms to comply with extended producer responsibility (EPR) rules and build sustainable business models that resonate with eco-conscious consumers. The integration of AI, digital twins, and life-cycle assessment tools into the product development process further shows how OBM enablers are leading the digital-circular convergence.

Finally, Chapter 9 brings together the future directions of OBM evolution. It emphasizes that the success of OBM transformation depends not only on firm-level capabilities but also on supportive ecosystems—policy, education, finance, and digital infrastructure. Governments can accelerate OBM growth through tax incentives for circular R&D, sustainability-linked loans, and alignment with global ESG standards. OBM enablers are central to this future, acting as bridges between global trends and local implementation. COSMAX's case exemplifies how an OBM enabler can shape global supply chains, co-develop eco-standards, and institutionalize sustainability at scale. The chapter also introduces the concept of OBM ecosystems, in which enablers, suppliers, retailers, universities, and regulators collaborate to co-create value.

Across all nine chapters, a consistent theme emerges: the OBM enabler is not merely a manufacturer, but a platform architect, innovation accelerator, and strategic partner. It orchestrates resources, absorbs market signals, digitizes operations, and redefines value beyond profit—to include environmental stewardship, social responsibility, and consumer trust. The book argues that as industries become more interconnected, regulations more demanding, and consumers more discerning, the role of OBM enablers will become ever more central. Firms like COSMAX offer a blueprint for the next generation of manufacturing—one that is brand-driven, purpose-led, digitally powered, and sustainability-oriented.

In conclusion, this book offers a theoretical and practical framework for understanding the rise of OBM in the digital era, with a strong emphasis on the enabling infrastructure that makes it possible. It combines academic insight with real-world examples to demonstrate how OBM enablers can empower firms to build not just brands, but ecosystems—and not just products, but futures. For researchers, policymakers, and business leaders, the lessons presented here point toward a new paradigm of industrial innovation—where brand ownership, platform collaboration, and circular value creation define the path forward. This work was supported by JSPS Fostering Joint International Research B Grant Number 22KK0019 and JSPS KAKENHI (Grant-in-Aid for Scientific Research (C) Grant Number 23K01578).

June 2025

Young Won Park
Geon-Cheol Shin
Kyung-Soo Lee

Competing Interests The authors have no competing interests to declare that are relevant to the content of this manuscript.

Contents

About the Authors

Dr. Young Won Park is a Professor of the Faculty of Economics, Graduate School of Humanities and Social Sciences at Saitama University and an Endowed Chair Professor of the Management Education and Research Center at the University of Tokyo, Japan. He holds a Ph.D. degree in the Department of Advanced Social and International Studies from the University of Tokyo, Japan. His articles have been published in journals including *Management Decision, International Journal of Production Economics, International Journal of Technology Management, International Journal of Information Management, Business Horizons, Journal of Business Research, Journal of Purchasing and Supply Management, Benchmarking: An International Journal, International Journal of Services and Operations Management, International Journal of Logistics Systems and Management, International Journal of Business Excellence, International Journal of Procurement Management, Akamon Management Review, Japan Academy of International Business Studies, Japanese Society for Science and Technology Studies, and the Japan Society of Information and Communication Research.* He has received research awards including a Certificate for Highly Cited Research in Business Horizons, Dissertation Paper Awards from the Japan Association for Social Informatics (JASI), Best Paper Awards from The Japan Society of Information and Communication Research (JSICR), Research Awards of the Social Science Field from The Telecommunications Advancement Foundation (TAF) and Research Students Awards of the Social Science Field from The Telecommunications Advancement Foundation (TAF). His research interests are in technology management, global strategy and IT strategy, and global supply chain management.

Dr. Geon-Cheol Shin (Ph.D., Georgia State University, 1992) is the Vice President for Global Engagement at aSSIST University in Seoul, Korea. He currently serves as the Country Director for Korea at the Academy of International Business (AIB) and was the host of the 66th Annual AIB Conference in Seoul. Professor Shin has also held presidencies at the Korean Academy of International Business and the Association of APEC Studies. Previously, he was a Professor at the School of Management and Director of the Center for Global Innovation & Entrepreneurship at Kyung Hee University, also located in Seoul. Dr. Shin has published more than 100 scholarly articles in leading journals, including Korean Management Review, Korean Journal of International Business, Journal of Korea Trade, Journal of Business Research, Industrial Marketing Management, Journal of Product Innovation Management, International Business Review, International Marketing Review, Asia Pacific Business Review, Global Economic Review, European Journal of Purchasing and Supply Management, and Service Business: An International Journal. He is also the author of The Korean Wave in a Post-Pandemic World, published by Springer in 2023.

Chairman Kyung-Soo Lee is the founder and leader who has developed Cosmax into the world's No. 1 cosmetics ODM company. Chairman Lee graduated from Seoul National University College of Pharmacy in 1970. After graduation, he worked at leading pharmaceutical companies in Korea including Dong-A Pharmaceutical and Daewoong Pharmaceutical. In 1992 he founded Cosmax. Chairman Lee has received numerous awards and accolades, including the Presidential Commendation on Trade Day 2010, the Silver Tower Industrial Medal in 2015, the "200 Million Dollar Export Tower" on Trade Day 2024. He completed the AMP (Advanced Management Program) at Seoul National University Graduate School of Business in 1990 and the course of Wharton-KMA CEO Institute in 2008. He has been listed among the top 100 CEOs of South Korea for several times, and he continues to demonstrate the power of Korean cosmetics in the global market with unparalleled technology and quality.

Chapter 1
The Evolution of OEM, ODM, and OBM Business Models

1 Introduction: Rethinking Value Creation in the Age of OBM

The transformation from Original Equipment Manufacturing (OEM) to Original Brand Manufacturing (OBM) represents a pivotal shift in how firms create and capture value in global markets. This book opens by exploring this evolution through the lens of firm behavior, innovation strategies, and competitive dynamics, with a particular focus on the cosmetics industry. Rather than following a linear path, the transition to OBM is often characterized by hybrid experimentation, resource reconfiguration, and digital adaptation, as evidenced by both empirical research and real-world case studies.

Lee et al. (2015) revealed that Korean SMEs navigating the OEM–OBM shift did not simply replicate existing business models but crafted distinct strategies informed by trial-and-error learning, tacit knowledge, and responses to external pressures—including litigation and industry competition. This insight underscores one of the book's core themes: OBM transformation is not a standardized process but a strategic reorientation that demands innovation, leadership, and resilience.

This complexity is echoed in a study of emerging economy firms, which emphasized the necessity of "path-breaking" capabilities—often cultivated through external partnerships and global subsidiaries—to facilitate meaningful OBM transitions (Kittilaksanawong, 2015). These capabilities lie at the heart of this book, which focuses on organizational learning, R&D, branding, and supply chain innovation.

In addition, Guo et al. (2020) explored how OBM sourcing decisions in the apparel sector hinge on the interplay between investment cost and technological spillover. Their findings suggest that OBM success is context-sensitive and strategically nuanced. Similarly, Ng et al. (2014) demonstrated that while total quality management and branding are often viewed as separate domains, their interaction is essential for sustaining OBM competitiveness. Their conclusion—that operational

Y. W. Park et al., *Original Brand Manufacturing Business Model*,
https://doi.org/10.1007/978-981-95-0253-0_1

and marketing investments must be integrated—offers a central premise for this book's third section on sustainable OBM practices and circular value creation.

Economic shocks such as the 2008 global financial crisis have also played a catalytic role in motivating firms to reassess their reliance on OEM strategies. Tang (2011) showed how Chinese textile OEMs, once locked into low-margin manufacturing, began pivoting toward OBM in response to financial instability, talent constraints, and global supply chain pressures. The implication is clear: macroeconomic volatility often accelerates strategic shifts in business models.

Leadership and entrepreneurship further shape OBM outcomes. Yan et al. (2011) found that Taiwanese firms with visionary leaders—capable of balancing structural control with market-oriented agility—were more likely to evolve toward OBM. This reflects a key argument made throughout the book: the OBM transformation is as much about internal capability development and leadership orientation as it is about external market factors.

Recent studies, such as Dinh et al. (2024), show how social responsibility and compliance have become central to strategic supplier selection in Vietnamese textile and garment firms transitioning toward OBM. This mirrors global trends in cosmetics, where OBM firms are increasingly evaluated on their CSR credentials, eco-certifications, and ethical sourcing—topics expanded upon in later chapters addressing circular economy integration.

The cosmetics industry serves as this book's primary empirical context due to its unique convergence of rapid product cycles, brand loyalty, sensory engagement, and regulatory complexity. Once dominated by contract manufacturers, the industry has experienced a surge in OBM initiatives. Firms like COSMAX have redefined their role within the global value chain by leveraging digital innovation, consumer analytics, and proprietary branding (Park et al., 2023).

Chu (2009) argued that cosmetics OBMs must develop competencies that span both upstream and downstream value creation—from formulation and packaging to storytelling and regional adaptation.

Multiple scholars support this strategic imperative. Liang et al. (2013), Sun and Zhao (2010), and Lin and Chen (2007) have shown that successful OBM firms in the personal care sector consistently prioritize R&D, marketing innovation, and agile supply chain management. Lin and Wong (2016) further note that the proliferation of digital technologies—especially social media, e-commerce, and data analytics—has significantly reduced entry barriers and allowed OBMs to scale faster and connect with niche consumer segments.

This transformation is not uniform across regions. Korean firms such as COSMAX and AmorePacific have benefited from various state support, cultural diplomacy (e.g., K-beauty), and trend responsiveness. Meanwhile, Taiwanese firms often adopt hybrid strategies, balancing ODM operations with selective OBM branding efforts to hedge risks and preserve B2B relationships (Chu, 2009; Lin & Chen, 2007).

In sum, the OEM–OBM transition is a multifaceted journey shaped by industry characteristics, market signals, technological tools, and institutional environments. The cosmetics industry exemplifies how firms can move beyond cost leadership to embrace brand ownership, innovation, and sustainability. This book sets out to unpack the dynamics, strategies, and frameworks that enable this transformation, offering a comprehensive roadmap for firms aiming to thrive in the digital, consumer-centric economy of the future.

2 Theoretical Foundations and Historical Context

The shift from OEM to OBM can be contextualized within broader theories of industrial upgrading, value chain integration, and innovation management. The OEM–ODM–OBM transformation has been widely studied as a strategic pathway for latecomer firms, particularly in Asia, to escape the low-value-added trap and move up the global value chain (GVC).

Gereffi (1999) introduced the global value chain framework, emphasizing how developing-country firms often begin as OEMs and progressively move toward OBM by building capabilities in design, branding, and marketing. This theoretical lens explains why the OBM transformation is not merely a shift in business model, but a reconfiguration of a firm's position in the GVC hierarchy. OBMs control more profitable and strategic segments of the value chain, such as product development, brand positioning, and consumer engagement.

Innovation theory also plays a critical role in understanding the OBM shift. Schumpeterian perspectives on innovation emphasize the role of dynamic capabilities—namely, sensing, seizing, and reconfiguring resources to capture new opportunities (Teece, 2007). OBM firms are expected to possess a strong orientation toward product innovation, rapid market response, and continual brand adaptation.

In the cosmetics industry, the OBM model is particularly salient due to the sector's reliance on brand identity, design, and consumer loyalty. While OEMs and ODMs provide manufacturing and design services respectively, OBMs in cosmetics own and manage the entire value proposition, from product ideation to consumer marketing. This strategic control enables them to build brand equity, differentiate offerings, and respond flexibly to market trends.

Historically, cosmetics manufacturing has been dominated by OEMs that served global brands. However, changes in market dynamics, technological tools, and consumer expectations have opened the door for OBMs. For instance, digital platforms have democratized brand creation and allowed smaller firms to reach global audiences without traditional retail intermediaries.

The rise of OBMs in cosmetics can be traced to three interrelated trends.

- Digital Transformation: Social media, e-commerce, and digital marketing have revolutionized consumer engagement. OBMs in cosmetics leverage platforms like Instagram, TikTok, and YouTube to build brand identity, co-create with influencers, and drive viral marketing campaigns. These tools reduce customer acquisition costs and increase the visibility of niche brands.
- Consumer-Centric Innovation: Modern consumers seek personalized, sustainable, and ethically produced products. OBMs differentiate themselves by embedding

CSR, natural ingredients, cruelty-free testing, and eco-friendly packaging into their brand narrative. This focus on authenticity and transparency aligns with the preferences of Gen Z and millennial shoppers.
- Agile Product Development: The cosmetics industry operates on short product life cycles and rapid trend changes. OBMs benefit from streamlined decision-making and in-house innovation teams that can quickly prototype, test, and launch new products. By controlling branding and distribution, OBMs can pivot faster than traditional OEMs reliant on brand clients.

Scholars such as Park et al. (2023) highlight the strategic transition of COSMAX, a Korean cosmetics firm, from a global ODM to a leading OBM. COSMAX utilized its R&D infrastructure and market insights to create proprietary brands that align with global beauty trends. Their transition was facilitated by organizational restructuring, digital tool adoption, and collaboration with e-commerce platforms.

Comparative studies further illuminate how OBM strategies vary across countries. Korean OBMs benefit from strong government support and a robust domestic market. Policies promoting the "K-Beauty" brand have fueled international demand, creating fertile ground for OBM growth. In contrast, Taiwanese OBMs often pursue hybrid strategies, maintaining ODM contracts while gradually developing their own brands.

In Vietnam, the transition toward OBM is shaped by foreign investment, knowledge transfer, and supply chain upgrading. Studies by Le et al. (2019) and Dinh et al. (2024) show that Vietnamese firms recognize OBM as a pathway to higher value capture but face barriers such as weak brand recognition and limited R&D capabilities. To overcome these, Vietnamese cosmetics OBMs are increasingly investing in branding, CSR, and digital tools.

Another critical theoretical perspective comes from the lens of knowledge accumulation and learning. Liu and Zhang (2014) describe alliance learning as a key driver of OBM transformation. Firms accumulate capabilities through interfirm collaborations, cross-border partnerships, and learning-by-doing. In cosmetics, this includes joint ventures with dermatologists, packaging firms, and influencers.

Furthermore, OBM strategies require strong internal alignment and cultural shifts. Lin and Chen (2007) argue that administrative innovation—such as decentralized decision-making, cross-functional teams, and performance-based incentives—is essential for nurturing OBM mindsets. In cosmetics firms, this manifests as agile R&D teams, customer experience units, and brand storytelling departments.

From a macroeconomic perspective, OBM development is closely tied to industrial policy. Countries like South Korea and China have integrated OBM promotion into their economic strategies. In contrast, countries without coordinated policy support may find OBM scaling more difficult. For example, Taiwan's lack of a "national champion" strategy has led to a slower OBM evolution despite its strong OEM and ODM base (Chu, 2009).

In conclusion, the theoretical foundations and historical context of the OEM to OBM transition, particularly in the cosmetics industry, illustrate a multi-dimensional process involving strategic, organizational, technological, and institutional change. OBMs represent not just a business model, but a capability configuration that allows firms to own the customer relationship, build lasting brand value, and capture a larger share of value within global production networks.

The cosmetics industry, with its emphasis on aesthetics, identity, and consumer engagement, provides a rich setting to explore these dynamics. As firms navigate this transformation, they draw upon a blend of dynamic capabilities, digital infrastructure, and policy support to evolve from behind-the-scenes manufacturers to brand-owning market leaders. The following sections will examine these themes in greater detail through empirical studies, case analyses, and comparative insights across regions.

3 Strategic Perspectives on OEM–OBM Transformation

The strategic transformation from Original Equipment Manufacturing (OEM) to Original Brand Manufacturing (OBM) is a complex, multifaceted evolution that involves deliberate positioning, investment in intangible assets, and a redefinition of competitive advantage. This transformation is especially critical in the cosmetics industry, where OBM has emerged as a vital path to sustainable growth, brand equity, and international market penetration. Figure 1 illustrates the value chain from product planning to the end customer, showing how each manufacturing model—OEM (Original Equipment Manufacturing), ODM (Original Design Manufacturing), and OBM (Original Brand Manufacturing)—engages with different stages. OEM involves only the production stage, where the manufacturer makes products based on client specifications without engaging in planning, research, or branding. ODM includes both research and production. The manufacturer develops the product design and formulation based on client needs. OBM covers the full value chain from planning and research to marketing and customer interface under the customer's brands.

At the heart of the OEM–OBM transformation lies the need for greater value capture. OEM firms traditionally rely on high-volume, low-margin production services for third-party brands. However, this model renders them vulnerable to

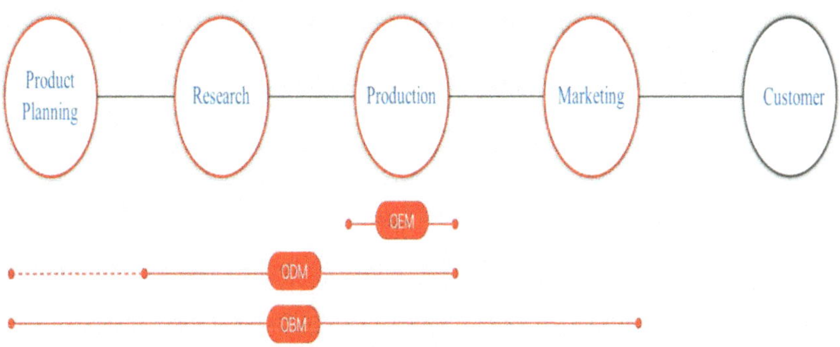

Fig. 1 Different stages of OEM–ODM–OBM

external shocks, pricing pressures, and client dependency. As such, the strategic imperative for OEMs is to transition toward OBM, where they can control the brand narrative, pricing, and customer relationships.

The cosmetics industry is particularly conducive to OBM strategies due to its branding-centric structure, rapid trend cycles, and direct consumer engagement. OBMs command premium pricing through differentiated brand identities. In cosmetics, where aesthetic appeal and emotional resonance dominate purchasing decisions, owning the brand allows firms to craft a compelling story, attract loyal customers, and build a consistent brand image across channels. Direct interaction with consumers provides OBMs with critical feedback loops for innovation, quality assurance, and personalization. This is increasingly relevant in cosmetics, where consumer preferences shift rapidly and demand for clean, sustainable, and customizable products is growing. OBMs are not bound by external contracts and can pivot quickly in response to trends, crises, or emerging markets. This agility is crucial in cosmetics, where viral products and influencer marketing can create demand spikes almost overnight.

Strategic transformation from OEM to OBM can be understood through several theoretical and applied frameworks. The Dynamic Capabilities Framework emphasizes the firm's ability to sense, seize, and reconfigure internal and external competencies. In cosmetics, OBMs must sense emerging beauty trends such as K-beauty or clean beauty, seize them via R&D and design, and reconfigure operations to launch timely offerings. Firms must shift from product or production orientation to brand orientation, where brand values guide decision-making across departments—from product development to customer service. OBMs must balance exploitation of current capabilities like OEM production knowledge with exploration of new markets, technologies, and customer needs. This dual capability supports long-term innovation without sacrificing short-term efficiency.

COSMAX, a South Korean cosmetics manufacturer, provides a compelling case of successful OBM enabler. Initially an ODM powerhouse producing for global giants, COSMAX recognized the limitations of its position in the value chain. It has increasingly evolved into a hybrid OBM enabler and platform-driven manufacturer, leveraging its R&D capabilities, industry insights, and government support. COSMAX's strategy involved investing in skin science and bioengineering to develop proprietary formulations that differentiated its OBM products from contract-manufactured ones. It utilized big data and AI to identify consumer trends and tailor marketing efforts, implementing real-time social listening tools to refine product concepts and launch cycles. COSMAX also targeted domestic and international markets simultaneously, utilizing Korea's global beauty appeal to enter markets such as China, Southeast Asia, and the United States, adapting its offerings to local tastes. The company's OBM success was not linear. However, through cross-functional alignment and top-down strategic commitment, COSMAX has emerged as a global OBM leader.

The path to OBM varies by country, shaped by institutional context, resource availability, and consumer culture. Korean firms benefit from strong state support, cultural exports like K-pop and K-drama, and a highly developed cosmetics ecosystem. This synergy allows for accelerated OBM scaling, especially for digitally native brands.

Taiwanese OBMs often follow a hybrid strategy, retaining ODM contracts for cash flow while gradually launching niche brands. Strategic alliances with foreign firms and emphasis on quality provide differentiation. OBM strategies in Vietnam are in the early stages. Firms focus on integrating local ingredients, promoting cultural identity, and leveraging e-commerce. However, strategic gaps exist in marketing expertise and brand positioning.

Despite its appeal, transitioning to OBM presents several strategic challenges. Developing brand equity requires long-term investment in marketing, design, and customer experience. Many OEMs underestimate the required resources. Existing relationships with global brand clients may limit distribution options or create conflict. Managing channel overlap without alienating partners is critical. OBM transformation requires new skills like digital marketing and retail management and mindsets. Resistance to change can hinder implementation. Unlike OEMs with guaranteed contracts, OBMs bear full market risk. Product failures, reputational damage, or competitive missteps directly affect the firm.

To navigate the transition effectively, OEM firms should consider phased transition strategies, beginning with co-branding or limited edition OBM launches to test the market while maintaining OEM revenues. They should engage directly with consumers through digital platforms, feedback mechanisms, and influencer collaborations to co-create products. It is essential to define a clear brand identity, positioning, and value proposition early. This includes selecting brand names, visual identity, and tone of voice aligned with target segments. Firms must also invest in branding, storytelling, and retail management capabilities. Upskilling internal teams or hiring external talent can bridge strategic gaps. Strategic partnerships with design studios, marketing agencies, and distribution platforms can accelerate brand visibility and reach.

Strategic transformation from OEM to OBM in the cosmetics industry is not a linear or risk-free process. It requires a rethinking of the firm's core value proposition, a commitment to building intangible assets, and the agility to respond to fast-changing consumer preferences. However, the rewards—greater value capture, brand autonomy, and long-term competitiveness—make this journey both essential and rewarding. By examining the strategies employed by firms like COSMAX and others, it becomes evident that OBM is not just about selling branded products—it is about owning the entire consumer experience, from ideation to after-sales service. COSMAX's approach shows that OBM does not need to mean owning a brand. It can mean owning the capability to create, enable, and scale brands. In this sense, COSMAX represents a new archetype: the OBM enabler as ecosystem architect. As competition intensifies and consumers demand authenticity, OEM firms that strategically invest in OBM capabilities will be best positioned to thrive in the global beauty market.

4 Innovation, Design, and Knowledge Integration

The shift from Original Equipment Manufacturing (OEM) to Original Brand Manufacturing (OBM) in the cosmetics industry is deeply rooted in innovation, design, and the strategic integration of knowledge across global value chains. Drawing on the literature from recent research, this section unpacks how firms harness technological, organizational, and market knowledge to facilitate this transformation, focusing particularly on latecomer economies in Asia such as South Korea, Taiwan, Vietnam, and China.

Innovation capability is central to the OBM transition. Firms must not only produce efficiently but also engage in product innovation, brand differentiation, and knowledge accumulation. Fan (2006) emphasizes that Chinese telecom firms like Huawei prioritized building in-house R&D capacity to enhance competitiveness, a strategy equally pertinent to the cosmetics industry. Likewise, Lin and Chen (2007) find that Taiwanese SMEs rely heavily on innovation—both technological and administrative—to drive performance, a necessity for firms aiming to escape the OEM trap.

Cosmetics firms transitioning to OBM are often latecomers in global production networks. Hobday (1998, 2001) shows how Acer and Samsung strategically acquired foreign technology and moved backward along the value chain to innovate and create their own brands. Similar patterns are observed in the cosmetics sector. Park et al. (2023) explore COSMAX's evolution through the integration of digital technologies such as AI and big data, illustrating how innovation is central to managing ODM/OBM models in a post-pandemic era.

Szeto (2000) argues that innovation capacity stems from inter-organizational networks. In cosmetics, these networks include ingredient suppliers, R&D labs, marketing agencies, and e-commerce platforms. Liu and Zhang (2014) highlight the role of alliance learning in knowledge transfer and capability formation, particularly in Taiwanese technological firms. This framework can be applied to cosmetic firms that often rely on partnerships to acquire new capabilities while maintaining flexibility in uncertain environments (Yi et al., 2011).

The ability to explore and exploit knowledge—what Kuo et al. (2018) term "innovation ambidexterity"—is vital for OBM firms. In their study of Acer, they show how dual strategies helped balance risk and speed, enabling successful brand creation. Chiu et al. (2016) further argue that dynamic capabilities such as sensing, seizing, and reconfiguring resources are essential for radical innovation performance. For cosmetic firms, this means constantly scanning beauty trends (e.g., clean beauty, K-beauty), investing in R&D, and rapidly adapting product portfolios.

Design, as both a functional and symbolic activity, plays a crucial role in OBM strategies. Tam et al. (2005) propose that Hong Kong's aspiration to become Asia's fashion hub hinges on OBM and the design of branded goods. Bolton (2009) reinforces this in the context of Chinese SMEs, suggesting that design-led innovation frameworks help firms navigate the transition from OEM to OBM. Similarly, Hsu and Fang (2009) maps product design strategies in Taiwanese IT firms, revealing the alignment between product design and new product development (NPD) across strategic groups. In cosmetics, design is not only about packaging aesthetics but also sensory experience, branding, and emotional connection with consumers.

Knowledge integration is also shaped by institutional and policy frameworks. Chu (2009) analyzes Taiwan's second movers and concludes that the lack of a national champion strategy limits OBM development. Conversely, South Korea's support for chaebol conglomerates has fostered globally competitive OBMs. Gereffi (1995) and Lee et al. (2014) both emphasize the role of industrial policy and innovation capabilities for sustainable development. For cosmetic firms, public investment in R&D and branding can be catalytic.

Case studies from Vietnam (Dinh et al., 2024; Le et al., 2019) demonstrate the increasing importance of CSR, innovation, and self-sufficiency in raw materials for OBM success. The shift from CMT to FOB, ODM, and OBM requires data-driven approaches to supplier selection and ethical branding. This aligns with findings from Tuntariyanond et al. (2017), who show that value creation in the Thai garment industry relies on strategic supplier–buyer relationships and interactive learning.

Moreover, OBM strategies are increasingly intertwined with digitalization. Zhou et al. (2019) describe how rural enterprises in China leverage ICTs to transform their operations and knowledge base. In cosmetics, this includes adopting e-commerce platforms, using customer data analytics, and creating immersive digital branding. Lin and Lin (2010) propose a framework for turning cultural digital archives into e-business assets—a strategy relevant to cosmetics OBMs that rely on heritage, natural ingredients, or cultural identity in brand storytelling.

Globalization further complicates the innovation landscape. Buckley (2009) frames the global factory as both an opportunity and a constraint, depending on a firm's ability to upgrade. Asian firms often struggle to transition from low-value functions to OBM due to limited knowledge accumulation (Yap & Rasiah, 2017). However, De Marchi et al. (2017) find that industrial districts with embedded lead firms and dynamic local actors are more resilient, suggesting that OBM success is more likely where localized innovation systems support experimentation.

Cross-functional integration is another determinant of OBM innovation. Lu and Yang (2004) show that R&D-marketing cooperation enhances NPD in Taiwan's IT sector. Sun et al. (2009) confirm that TQM tools like QFD and value analysis improve NPD speed, thus contributing to OBM efficiency. These insights apply directly to cosmetics firms that must synchronize formulation development, marketing campaigns, and supply chain responsiveness.

Cultural design also plays a pivotal role. Lin (2007) emphasizes the need to design culture into modern products through cross-cultural evaluation. For cosmetic OBMs, this involves aligning packaging, scent, and brand message with local and global tastes. Yodwangjai (2014) illustrates how semantic differential techniques can bridge designer-consumer perception gaps in furniture design—an approach applicable to cosmetic product design as well.

Economic pressures and environmental shocks, like the COVID-19 pandemic, have intensified the need for rapid innovation. Shih and Lin (2022) argue that co-locating marketing and production functions improves agility during crises. Park et al.

(2023) demonstrate how COSMAX thrived post-COVID-19 by digitizing its R&D and marketing functions. These examples highlight the critical role of organizational adaptability (Seah et al., 2014) and strategic resilience in OBM models.

Finally, the cosmetics OBM transformation must consider the embeddedness of local firms in global value chains. Poon et al. (2006) and Chin (2013) note that global production networks and FDI can either support or hinder upgrading depending on the firm's absorptive capacity and leadership. The literature supports hybrid strategies—OEM cash flow with OBM investment—as a viable path for many Asian SMEs (Lee et al., 2015).

In sum, innovation, design, and knowledge integration are not merely operational enhancements—they are the strategic levers through which OEMs evolve into OBMs. The cosmetics industry, with its branding intensity and dynamic consumer demands, exemplifies the need for a holistic approach to innovation that combines internal capabilities, external collaborations, and institutional support. The next section will delve into the operational and organizational capabilities that enable firms to implement these strategies effectively.

5 Organizational Capabilities and Firm-Level Transformation

The transformation from Original Equipment Manufacturing (OEM) to Original Brand Manufacturing (OBM) in the cosmetics industry is deeply dependent on the development and deployment of organizational capabilities. These capabilities encompass a wide array of firm-level processes, including leadership vision, dynamic capabilities, cross-functional coordination, learning mechanisms, and the ability to reconfigure resources in response to market shifts. Drawing from an extensive review of recent scholarly sources, this section explores how organizational capabilities shape and sustain firm-level transformation in the context of the cosmetics industry's OBM trajectory.

Organizational transformation begins with leadership intent. Li et al. (2018) assert that enterprise upgrading is not merely a function of external market conditions but is driven by internal measurement standards and strategic decision-making. In the cosmetics sector, leaders who prioritize OBM must articulate a vision that shifts the firm's identity from a low-profile contract manufacturer to a consumer-facing brand with global aspirations. Seah et al. (2014) further stress the role of adaptive leadership in facilitating co-evolution between organizational culture and market responsiveness. In cosmetics, this entails a deep cultural shift—from efficiency-focused operations to design-led innovation, branding, and consumer engagement.

The development of dynamic capabilities is a cornerstone of OBM transition. According to Chiu et al. (2016), capabilities such as sensing opportunities, coordinating assets, and reconfiguring processes are fundamental to radical innovation. For cosmetic firms, this means scanning global beauty trends, forging supply chain agility, and responding rapidly with new product offerings. These capabilities are not innate; they emerge from deliberate investment in talent, infrastructure, and cross-functional integration. Lin and Chen (2007) show that Taiwanese SMEs succeed through administrative innovation, suggesting that internal structures and routines must evolve alongside external products.

Team coordination and cross-functional integration are also vital. Lu and Yang (2004) demonstrate that R&D-marketing cooperation significantly improves new product development (NPD) performance in Taiwan's IT firms. This insight is directly transferable to cosmetic OBMs, where collaboration between marketing, formulation science, and packaging design is essential to delivering cohesive and appealing products. Sun et al. (2009) confirm that quality management tools such as teamwork, value analysis (VA), and quality function deployment (QFD) enhance the speed of NPD, helping OBMs reduce time-to-market.

Organizational learning is another pillar of OBM capability. Liu and Zhang (2014) propose a model of alliance learning where knowledge flows both within and between organizations. In cosmetics, firms that collaborate with ingredient suppliers, branding agencies, or e-commerce platforms gain access to new capabilities. This aligns with Szeto (2000), who argues that continuous innovation requires resource sharing within inter-organizational networks. COSMAX's success, for instance, lies in its ability to integrate external technological inputs while maintaining internal coherence (Park et al., 2023).

Strategic flexibility and responsiveness to environmental change are necessary for sustained transformation. Yi et al. (2011) categorize Chinese garment firms based on their flexibility strategies—laggard, conservative, agile, and aggressive—suggesting that agility correlates strongly with competitiveness. OBMs in cosmetics must cultivate organizational flexibility to respond to shifting consumer demands, regulatory changes, and technological disruption. Zhou et al. (2019) show that ICT adoption in rural Chinese enterprises enabled transformation by enhancing information flow, coordination, and responsiveness—qualities that are crucial for OBM firms navigating global markets.

The structure of the firm must also support transformation. Recent studies emphasize flat organizational structures and open innovation systems in the successful OBM case of Franz in Taiwan's gift industry (Jian Chung Seah et al., 2014; Yuan et al., 2009). Their findings suggest that decision-making autonomy, open communication channels, and a culture of creativity are essential for OBM success. In the cosmetics sector, firms must break down silos between departments and empower employees to contribute to innovation and brand development.

Resource allocation strategies further reflect a firm's readiness for OBM. Wang and Wu (2016) argue that R&D investments yield greater performance gains for OBMs than for OEMs, especially when aligned with downstream activities in the industry value chain. This is particularly true in cosmetics, where R&D drives differentiation in formulation, sustainability, and sensory experience. Firms that rely solely on OEM strategies underinvest in these areas, missing opportunities to build brand equity and customer loyalty.

Capability upgrading also involves a shift in performance metrics. Traditional OEMs prioritize cost, efficiency, and volume, while OBMs must measure success through brand equity, customer satisfaction, and innovation output. Kuo et al. (2018) emphasize the dual imperative of exploration and exploitation—OBMs must innovate while maintaining operational excellence. This tension requires new metrics and incentive systems, aligning employee goals with long-term brand performance.

Human capital development is central to building OBM capabilities. Recent studies highlight the importance of training, absorptive capacity, and tacit knowledge in firm upgrading (Poon & MacPherson, 2005; Poon et al., 2006; Yap & Rasiah, 2017). In cosmetics, this includes hiring brand strategists, product designers, and digital marketers who can translate technical knowledge into consumer value. Government support for skills development, as seen in South Korea and Taiwan, can accelerate this process.

Institutional embeddedness also shapes firm-level transformation. Chu (2009) observes that Taiwan's lack of a national champion policy has limited OBM progress, while South Korea's state-led industrial policy has nurtured global OBMs like AmorePacific and LG H&H. Gereffi (1995) and Lee et al. (2014) argue that supportive institutions—such as export promotion agencies, R&D grants, and branding subsidies—can catalyze OBM transformation by lowering risk and enhancing competitiveness.

In sum, organizational capabilities are the backbone of the OBM transition in the cosmetics industry. These capabilities span leadership, dynamic reconfiguration, cross-functional integration, learning, flexibility, and institutional alignment. Firms that build and deploy these capabilities are better positioned to move up the value chain, differentiate their offerings, and achieve long-term competitive advantage in the global cosmetics market. The next section will explore how digital transformation amplifies these capabilities and reshapes the OBM landscape.

6 The Impact of Digital Transformation

Digital transformation is fundamentally reshaping the global cosmetics industry, especially in the context of the transition from Original Equipment Manufacturing (OEM) to Original Brand Manufacturing (OBM). As digital technologies redefine production, marketing, distribution, and customer engagement, they simultaneously serve as catalysts and enablers for OBM development. Drawing upon insights from recent academic sources, this section explores how digital transformation impacts OBM strategies, capabilities, and outcomes within the cosmetics industry.

Digitalization reconfigures the operational backbone of cosmetics firms. Zhou et al. (2019) propose a three-layered model of firm transformation driven by ICTs: operation mode, open innovation, and actor networks. In the OBM context, digital tools enable firms to develop agile supply chains, automate production, and enhance product traceability. For example, ERP systems, AI-powered inventory management, and blockchain for supply transparency are now key enablers for OBM brands seeking to meet consumer demands for sustainability and speed.

Digital technologies also play a critical role in branding and consumer interaction. COSMAX, a major Korean ODM/OBM firm, effectively utilizes digital platforms to sense consumer trends, personalize products, and manage customer relationships (Park et al., 2023). E-commerce, social media marketing, influencer partnerships, and virtual try-on technologies allow OBMs to directly engage with consumers, bypassing traditional retail intermediaries. This shift is crucial for brand building, a core component distinguishing OBM from OEM models.

Moreover, data analytics enhances product innovation and customer-centricity. Firms employing digital platforms gather vast amounts of consumer data through online behavior tracking, product reviews, and loyalty programs. Yap and Rasiah (2017) emphasize knowledge accumulation as a critical enabler of firm upgrading. In cosmetics, such data informs R&D by identifying unmet needs, preferred ingredients, or new aesthetics. Digital tools thus connect back-office formulation labs with front-end customer preferences in real time.

Digital transformation also fosters internal cultural and organizational change. Seah et al. (2014) describe how open innovation and flat organizational structures enable rapid knowledge sharing and cross-functional collaboration—qualities essential for digital-era OBMs. By breaking down departmental silos, cosmetics firms can accelerate product development cycles, experiment with new branding strategies, and reduce time-to-market.

From a strategic standpoint, digital transformation lowers entry barriers for OBMs. Traditional OEMs needed vast capital to build distribution and retail channels. Today, platforms like Amazon, Tmall, and Instagram Shopping offer low-cost access to global markets. This democratization of market access empowers emerging cosmetic OBMs from developing regions, such as Vietnam and Bangladesh, to compete internationally (Fouji & Hoque, 2021; Le et al., 2019).

The digital shift also enables new forms of co-creation and customization. Semantic differential and Kansei engineering techniques, as demonstrated by Yodwangjai (2014), are now integrated into AI-driven consumer feedback loops. Consumers can co-design products through digital interfaces, increasing satisfaction and brand loyalty. OBM firms thus create unique, data-informed value propositions—an impossible feat under the OEM model.

Simultaneously, digital transformation introduces new challenges. Cybersecurity, intellectual property theft, and managing digital platforms' algorithms become strategic concerns. As seen in the counterfeit lithium-ion battery study by Kong et al. (2022), digital openness must be balanced with quality control and brand protection—especially critical for cosmetics, where consumer trust is paramount.

To manage this complexity, OBM firms need to develop digital capabilities. Chiu et al. (2016) emphasize the importance of sensing and reconfiguring capabilities—skills that translate directly into managing digital disruptions. Firms must hire data analysts, digital marketers, UX designers, and AI engineers. This shift represents a reallocation of resources and retraining of personnel, as seen in the talent strategies of Taiwan's IT and cosmetics firms (Lin & Chen, 2007).

Digital transformation also shapes strategic alliances. Cross-border partnerships, driven by digital integration, allow OBMs to tap into global innovation ecosystems. However, it also requires strategic investments in digital infrastructure, talent, and cybersecurity. Firms that embrace digital transformation holistically—integrating it into production, branding, and organizational culture—are better positioned to succeed as OBMs in the dynamic global cosmetics landscape. Liu and Zhan (2014) highlight alliance learning in cross-border supply chains, where OBMs collaborate with tech startups, logistics platforms, and content creators. These alliances expand organizational boundaries, embedding OBM firms in global networks of design, technology, and marketing.

In conclusion, digital transformation is both a driver and a differentiator in the OEM–OBM transition in cosmetics. It enables faster, consumer-driven innovation; lowers market entry costs; and enhances brand building through direct digital engagement.

7 Policy and Institutional Enablers

The transformation from Original Equipment Manufacturing (OEM) to Original Brand Manufacturing (OBM) in the cosmetics industry is not solely a firm-level phenomenon but one that is deeply embedded in the broader institutional and policy context. National innovation systems, industrial policies, and public–private collaborations play a decisive role in shaping the environment in which firms operate and evolve. Drawing on insights from the recent referenced studies, this section explores how institutional structures, government policies, and industrial ecosystems enable or constrain OBM transitions in the global cosmetics sector.

Institutional support is a foundational enabler of OBM development. Gereffi (1995) emphasizes that successful industrial upgrading in East Asia has been underpinned by state-led initiatives that integrate microeconomic upgrading strategies with macroeconomic development goals. In the cosmetics industry, this means that governments must not only support R&D and export activities but also facilitate branding, design innovation, and international marketing—areas traditionally underdeveloped in OEM-dominated economies.

East Asia offers numerous examples of policy-driven OBM transitions. In South Korea, the Ministry of Trade, Industry, and Energy has historically supported OBM growth through industrial policy instruments that include R&D subsidies, export promotion, and support for K-beauty branding initiatives. Park et al. (2023) describe how COSMAX and other Korean ODM–OBM hybrids benefited from government-backed innovation labs, supply chain digitization incentives, and partnerships with universities to foster product innovation and marketing capabilities. These public investments reduced barriers for cosmetic firms to invest in upstream design and downstream branding.

In contrast, Taiwan's OBM evolution has been more restrained. Chu (2009) argues that the absence of a "national champion" policy—unlike Korea's chaebol system—has limited Taiwan's OBM progress. The Taiwanese government has focused on supporting SMEs through incremental innovation and export-oriented manufacturing, which are more conducive to OEM and ODM models. However, as Seah et al. (2014) show in their case study of Franz (a Taiwanese gift brand), public support for open innovation, flat organizational structures, and design education has helped some firms make the leap to OBM by nurturing a creative workforce and entrepreneurial culture.

Vietnam presents a more recent example of an evolving policy environment. Le et al. (2019) and Dinh et al. (2024) discuss how Vietnamese textile and cosmetic firms are incentivized to develop OBM capabilities through preferential tax regimes for firms that comply with Corporate Social Responsibility (CSR) standards and source materials locally. While these policies were initially targeted at enabling compliance with free trade agreements, they have had the secondary effect of encouraging branding and supply chain independence—critical features of OBM transformation.

Government support for skills development is another institutional lever. Yap and Rasiah (2017) highlight the role of training programs in knowledge-intensive industries, arguing that human capital is the most critical constraint in latecomer OBM transitions. In the cosmetics sector, workforce development programs that focus on branding, design thinking, marketing analytics, and formulation science are essential to create a pipeline of OBM-ready talent. As the study by Lin and Chen (2007) in Taiwan shows, SMEs that engage in daily innovation practices—especially non-technological ones—are more likely to translate internal innovation into brand performance.

Public–private partnerships also facilitate OBM upgrading. The experience of COSMAX, as detailed by Park et al. (2023), demonstrates how firms can collaborate with state-backed digital innovation labs to experiment with artificial intelligence (AI) in product development and marketing. These collaborations reduce the financial and technological burden of innovation for individual firms and enable collective learning across the sector. Similarly, the findings of Szeto (2000) emphasize the importance of inter-organizational networks in building long-term innovation capacity.

Infrastructure and logistics also form part of the institutional landscape that supports OBM. The Belt and Road Initiative (BRI), as analyzed by Le et al. (2019), indirectly promotes OBM by improving Vietnam's logistics networks, reducing delivery times, and expanding market access. Better infrastructure enables cosmetic OBMs to engage in direct-to-consumer e-commerce and manage global inventory flows—functions essential for brand-building and customer service excellence.

The intellectual property (IP) regime is another crucial institutional determinant. For OBMs, IP protection ensures that investments in branding, packaging, and product innovation are safeguarded. Zhu (2009) argues that indigenous innovation strategies in China depend on strong legal frameworks to protect firm-specific capabilities. In the cosmetics sector, this includes trademarks, packaging designs, and proprietary formulations. In countries where IP enforcement is weak, firms may be discouraged from pursuing OBM strategies due to fears of imitation and brand dilution.

Export promotion and market access policies also influence OBM success. Jian Chung Yuan et al. (2009) discuss how Taiwanese firms in the gift industry leveraged government-sponsored trade shows, diplomatic networks, and branding consultancies to penetrate high-value export markets. Similarly, Tan (2017) identifies different generic internationalization strategies adopted by Chinese firms—ranging from low-cost suppliers to global consolidators—shaped by their home country's strategic direction and export policy frameworks.

Fiscal and regulatory incentives can be aligned with OBM objectives. Wang and Wu (2016) note that OBMs derive greater returns from R&D investments compared to OEMs, especially when supported by targeted tax breaks and co-financed innovation grants. Countries like South Korea and Singapore have implemented matching grants for branding expenditures, helping firms offset the high costs of entering premium markets and establishing brand recognition.

Finally, the institutional environment shapes societal attitudes toward branding and innovation. In their study on Africa's fashion economy, Karami and Read (2021) emphasize how local cultural narratives and creative entrepreneurship can be supported through policy frameworks that value local identity. Cosmetics firms benefit from similar institutional validation—when national discourse celebrates beauty innovation and homegrown brands, OBM efforts receive social legitimacy alongside financial incentives.

In conclusion, the transition from OEM to OBM in the cosmetics industry is inseparable from its institutional context. Governments and public institutions play a pivotal role in enabling OBM transformation through policy instruments, education, infrastructure, IP protection, and cultural validation. The experience across East and Southeast Asia demonstrates that where industrial policy is coherent, inclusive, and future-facing, OBM strategies in the cosmetics sector are more likely to flourish. The next section will explore the emerging themes associated with this complex transformation process.

8 Emerging Themes and Future Research Directions

The global cosmetics industry's ongoing transformation from Original Equipment Manufacturing (OEM) to Original Brand Manufacturing (OBM) has catalyzed a wide array of strategic, technological, and institutional shifts. Drawing upon the rich body of literature comprising recent scholarly studies, several emerging themes surface from this transformation, reflecting broader industrial patterns, sectoral trends, and evolving firm-level behaviors. These themes not only offer valuable insights for current practitioners and policymakers but also highlight promising avenues for future academic inquiry. This section outlines key thematic developments and proposes targeted research directions that can deepen our understanding of OBM transformation dynamics in the cosmetics industry and beyond.

8.1 Hybridization of Business Models: OEM-ODM-OBM Synergies

One significant emerging theme is the increasing fluidity between OEM, ODM (Original Design Manufacturing), and OBM models. Rather than linear transitions from OEM to OBM, many cosmetic firms are adopting hybrid models that leverage the advantages of multiple modes simultaneously. Studies by Chu (2009), Wang and Wu (2016), and COSMAX's case (Park et al., 2023) suggest that firms strategically retain ODM contracts while developing OBM lines, thereby ensuring stable revenue streams while building brand equity. Future research should examine how firms manage these hybrid identities, particularly how resource allocation, organizational culture, and supply chain governance adapt to support dual or triple model strategies.

8.2 The Rise of Design-Led Innovation in Emerging Markets

A recurring insight across studies (e.g., Bolton, 2009; Lin & Lin, 2010) is the central role of design in OBM success. Design-led innovation enables firms to differentiate in saturated markets, resonate with consumers emotionally, and establish brand narratives. While traditionally associated with Western brands, emerging market firms in Korea, Vietnam, and Taiwan are increasingly investing in local design capabilities. As design becomes a competitive advantage, future research should explore how local design ecosystems—such as universities, design incubators, and cultural institutions—contribute to OBM capacity-building in non-Western contexts.

8.3 Consumer Co-Creation and Personalization

Consumer engagement has become a cornerstone of OBM differentiation. Enabled by digital technologies, co-creation platforms, and AI-powered customization (Kong et al., 2022; Yodwangjai, 2014; Yodwangjai & Pimapunsri, 2011), OBMs now invite customers to shape product development, branding, and marketing. Future studies could explore how firms balance co-creation with brand control, what types of consumer participation yield the highest returns, and how these dynamics vary across cultural contexts. Moreover, examining how co-creation contributes to consumer loyalty and long-term brand equity in the cosmetics sector would yield valuable managerial insights.

8.4 Institutional and Policy Anchors for OBM Scaling

The critical role of national innovation systems and policy frameworks in facilitating OBM transitions is well established (Chu, 2009; Gereffi, 1995; Le et al., 2019). However, comparative studies across institutional regimes remain limited. Future research should delve into the specific mechanisms—e.g., export subsidies, IP protection, branding grants—that prove most effective for OBM growth. Moreover, longitudinal studies assessing the long-term impacts of such interventions could provide evidence-based guidance for policymakers seeking to cultivate OBM industries in developing economies.

8.5 Organizational Learning and Capability Deepening

The evolution of organizational capabilities—dynamic capabilities, absorptive capacity, and inter-organizational learning—has emerged as a defining feature of successful OBM firms (Chiu et al., 2016; Liu & Zhang, 2014; Sun & Zhao, 2010). Yet, the granular processes by which firms build and institutionalize these capabilities remain underexplored. Future studies could employ ethnographic and longitudinal methods to trace how capabilities are developed, embedded, and transferred within and across cosmetic firms. Particular attention should be paid to the role of cross-functional teams, informal knowledge sharing, and leadership in shaping learning trajectories.

8.6 OBM Performance Metrics and Evaluation Frameworks

As firms transition toward OBM, traditional metrics—such as production volume or cost efficiency—become less informative. Instead, new measures of success, including brand equity, consumer engagement, innovation speed, and ESG (environmental, social, governance) performance, gain prominence. The literature (Wang & Wu, 2016; Yap & Rasiah, 2017) suggests the need for holistic frameworks that capture the multi-dimensional nature of OBM value creation. Future research could develop and validate such frameworks, integrating qualitative and quantitative indicators and assessing their relevance across different firm sizes, markets, and maturity stages.

8.7 Sustainability and Ethical Branding as Differentiators

As consumer expectations evolve, sustainability and ethics are becoming core elements of OBM strategy. CSR factors, once peripheral, are now decisive in supplier selection (Dinh et al., 2024), consumer trust, and even regulatory compliance. Cosmetic OBMs increasingly compete on their ability to source responsibly, reduce environmental impact, and support inclusive representation. Future research should investigate how firms embed sustainability in their branding narratives, how consumers perceive these efforts, and how sustainability-driven innovation affects supply chain configurations and product development cycles.

8.8 Digital Ecosystems and OBM Acceleration

Digital transformation is not just a facilitator but a catalyst for OBM growth. As seen in COSMAX's digital integration (Park et al., 2023) and ICT layers (Zhou et al., 2019), digital platforms enable OBMs to bypass traditional barriers, engage directly with consumers, and gather real-time data for strategic decision-making. However, the digital divide, platform dependency, and algorithmic opacity also introduce new vulnerabilities. Future studies should explore how OBMs can build resilient digital strategies, negotiate power asymmetries with platform owners, and use digital ecosystems to foster innovation and global expansion.

8.9 Cross-Sectoral Learning and Industry Convergence

Several papers (e.g., Fan, 2006; Jin & von Zedtwitz, 2008) suggest that lessons from other industries—IT, telecom, and fashion—can inform OBM strategies in cosmetics. As the lines between beauty, wellness, and technology blur, cross-sectoral learning becomes increasingly relevant. Research could explore how OBMs adopt strategies from tech firms (e.g., agile innovation, D2C models), how convergence reshapes value chains, and how consumer expectations co-evolve across sectors.

8.10 Regional Value Chains and Local Clusters

Finally, the spatial dimensions of OBM transformation merit greater attention. Studies by De Marchi et al. (2017) and Buckley (2009) highlight the role of regional clusters and global factories in shaping firm upgrading. In cosmetics, geographic proximity to ingredient suppliers, design studios, and e-commerce hubs can accelerate OBM development. Future research should map regional OBM ecosystems, assess cluster competitiveness, and explore how regional policy can support integrated value chain upgrading.

The transformation from OEM to OBM in the cosmetics industry is an unfolding narrative rich with complexity and opportunity. Emerging themes point to the convergence of design, digitalization, sustainability, and institutional support as key levers for success. As the boundaries between manufacturing, branding, and consumer engagement blur, future research must adopt interdisciplinary, multi-level approaches to unpack the nuances of this transformation. By exploring the themes outlined above, scholars and practitioners alike can contribute to building a more innovative, inclusive, and resilient cosmetics industry.

9 Conclusion

This book set out to explore the transition from Original Equipment Manufacturing (OEM) and Original Design Manufacturing (ODM) to Original Brand Manufacturing (OBM), emphasizing the potential for firms to elevate their position in global markets by embracing innovation, branding, and sustainability. The transformation is not just a change in business models—it is a redefinition of value creation, fueled by digital technologies, customer-centric design, and evolving institutional frameworks.

The historical evolution of OEM, ODM, and OBM reveals a progressive shift in firm autonomy and value capture. OEMs primarily focus on efficient production for third-party brands, while ODMs add design capabilities. OBMs, however, fully own the value proposition—controlling brand, marketing, consumer experience, and innovation. This evolution is especially relevant in consumer-facing industries like cosmetics, where brand identity and product differentiation drive profitability. Our case studies demonstrate that the OBM path is neither linear nor universal but context-dependent, often requiring hybrid strategies and deep organizational change.

This chapter positions this evolution in historical and theoretical context, showing how GVC theory, dynamic capabilities, and national innovation systems explain the structural logic of upgrading. Countries like South Korea, Taiwan, and Vietnam have followed diverse paths to OBM, depending on their industrial policy, innovation infrastructure, and cultural narratives. In the cosmetics industry, this shift has been accelerated by market fragmentation, digitalization, and consumer demand for authenticity and sustainability.

Chapter 2 explores the digital transformation that underpins OBM success in the twenty-first century. Technologies like AI, IoT, and big data analytics empower firms to gather insights, personalize offerings, and scale operations efficiently. Digital platforms have dramatically reduced market entry barriers, allowing even small firms to engage directly with consumers and build loyal communities. In cosmetics, OBMs use tools like virtual try-ons, social listening, and automated logistics to deliver seamless customer experiences.

Chapter 3 discusses how OBM firms craft a global vision through purpose management. Unlike OEMs, OBMs must articulate clear brand values and mission-driven narratives. Purpose-driven brands often outperform competitors by resonating with consumers' ethical and lifestyle preferences. Case studies show that successful OBM firms embed their purpose into every aspect of their operations—from product design to supply chain sourcing.

In Chapter 4, innovation is placed at the core of OBM transformation. R&D is no longer confined to labs—it is integrated with marketing, consumer feedback, and open innovation networks. Cosmetics OBMs have been especially agile in leveraging trends like clean beauty, vegan formulations, and biotech ingredients. Firms like COSMAX have combined internal R&D with external partnerships, creating iterative learning loops that speed up product development.

Chapter 5 delves into marketing strategies, highlighting that OBMs must build brand power through storytelling, design management, and multi-channel engagement. Digital platforms, influencer partnerships, and community co-creation are critical for OBMs. The ability to emotionally connect with consumers sets OBMs apart in an era of product commodification. Branding is not a peripheral activity—it is the very core of value creation.

Chapter 6 emphasizes how production must evolve to support brand-led strategies. OBMs need flexibility, speed, and quality—often requiring reconfiguration of manufacturing processes. Technologies like smart factories and automation enhance efficiency while supporting small-batch customization. OBMs also focus on traceability, ensuring alignment between brand promises and operational practices.

Chapter 7 presents supply chain management as both a strategic asset and a source of resilience. OBMs invest in supply chain transparency, strategic sourcing, and ethical compliance to meet the expectations of modern consumers and regulators. Supplier relationships shift from transactional to collaborative, as OBMs co-develop innovations and share market intelligence with upstream partners.

Chapter 8 turns to sustainability and the circular economy, showcasing how OBMs embed environmental and social values into their operations. From eco-friendly packaging to zero-waste production, OBMs lead in redefining what it means to be responsible brands. Regulations and consumer activism alike demand this shift, making sustainability not a cost but a competitive advantage.

Chapter 9 concludes the main body by outlining trends and strategic outlooks for OBM evolution. The convergence of wellness, technology, and aesthetics is blurring industry boundaries. OBMs must embrace agility, global–local hybridity, and cross-sectoral collaboration. Institutional support remains vital—governments and international organizations can facilitate OBM growth through R&D incentives, trade facilitation, and branding promotion.

Throughout the book, the cosmetics industry serves as a rich empirical context. It illustrates the interplay of branding, innovation, design, and digital engagement in shaping OBM strategies. OBM enabler firms like COSMAX have provided critical lessons in navigating this transformation. Several cross-cutting insights emerge.

First, digital technologies are accelerators, not just tools. They enable real-time innovation, reduce asymmetries between large and small firms, and create new value spaces through personalization and co-creation.

Second, branding is strategic capital. In OBM, intangible assets—brand equity, consumer trust, and narrative—are more valuable than physical assets. Building this capital requires long-term investment, creativity, and strategic alignment.

Third, organizational capabilities matter. Firms must develop dynamic capabilities to sense market changes, seize innovation opportunities, and reconfigure resources.

Cross-functional collaboration, leadership commitment, and learning culture are prerequisites.

Fourth, sustainability is non-negotiable. From ESG reporting to green logistics, OBMs are judged by their ethical footprint. Firms that integrate sustainability into their DNA gain access to new markets, investor support, and consumer loyalty.

Fifth, institutions shape outcomes. National policy frameworks, IP protection, education systems, and trade infrastructure influence the ease and speed of OBM transitions. Government support for branding, R&D, and digital inclusion is crucial.

For future research and practice, several directions stand out. More longitudinal and cross-national studies are needed to track OBM transitions over time. The role of AI in OBM personalization, the ethics of algorithmic branding, and the dynamics of regional clusters all warrant deeper inquiry. Practitioners need tools to assess OBM readiness, allocate resources effectively, and manage hybrid OEM-OBM operations.

In conclusion, OBM is not merely a business model—it is a mindset and a strategic orientation. It represents the aspiration to not just manufacture products, but to own meaning, identity, and experience in the global marketplace. This book offers a roadmap for that journey, equipping firms, policymakers, and researchers with the frameworks, case studies, and tools to navigate the complex yet rewarding path to OBM transformation.

References

Bolton, S. (2009). The value of design-led innovation in Chinese SMEs. In *Proceedings of the 19th CIRP Design Conference – Competitive Design* (30–31, p. 369).

Buckley, P. J. (2009). The impact of the global factory on economic development. *Journal of World Business, 44*(2), 131–143.

Chiu, W. H., Chi, H. R., Chang, Y. C., & Chen, M. H. (2016). Dynamic capabilities and radical innovation performance in established firms: A structural model. *Technology Analysis & Strategic Management, 28*(8), 965–978.

Chu, W. W. (2009). Can Taiwan's second movers upgrade via branding? *Research Policy, 38*(6), 1054–1065.

De Marchi, V., Gereffi, G., & Grandinetti, R. (2017). Evolutionary trajectories of industrial districts in global value chains. In *Local clusters in global value chains* (pp. 33–50). Routledge.

Dinh, T. H., Nguyen, T. T. T., Do, T. T. T., Nguyen, T. V. T., & Nguyen, H. L. (2024). Selection supplier for Textile and Garment enterprises in Vietnam using association rules. *The Asian Journal of Shipping and Logistics, 40*(4), 206–212.

Fan, P. (2006). Catching up through developing innovation capability: Evidence from China's telecom-equipment industry. *Technovation, 26*(3), 359–368.

Fouji, M. H., & Hoque, I. (2021). Supplier internationalization through upgrading in global supply chain: Evidence from the garments industry of Bangladesh. *International Journal of Global Business and Competitiveness, 16*(2), 116–129.

Gereffi, G. (1995). Global production systems and third world development. In B. Stallings (Ed.), *Global change, regional response: The new international context of development* (pp. 100–142). Cambridge University Press.

Gereffi, G. (1999). International trade and industrial upgrading in the apparel commodity chain. *Journal of International Economics, 48*(1), 37–70.

Guo, J., Wu, J., & Dai, J. (2020). Production sourcing strategy for an apparel original brand manufacturer in the presence of technology spillover. *IEEE Transactions on Engineering Management, 70*(4), 1283–1294.

Hobday, M. (1998). Latecomer catch-up strategies in electronics: Samsung of Korea and ACER of Taiwan. *Asia Pacific Business Review, 4*(2–3), 48–83.

Hobday, M. (2001). The electronics industries of the Asia–Pacific: Exploiting international production networks for economic development. *Asian-Pacific Economic Literature, 15*(1), 13–29.

Hsu, Y. H., & Fang, W. (2009). Intellectual capital and new product development performance: The mediating role of organizational learning capability. *Technological Forecasting and Social Change, 76*(5), 664–677.

Jian Chung Yuan, B., Tai Ping Chiu, H., Ming Kao, K., & Wei Lin, C. (2009). A new business model for the gift industry in Taiwan. *European Business Review, 21*(5), 472–480.

Jin, J., & von Zedtwitz, M. (2008). Technological capability development in China's mobile phone industry. *Technovation, 28*(6), 327–334.

Karami, M., & Read, S. (2021). Co-creative entrepreneurship. *Journal of Business Venturing, 36*(4), Article 106125.

Kittilaksanawong, W. (2015). How do emerging economy firms learn to evolve from contract manufacturing to own brand management? *Global Enterprise Management, 2*, 1–17.

Kong, L., Das, D., & Pecht, M. G. (2022). The distribution and detection issues of counterfeit lithium-ion batteries. *Energies, 15*(10), 3798.

Kuo, T. K., Lim, S. S., & Sonko, L. K. (2018). Catch-up strategy of latecomer firms in Asia: A case study of innovation ambidexterity in PC industry. *Technology Analysis & Strategic Management, 30*(12), 1483–1497.

Le, Q. A., Tran, V. A., & Duc, B. L. N. (2019). The belt and road initiative and its perceived impacts on the textile and garment industry of Vietnam. *Journal of Open Innovation: Technology, Market, and Complexity, 5*(3), 59. https://doi.org/10.3390/joitmc5030059

Lee, K., Park, T. Y., & Krishnan, R. T. (2014). Catching-up or leapfrogging in the Indian IT service sector: Windows of opportunity, path-creating, and moving up the value chain. *Development Policy Review, 32*(4), 495–518.

Lee, K., Song, J., & Kwak, J. (2015). An exploratory study on the transition from OEM to OBM: Case studies of SMEs in Korea. *Industry and Innovation, 22*(5), 423–442.

Li, L., Su, F., Zhang, W., & Mao, J. Y. (2018). Digital transformation by SME entrepreneurs: A capability perspective. *Information Systems Journal, 28*(6), 1129–1157.

Liang, C., Chen, T., & Lin, Y. (2013). How do different business models affect intellectual capital? *Journal of Intellectual Capital, 14*(2), 176–191.

Lin, H. F. (2007). Knowledge sharing and firm innovation capability: An empirical study. *International Journal of Manpower, 28*(3/4), 315–332.

Lin, M. C. Y., & Wong, P. (2016). Recapturing the Taiwan miracle diversifying the economy through innovation and collaboration. Milken Institute Asia Center, June, 1–11. https://milkeninstitute.org/sites/default/files/reports-pdf/Recapturing-the-Taiwan-Miracle_0.pdf

Lin, R., & Lin, C. L. (2010, July). From digital archives to E-business: A case study on turning "art" into "business". In *2010 International Conference on e-Business* (ICE-B) (pp. 1–8). IEEE.

Lin, Y. Y., & Chen, Y. C. (2007). Does innovation lead to performance? An empirical study of SMEs in Taiwan. *Management Research News, 30*(2), 115–132.

Liu, C. L. E., & Zhang, Y. (2014). Learning process and capability formation in cross-border buyer–supplier relationships: A qualitative case study of Taiwanese technological firms. *International Business Review, 23*(4), 718–730.

Lu, L. Y. Y., & Yang, C. (2004). The R&D and marketing cooperation across new product development stages: An empirical study of Taiwan's IT industry. *Industrial Marketing Management, 33*(7), 593–605.

Ng, S. C. H., Zhao, X., Fan, X., & Rungtusanatham, J. M. (2014). TQM and brand-building by Chinese original brand manufacturers: Impact on business performance. *International Journal of Production Research, 52*, 825–846.

Park, H., Hong, S., & Shin, H. (2023). Rising and thriving in the post COVID-19 era: A case study of COSMAX, a leader of the Korean cosmetic industry. *Asia Pacific Business Review, 29*(4), 1105–1124.

Poon, J. P., & MacPherson, A. (2005). Technology acquisition among Korean and Taiwanese firms in the United States. *International Business Review, 14*(5), 559–575.

Poon, J. P., Hsu, J. Y., & Jeongwook, S. (2006). The geography of learning and knowledge acquisition among Asian latecomers. *Journal of Economic Geography, 6*(4), 541–559.

Seah, M., Hsieh, M. H., & Huang, H. Y. (2014). Leader driven organizational adaptation. *Management Decision, 52*(8), 1410–1432.

Shih, Y. Y., & Lin, C. A. (2022). Co-location with marketing value activities as manufacturing upgrading in a COVID-19 outbreak era. *Journal of Business Research, 148*, 410–419.

Sun, H., & Zhao, Y. (2010). The empirical relationship between quality management and the speed of new product development. *Total Quality Management & Business Excellence, 21*, 351–361.

Sun, H., Zhao, Y., & Yau, K. (2009). The relationship between quality management and the speed of new product development. *The TQM Journal, 21*(6), 576–588.

Szeto, E. (2000). Innovation capacity: Working towards a mechanism for improving innovation within an inter-organizational network. *The TQM Magazine, 12*(2), 149–158.

Tam, F. Y., Chan, T. S., Chu, P. W., Lai, T. C., & Wang, L. L. (2005). Opportunities and challenges: Hong Kong as Asia's fashion hub. *Journal of Fashion Marketing and Management: An International Journal, 9*(2), 221–231.

Tan, K. (2017). Generic internationalization strategies of emerging market multinationals: The case of Chinese firms. *Advances in Economics and Business, 5*(2), 83–94.

Tang, H. (2011). The route choice of the brand creation of Chinese textile original equipment manufacturers in the post-financial crisis era. In *2011 International Conference on Management and Service Science*.

Teece, D. J. (2007). Explicating dynamic capabilities: The nature and microfoundations of (sustainable) enterprise performance. *Strategic Management Journal, 28*(13), 1319–1350.

Tuntariyanond, P., Anuntavoranich, P., Mokkhamakkul, T., & Wichian, S. N. (2017). Value creation logic in buyer-seller relationships in garment industry in Thailand. *International Journal of Economic Policy in Emerging Economies, 10*(1), 31–46.

Wang, C. C., & Wu, A. (2016). Geographical FDI knowledge spillover and innovation of indigenous firms in China. *International Business Review, 25*(4), 895–906.

Yan, H. D., Chiang, C., & Chien, C. S. (2011). From original equipment manufacturing to branding: Entrepreneurship, strategic leadership, and Taiwan's firm transformation. *International Entrepreneurship and Management Journal, 10*, 81–102.

Yap, X. S., & Rasiah, R. (2017). Catching up and leapfrogging in a high-tech manufacturing industry: Towards a firm-level taxonomy of knowledge accumulation. *Knowledge Management Research & Practice, 15*(1), 114–129.

Yi, C. Y., Ngai, E. W. T., & Moon, K. L. (2011). Supply chain flexibility in an uncertain environment: Exploratory findings from five case studies. *Supply Chain Management: An International Journal, 16*(4), 271–283.

Yodwangjai, S. (2014). Product design and development for dinner chair of Kansei engineering. *Engineering and Applied Science Research, 41*(2), 191–200.

Yodwangjai, S., & Pimapunsri, K. (2011). Application of semantic differential technique and statistical approach to evaluate designer's and consumer's perception in furniture design. *Applied Science and Engineering Progress, 4*(1), 23–30.

Zhou, Q., Gao, P., & Chimhowu, A. (2019). ICTs in the transformation of rural enterprises in China: A multi-layer perspective. *Technological Forecasting and Social Change, 145*, 12–23.

Zhu, Z. (2009). Transferring management knowledge into China: A conceptual model and case study. *Human Systems Management, 28*(1–2), 19–34.

Chapter 2
Navigating the Digital Shift: OBM Business Model in the Era of Digital Transformation

1 Introduction: The Digital Imperative for OBM

The rise of digital technologies has fundamentally transformed how companies create, deliver, and capture value. For Original Brand Manufacturers (OBMs), particularly those emerging from the traditional OEM (Original Equipment Manufacturing) and ODM (Original Design Manufacturing) models, digital transformation is not just an opportunity—it is a strategic imperative. The cosmetics industry, with its reliance on branding, aesthetics, and consumer experience, sits at the forefront of this shift.

Digital transformation enables OBM firms to build intimate, data-driven relationships with consumers, scale personalized offerings, and iterate product lines in near real time. This transition is powered by a suite of digital tools—artificial intelligence (AI), the Internet of Things (IoT), cloud infrastructure, big data analytics, and e-commerce platforms—that together redefine the dynamics of competition. Brands can now collaborate directly with consumers, predict trends using machine learning, and operate across borders with minimal physical presence.

This chapter explores how digital technologies are reshaping the OBM landscape through the lens of five pioneering firms in the K-beauty sector: COSMAX, Anua, APR, Manyo Factory, and Olive Young. These firms exemplify different models of digital adaptation—from tech-enabled manufacturing to direct-to-consumer scaling—and offer a roadmap for how OBMs can compete and thrive in the digital age.

COSMAX, a global manufacturing powerhouse, has transitioned into a digital OBM enabler. Its investment in AI-driven R&D, regulatory compliance infrastructure, and platform services allows client brands to shorten development cycles, meet international standards, and scale globally. COSMAX's hybrid approach demonstrates that manufacturing leadership and digital sophistication are not mutually exclusive but mutually reinforcing.

Anua represents a digital-native brand built on obsessive customer focus. Through constant engagement, real-time NPS monitoring, and AI-powered sentiment analysis,

Y. W. Park et al., *Original Brand Manufacturing Business Model*,
https://doi.org/10.1007/978-981-95-0253-0_2

Anua has refined its product-market fit with unparalleled speed. Its ability to use data to co-create with consumers exemplifies a modern OBM strategy grounded in empathy and analytics.

APR, a beauty-tech firm, blends software, hardware, and skincare into a seamless user experience. Its smart devices, app-linked diagnostics, and AI-recommended skincare routines illustrate how OBMs can generate stickiness and differentiation through convergence. APR's model highlights how OBMs can redefine categories by integrating physical products with digital ecosystems.

Manyo Factory started as a D2C skincare brand and scaled through TikTok virality and Amazon success. Its evolution from niche e-commerce to mass offline retail—now stocked in Costco, Target, and Ulta—reflects the power of omnichannel agility. Manyo's hybrid model, supported by modular product development and agile operations, enables it to respond quickly to market feedback and scale efficiently.

Olive Young, though not a brand manufacturer itself, plays a critical OBM-enabling role. As Korea's leading health and beauty (H&B) retailer, it offers indie brands shelf space, customer insights, and digital infrastructure. With its discovery-based shopping format and global expansion initiatives, Olive Young demonstrates how retail platforms can incubate and accelerate OBM brands domestically and abroad.

Together, these five case studies highlight how digital transformation redefines the strategic toolkit of OBM firms. Beyond technology adoption, successful digital OBMs cultivate data-driven cultures, form ecosystem partnerships, and build feedback-driven innovation loops. They no longer merely launch products—they manage consumer experiences, build communities, and deliver value as platforms.

The implications of this shift are profound. OBM firms must embed digital strategy into every layer of their operations. They must transform R&D from intuition-based to insight-driven, branding from monologue to dialogue, and supply chains from linear pipelines to responsive networks. Moreover, they must build new organizational capabilities in data science, UX design, compliance, and digital marketing—often in collaboration with external partners.

As global markets become more competitive and fragmented, digital fluency becomes the foundation for brand equity and consumer loyalty. The future of OBM lies in dynamic, interconnected value creation—where speed, personalization, and relevance define success. By learning from the pioneers of digital OBM, emerging firms can chart a path toward sustainable, scalable growth.

In this digital era, OBM is not simply about owning a brand—it is about orchestrating ecosystems, capturing hearts, and delivering experiences that evolve with the consumer. The K-beauty sector, through its innovation, agility, and cultural resonance, provides a vivid blueprint for this transformation. As more firms embrace this shift, the OBM model will continue to evolve—from manufacturing and marketing to storytelling and community-building—toward a future where technology, creativity, and consumer connection converge.

2 Digitalization and OBM Value Creation

Digital transformation is reshaping how OBM firms create, deliver, and capture value across the entire business model. In contrast to OEMs and ODMs that prioritize manufacturing efficiency or design services, OBMs are increasingly expected to innovate at the brand level and respond directly to end-consumer needs. The infusion of digital technologies into this process has given rise to what scholars describe as a multi-scalar transformation—one that operates at the organizational, technological, and market engagement levels simultaneously.

From a theoretical standpoint, Teece's (2007) dynamic capabilities framework offers a useful lens. OBM firms must constantly sense emerging consumer trends, seize innovation opportunities, and reconfigure internal assets. In a digital context, this involves leveraging real-time analytics, adopting modular and scalable platforms, and building cross-functional teams that can integrate R&D, marketing, and logistics. Digitalization transforms OBMs into agile, learning organizations that can prototype rapidly, test markets efficiently, and scale innovations globally.

Digital branding is one of the most visible transformations. As noted by Lin and Wong (2016), OBMs now operate in an attention economy, where their ability to craft compelling narratives across multiple digital touchpoints determines consumer engagement. In the cosmetics industry, where visual and emotional appeal is central, social media platforms such as Instagram, TikTok, and YouTube have become key arenas for brand development. Influencer marketing, user-generated content, and viral challenges are tools through which OBMs build credibility and trust. These strategies are not just promotional but foundational to the OBM model in a digital age.

The integration of AI and big data analytics further supports innovation and customization. As Park et al. (2023) document in their study of COSMAX, the use of predictive analytics enables OBMs to identify product trends, forecast demand, and customize formulations at scale. AI-powered tools also allow firms to experiment with product recommendations, packaging variations, and dynamic pricing. In turn, this data-driven approach enables personalization—a key differentiator for OBM brands targeting niche consumer segments.

Digital platforms such as Amazon and Alibaba offer OBM firms unprecedented access to global markets. As Slama (2023) discusses in his Digital OEM framework, firms can integrate software-as-a-service with physical product development to deliver smart, connected products. This applies equally to OBM brands that must now think of their products not just as commodities but as data points within larger consumer ecosystems. Amazon's algorithmic rankings, for example, reward high engagement and positive feedback, encouraging OBMs to invest in continuous customer satisfaction and iterative product improvement.

Another key shift is in manufacturing and logistics. IoT-enabled production systems, combined with ERP and CRM software, allow OBM firms to streamline supply chains and ensure traceability. In the cosmetics sector, where regulatory compliance and quality assurance are paramount, such systems are critical. COSMAX's adoption of modular manufacturing, for instance, enables rapid switching between product lines based on market demand. This agility is further enhanced by real-time inventory tracking and automated fulfillment systems that minimize stockouts and reduce lead times.

E-commerce also reshapes customer journeys. As documented by Ng et al. (2014), the integration of TQM and branding is vital for sustained OBM performance. Digital OBM firms engage with customers beyond point-of-sale, using CRM tools to monitor feedback, encourage reviews, and manage loyalty programs. This lifecycle engagement fosters brand loyalty and supports upselling and cross-selling strategies. Moreover, OBMs can track customer lifetime value (CLV), segment audiences more effectively, and personalize communication to drive repeat purchases.

Importantly, digital transformation also affects organizational structure and capability building. As Chiu et al. (2016) emphasize, OBMs require reconfigured internal routines and competencies to manage digital tools effectively. This includes building in-house data science teams, upskilling marketers in search engine optimization (SEO) and analytics, and retraining product managers to work in agile sprints. OBMs must also invest in cybersecurity, privacy compliance (e.g., GDPR), and platform governance to maintain consumer trust and data integrity.

Furthermore, OBM firms increasingly engage in co-creation and open innovation. Consumer feedback, social media sentiment, and online communities provide rich sources of ideation. OBMs often run crowdsourcing campaigns, beta tests, and influencer collaborations to co-develop new products. This participatory approach not only enhances product relevance but also strengthens brand authenticity. As Liu and Zhang (2014) argue, alliance learning and inter-organizational networks are central to building sustainable innovation capabilities.

Regional ecosystems also play a significant role. Chu (2009) notes that OBM success is often shaped by institutional support and local innovation systems. In Korea, for example, the K-beauty boom was supported by government branding initiatives, R&D subsidies, and export facilitation. Korean OBMs have benefited from these programs, leveraging state-backed platforms to experiment with AI, develop eco-friendly packaging, and access global certification schemes.

Sustainability and CSR are also embedded into digital OBM practices. Firms now use blockchain to ensure ingredient traceability, AI to optimize sustainable packaging, and digital storytelling to communicate their ESG commitments. As Dinh et al. (2024) show, CSR is not only a compliance issue but a source of competitive advantage in OBM supplier selection and consumer preference.

In sum, digital transformation reshapes every facet of the OBM value chain—from ideation and production to branding and customer service. It demands a fundamental rethinking of strategy, capability, and organization. OBM firms that embrace this shift are better positioned to build resilient, scalable, and emotionally resonant brands.

They not only respond to market trends—they shape them, leveraging digital tools to engage, learn, and evolve in real time.

3 Case Studies of K-Beauty Firms Leveraging Digital OBM

3.1 COSMAX: From ODM to Digital OBM Ecosystem Leader

COSMAX, once a traditional ODM giant, has increasingly evolved into a hybrid OBM enabler and platform-driven manufacturer. COSMAX's transformation demonstrates how digital technologies can be leveraged not only to improve production efficiency but also to enable customer firms to launch their customers' products more effectively.

COSMAX has built a global digital infrastructure that connects its R&I (Research and Innovation) centers in Korea, the United States, China, Indonesia, and Thailand. With investments in AI-powered trend analysis tools and data analytics platforms, COSMAX offers predictive consumer insights to its clients. Figure 1 shows researchers at the COSMAX R&I Center developing a new product for an indie brand client. Moreover, COSMAX employs a range of tools to analyze emerging trends across social media, search engines, and e-commerce platforms, enabling the development of products tailored to both local and global consumer preferences.

In the United States, COSMAX has established a robust presence with a research hub and factory operations that comply with the latest regulatory frameworks, including MoCRA and OTC rules. Its New Jersey plant serves as a launchpad

Fig. 1 Researchers at the COSMAX R&I center developing a new product

for K-beauty products customized for the North American market. According to a 2025 analyst report, COSMAX benefits from a dual-market momentum—leveraging both Chinese consumption recovery and increased exports to Western markets (Kim, 2025). Its US operations, strengthened by a new West Coast sales office and advanced regulatory compliance teams, are attracting indie brands looking to scale through OBM offerings.

COSMAX also provides a full-service OBM enablement platform. Clients can choose from thousands of base formulas and packaging options, customize their SKUs using AI-driven personalization engines, and launch directly through integrated e-commerce support. COSMAX offers branding kits, digital content solutions, social media campaign templates, and even logistics infrastructure. This aligns with Slama's (2023) concept of the "Digital OEM," where manufacturers support their clients' entire go-to-market process through digital tools and services.

Notably, COSMAX's strategy avoids direct competition with client OBM brands by positioning itself as a digital ecosystem partner rather than a brand owner. Its value proposition lies in the ability to accelerate time-to-market, reduce innovation risk, and lower entry barriers for new brands. The firm's investments in sustainable formulation, halal compliance (especially important in Southeast Asia), and traceability have positioned it as a global OBM enabler attuned to both local and global market demands.

By integrating AI, IoT systems, modular production, digital product lifecycle management, and B2B e-commerce platforms, COSMAX has transformed from a contract manufacturer to a digital-first innovation partner. Its continued success underscores the strategic imperative for OBM firms and their partners to embrace digital capabilities not only for operational efficiency but for co-creation, rapid iteration, and market responsiveness.

3.2 Anua: Customer Obsession and Digital Scaling

Anua, the flagship skincare brand of global commerce startup The Founders, represents a quintessential case of digital-native OBM strategy that integrates product development, consumer insight, and omnichannel branding. Founded with a mission of "customer-obsessed innovation," Anua rapidly ascended in the global K-beauty landscape through its hero product, the Heartleaf 77 Soothing Toner. The product, based on Houttuynia Cordata extract, exemplifies the company's commitment to clean beauty, minimalism, and high-function formulation.

At the core of Anua's strategy is an obsessive commitment to consumer satisfaction. Each product undergoes a development lifecycle of over 2,000 h, during which Anua conducts extensive consumer testing, collects Net Promoter Score (NPS) feedback, and iterates based on real-time sentiment data. Using digital sentiment analysis and AI-powered survey tools, Anua creates high-fidelity feedback loops that allow rapid reformulation, packaging redesign, and marketing message adjustments.

This iterative model of product co-creation establishes a deep emotional bond with consumers while minimizing product-market misfit.

Anua's digital strategy thrives across multiple channels. Its success on Amazon United States underscores the firm's ability to scale digitally: the brand achieved the No.1 beauty product ranking during Prime Day 2024 with a 537% year-on-year growth. Strategic use of TikTok as a content seeding platform has further amplified brand exposure, particularly among Gen Z and Millennial consumers. The brand leverages micro-influencer campaigns, authentic storytelling, and viral content formats, ensuring wide organic reach without overreliance on paid ads.

Beyond online platforms, Anua has successfully entered the physical retail space. Its partnership with Ulta Beauty, one of the largest cosmetics retailers in the United States, marked a significant milestone—Anua became one of the first K-beauty indie brands to be stocked across all Ulta outlets. This omnichannel expansion is managed through centralized inventory, AI-based demand forecasting, and digital retail dashboards that align stock levels with geo-located demand patterns.

From an organizational perspective, Anua exhibits a flat, agile structure. Cross-functional teams bring together R&D, digital marketing, and customer experience (CX) functions, allowing seamless integration of insight and execution. AI tools analyze product reviews, social media comments, and customer service logs to surface emerging pain points and preferences, which are then addressed in the next product iteration.

Anua's digital OBM model aligns closely with contemporary academic insights. As Liu and Zhang (2014) highlight, the success of OBMs depends on inter-functional learning and knowledge integration. Anua's internal systems support rapid knowledge transfer, while its brand-building tactics mirror those emphasized by Ng et al. (2014)—combining product excellence with emotionally resonant narratives.

Moreover, Anua's product development model exemplifies what Sun et al. (2009) identify as the synergy between quality management and new product speed. By shortening feedback loops and integrating TQM tools with digital interfaces, Anua consistently outpaces competitors in launching high-demand SKUs.

In sum, Anua's case shows how digital OBM firms can elevate consumer satisfaction into a core capability. Through an integrated strategy of customer listening, data-informed innovation, and omnichannel scaling, Anua has become a leading example of how digital-native OBMs can grow quickly, adapt efficiently, and compete globally without relying on traditional advertising or distribution infrastructure.

3.3 APR: Beauty-Tech Convergence and Omnichannel Success

APR Corporation exemplifies the fusion of skincare, consumer electronics, and platform-driven D2C commerce. Its leading brands—Medicube and AGE-R—have captured top positions in Amazon's anti-aging and skincare device categories.

APR's trajectory demonstrates how digital OBM firms can succeed through full-stack integration of physical products, software systems, and personalized consumer interfaces.

Founded with a dual focus on cosmetics and home-use beauty devices, APR's OBM strategy is deeply rooted in R&D and technological differentiation. Medicube, the company's skincare line, is backed by clinical data and dermatologist partnerships, while AGE-R, its line of skincare devices, integrates IoT functions, app-based customization, and AI-powered skin diagnostics. These features enable consumers to personalize their skincare routines, track progress, and receive adaptive treatment suggestions via the Medicube+ app.

The synergy between devices and skincare represents a new paradigm in OBM: convergence-based ecosystems. APR's value proposition is not limited to a product—it's a lifestyle platform. As Chiu et al. (2016) argue, radical innovation performance depends on dynamic capabilities such as sensing and reconfiguring. APR exemplifies this by responding quickly to trends (e.g., anti-aging, DIY aesthetics), adjusting device algorithms, and aligning skincare ingredients with dermatological findings.

APR's marketing success hinges on omnichannel fluency. The company operates a robust D2C site that offers exclusive promotions, loyalty rewards, and cross-category bundles. Simultaneously, APR ranks high on Amazon due to well-optimized product pages, review management, and seasonal promotional campaigns. Its Black Friday 2024 campaign recorded a 2,343% year-over-year growth, underscoring the brand's resonance with digitally native consumers.

Offline expansion is equally aggressive. APR products are available in major US and Asian retailers, with flagship stores and pop-up booths showcasing the synergy between skincare and devices. The company's participation in global expos such as CES underscores its identity as a beauty-tech innovator. These events also serve as platforms for B2B deal-making and investor relations.

Behind the scenes, APR relies on an AI-powered CRM system that segments users, recommends SKUs, automates upselling, and measures campaign ROI. This system integrates with logistics and customer service to ensure seamless experience across touchpoints. For instance, real-time support bots and AI diagnostics reduce the need for human service agents, improving response time and operational efficiency.

APR's strategic outlook focuses on three growth levers: international expansion, product pipeline diversification, and tech innovation. Its entry into markets like the Middle East, Latin America, and Europe is facilitated through local distributors and regional compliance teams. The upcoming PDRN skincare line and advanced AGE-R models signal a continuous commitment to cutting-edge OBM innovation.

Academically, APR's approach reflects the principles of knowledge recombination (Yap & Rasiah, 2017) and open innovation. The company collaborates with dermatologists, electrical engineers, and behavioral scientists to develop multifunctional products. Its internal culture encourages cross-departmental experimentation and rapid iteration, mirroring the agile models promoted by Lin and Chen (2007).

APR's success illustrates how OBMs can transcend conventional product categories by owning the entire user experience—from diagnosis and formulation to device use and lifestyle content. This ecosystem model enhances brand stickiness, raises switching costs, and enables scalable personalization. In doing so, APR sets a benchmark for how OBM can be reimagined through digital infrastructure, technological convergence, and strategic foresight.

3.4 *Manyo Factory: Expanding from Online to Offline*

Manyo Factory, a pioneering D2C skincare brand, epitomizes how digital-first OBMs can evolve into omnichannel powerhouses. The company initially gained traction through social media platforms like TikTok and Amazon, where its Pure Cleansing Oil frequently outperformed established global brands in sales rankings. The product's popularity stemmed from its clean formulation, sensory appeal, and resonance with the "glass skin" aesthetic popularized by K-beauty content.

The digital growth phase for Manyo Factory was marked by viral marketing and influencer collaborations. Key opinion leaders (KOLs) on TikTok and Instagram created user-generated content showcasing the product's texture and efficacy. These campaigns were augmented by strategic keyword optimization and Amazon SEO, resulting in multiple bestseller badges.

Recognizing the limits of online-only presence, Manyo Factory began its transition to offline channels in 2023. It has since secured distribution in over 3,000 physical locations across the United States, including retail giants such as Costco, Ulta Beauty, and Target. Notably, its products are not relegated to generic "K-beauty" shelves but are positioned as "fan favorites" alongside legacy brands. This reflects a broader strategic ambition: to be perceived not just as a Korean brand but as a global skincare authority.

The success of this transition lies in operational alignment. Manyo Factory has developed a modular product development framework, where each SKU is iteratively improved based on customer feedback. The firm's R&D, packaging, and marketing teams coordinate using shared dashboards and agile sprints. Weekly review sessions analyze sales data, NPS results, and social sentiment, enabling micro-adjustments in real time.

From a supply chain standpoint, Manyo leverages demand forecasting tools and ERP integration to manage inventory across e-commerce and offline channels. Its logistics partners provide real-time delivery tracking and automated restocking, ensuring consistent availability even during viral demand spikes.

Manyo's OBM evolution reflects broader themes in OBM literature. The firm's success supports findings by Sun and Zhao (2010) on the importance of quality-speed integration. Its transition from niche D2C to mainstream retail echoes the pathway mapped by Chu (2009), where second-mover firms leverage digital branding to upgrade within the global value chain.

Moreover, Manyo's collaborative partnerships with OEM/ODM/OBM firms such as COSMAX underscore the value of strategic outsourcing in OBM scalability. While retaining control over branding and innovation, Manyo benefits from manufacturing excellence and regulatory compliance provided by its partners.

The case of Manyo Factory underscores how OBM firms can harness digital traction to build sustainable offline footprints. Its strategic clarity, operational integration, and data-driven culture position it as a template for emerging indie brands seeking long-term global relevance.

3.5 Olive Young: Discovery-Based Retail and OBM Enablement

CJ Olive Young, Korea's leading health and beauty (H&B) retailer, has emerged as a pivotal player in enabling the digital OBM ecosystem. Unlike conventional OBM brands, Olive Young does not produce its own line of cosmetics (beyond private labels), but its strategic role as a retail enabler, market validator, and innovation platform positions it as a cornerstone of Korea's beauty export engine. Harvard Business School recognized Olive Young's retail model as a global benchmark, citing its "discovery-based shopping" model as a core innovation in experiential retail (Karp & Lin, 2025).

At the core of Olive Young's value creation is its hybrid "Half-Service" model. This model blends the intimacy of personalized service with the freedom of self-paced exploration. Consumers shop without pressure from store associates, enabled by a category-based layout that emphasizes trend-based discovery over brand loyalty. This design increases dwell time, encourages spontaneous purchases, and amplifies exposure for emerging OBM brands.

Olive Young plays a catalytic role for K-beauty OBM firms, particularly indie brands. According to company data, over 100 OBM brands surpassed KRW 10 billion (approx. USD 7.5 million) in annual revenue after entering Olive Young's distribution network. Indie brands such as Round Lab, Torriden, and Anua saw explosive sales during promotional events like "Ol-Yung Sale," where SMEs accounted for the top 10 products in daily revenue. In doing so, Olive Young democratizes shelf access, previously dominated by conglomerate-owned brands.

From a platform perspective, Olive Young functions as a real-world product validation ecosystem. In-store product trials, shopper behavior data, and consumer reviews provide critical insight for OBM firms to refine formulations, packaging, and messaging. Olive Young shares analytics dashboards with partner brands, offering category trend forecasts, shelf-to-basket conversion rates, and geo-demographic purchase patterns—tools that enable agile product management.

Digital integration further enhances Olive Young's OBM support. Its proprietary CRM and mobile app ecosystem allow brands to push targeted offers, collect direct feedback, and engage in loyalty-based co-marketing. The launch of Olive Young's Global Mall extended its OBM support to cross-border e-commerce, enabling direct-to-consumer exports to over 150 countries. Notably, over 80% of the 2,000+ brands sold in Olive Young are SME OBMs, many of whom operate without dedicated offline stores.

Olive Young's global ambitions include the 2025 launch of its first US retail location in Los Angeles, under the newly established CJ Olive Young United States. This move positions Olive Young as a physical OBM accelerator in international markets. Unlike Sephora or Ulta, Olive Young's model emphasizes K-beauty curation, multi-brand community activation, and discovery-driven merchandising. These factors enable it to bridge online brand equity with offline consumer engagement.

Olive Young's success aligns with OBM-enabling ecosystems discussed in OBM literature. As noted by Lee et al. (2015), ecosystem actors—such as retailers and contract manufacturers—play instrumental roles in helping SMEs transition from OEM to OBM. Olive Young acts as the final-mile ecosystem partner, providing shelf space, retail intelligence, and global exposure that empower indie OBMs to scale.

Moreover, the platform's ability to coordinate logistics, regulatory compliance, and demand forecasting simplifies global expansion for OBM firms. Its collaboration with CJ Logistics ensures last-mile delivery efficiency, while its use of feedback analytics improves SKU planning across omnichannel settings.

In summary, Olive Young redefines the role of the retailer within the OBM model. Beyond sales, it functions as an ecosystem orchestrator—curating brands, incubating innovations, and facilitating export readiness. Through its customer-centric layout, advanced data capabilities, and global channel infrastructure, Olive Young represents a new generation of OBM enablers—one that combines commerce, community, and digital intelligence to support OBM success in the digital era.

4 Strategic Implications for OBM Firms

The rise of digital transformation in the cosmetics industry has opened a new strategic horizon for OBM (Original Brand Manufacturing) firms. By integrating digital technologies across product development, supply chains, marketing, and consumer engagement, OBM firms can capture greater value and operate with increased agility and intelligence. This section expands on four strategic pillars—speed to market, customer intimacy, operational agility, and brand equity development—and elaborates on the challenges and investment imperatives OBM firms must consider in the digital era.

4.1 Speed to Market: Acceleration Through Digitalization

Speed to market is a decisive competitive factor in the fast-paced cosmetics industry, where consumer preferences evolve rapidly, and product life cycles are short. Digital tools, particularly AI-driven R&D, predictive analytics, and cloud-based supply chain coordination, enable OBM firms to reduce time-to-launch from months to weeks.

AI-powered platforms such as trend-sensing tools scrape data from TikTok, Instagram, and beauty review forums to forecast micro-trends. Firms like COSMAX use these insights to guide rapid formulation development. Digital twin technologies allow for simulation-based testing, enabling faster prototyping without costly physical trials. Additionally, digital label management and e-packaging systems streamline regulatory compliance across international markets.

Furthermore, e-commerce platforms such as Amazon, Olive Young Global, and D2C brand websites offer OBM firms the ability to soft-launch products, gather feedback, and scale successful SKUs quickly. This feedback loop between development and consumer reaction compresses market validation timelines and enhances iterative product refinement.

4.2 Customer Intimacy: Building Emotional and Data-Driven Connections

OBM firms differentiate themselves by owning the brand-customer relationship. Digital touchpoints provide unprecedented opportunities to cultivate emotional loyalty and deliver personalized experiences. Data analytics platforms capture granular consumer behaviors, while AI-driven engines segment audiences by behavior, psychographics, and purchase intent.

For example, Anua's weekly NPS (Net Promoter Score) surveys, social media monitoring, and CRM analytics allow it to constantly tune its messaging and reformulate products based on real-time sentiment. Similarly, APR's skin-device pairing algorithms offer hyper-personalized skincare routines, deepening consumer trust and stickiness.

Customer intimacy is also facilitated through community engagement. OBM brands build tribes through brand storytelling, influencer partnerships, user-generated content campaigns, and social commerce. Platforms like TikTok and Instagram not only serve as promotional tools but also as co-creation spaces, where consumers contribute to trend validation and brand development.

4.3 Agility and Scalability: Modularization and Cloud-Enabled Growth

Agility and scalability are enhanced by cloud infrastructure, modular manufacturing, and decentralized distribution systems. Digital OBMs are able to pivot quickly—whether responding to supply chain shocks, regulatory changes, or viral demand spikes.

Firms like Manyo Factory exemplify this agility through their hybrid online-offline strategy. Starting as a D2C brand, Manyo scaled into over 3,000 physical US retail locations. Its modular development model allows for fast formulation tweaks based on market feedback. Similarly, COSMAX supports scalable OBM launches by offering plug-and-play formula libraries and real-time manufacturing dashboards.

Cloud-based ERP and MES (Manufacturing Execution Systems) facilitate real-time visibility and traceability across production nodes. This is especially crucial for OBM firms navigating MoCRA (Modernization of Cosmetics Regulation Act) and other jurisdiction-specific requirements.

Furthermore, omnichannel orchestration platforms integrate logistics, inventory management, and customer service across digital and physical channels. This ensures consistent experiences while enabling firms to meet consumers wherever they are.

4.4 *Brand Equity Development: Sustained Engagement in a Fragmented Media Environment*

In the attention economy, brand equity is no longer built solely on product performance—it depends on narrative consistency, authenticity, and ongoing engagement. OBMs must continually nurture their brand identity across touchpoints, from TikTok stories to retail shelf displays.

Digital transformation enables this continuity. Olive Young's data dashboards provide brands with shopper behavior insights that inform in-store merchandising, while CRM platforms allow for lifecycle-based communication. APR, through CES showcases and global D2C campaigns, builds an image of technological sophistication and clinical credibility.

Brand equity also benefits from sustainable and ethical storytelling. Transparency around ingredients, supply chain, and corporate values becomes easier with blockchain-enabled traceability and digital sustainability indices. OBMs that can align ESG narratives with digital touchpoints build deeper trust and long-term brand value.

4.5 *Investment and Risk Considerations: Human Capital, Security, and Regulation*

Despite the advantages, digital OBM transformation comes with significant investment requirements. Human capital remains a key constraint. Firms need talent in data science, UX design, regulatory affairs, digital marketing, and AI engineering. Upskilling, cross-functional integration, and organizational agility are essential.

Cybersecurity is another critical concern. As OBMs expand their digital footprint—from consumer databases to AI models—the risk of breaches increases. Investments in data encryption, compliance systems (e.g., GDPR, CCPA), and ethical AI governance are imperative.

Regulatory compliance is growing more complex. MoCRA in the United States imposes stringent rules on safety substantiation, ingredient labeling, and adverse event reporting. COSMAX's segmentation of compliance roles, such as having dedicated MoCRA and OTC regulation specialists, provides a model for other firms.

Firms must also navigate the digital divide. While larger OBMs can afford end-to-end digital stacks, SME OBMs may need to leverage platforms like COSMAX or Olive Young to access advanced tools and global infrastructure. Thus, ecosystem partnerships become not just enablers but strategic imperatives.

In conclusion, the strategic implications of digital transformation for OBM firms are profound. Digital tools accelerate speed to market, deepen customer relationships, enable agile scaling, and enhance brand equity. However, these benefits are contingent upon thoughtful investments in technology, talent, and trust. OBM firms that embrace digital transformation as a core strategic mindset—not just a technological upgrade—are best positioned to thrive in the volatile, value-driven global beauty marketplace.

5 Conclusion: Reimagining OBM in the Digital Era

Digital transformation is not simply a technological evolution; it is a foundational shift in how OBM firms define and deliver value. As the global beauty industry grows more connected, competitive, and fast-paced, OBM firms must operate not only as product innovators but also as digital natives—leveraging data, platforms, and partnerships to compete and thrive.

Through the lens of K-beauty pioneers like COSMAX, Anua, APR, Manyo Factory, and Olive Young, we see how success in the digital OBM space is increasingly shaped by agility, collaboration, and consumer-centric innovation. COSMAX has redefined its role from manufacturer to ecosystem enabler, supporting brand owners through AI-powered R&D, regulatory compliance, and e-commerce integration. Anua has built a strong global following through customer obsession, digital sentiment analysis, and continuous co-creation with its users.

APR has exemplified the convergence of skincare, technology, and personalization, creating an integrated OBM model that spans devices, content, and services. Manyo Factory's journey from online virality to brick-and-mortar presence illustrates the power of omnichannel agility. Meanwhile, Olive Young plays a crucial role in scaling OBM brands through discovery-based retail, data-enabled product validation, and global distribution.

From these case studies emerge five enduring principles:

Digital strategy must be embedded, not appended. OBM success requires digital tools and thinking across every business function—from R&D and branding to logistics and compliance.

Data is central to competitive advantage. From trend forecasting to customer feedback, the ability to gather and act on data swiftly enables innovation and personalization.

Ecosystem partnerships are essential. OBMs must build strategic alliances with manufacturers, retailers, and digital platforms to expand reach and capability while sharing risk.

Emotional engagement drives loyalty. Today's consumers want more than performance—they seek purpose, transparency, and authenticity. OBMs must invest in storytelling and community-building.

Operational agility ensures resilience. The ability to pivot in response to market shifts, regulations, or emerging trends is a core competency for digital-first OBMs.

Ultimately, digital transformation requires more than adopting tools—it demands a shift in mindset. OBM firms must evolve from linear product developers into agile, experience-focused organizations. They must be ready to experiment, iterate, and co-create continuously.

The journey of digital OBM is not a destination but an ongoing process. Those who embrace it will shape the future of beauty—where technology meets creativity, and data fuels emotional resonance. For OBMs, the future is not just about going digital—it's about becoming digitally fluent, customer-obsessed, and globally scalable from day one.

References

Chiu, W. H., Chi, H. R., Chang, Y. C., & Chen, M. H. (2016). Dynamic capabilities and radical innovation performance in established firms: A structural model. *Technology Analysis & Strategic Management, 28*(8), 965–978.

Chu, W. W. (2009). Can Taiwan's second movers upgrade via branding? *Research Policy, 38*(6), 1054–1065.

Dinh, T. H., Nguyen, T. T. T., Do, T. T. T., Nguyen, T. V. T., & Nguyen, H. L. (2024). Selection supplier for textile and garment enterprises in Vietnam using association rules. *The Asian Journal of Shipping and Logistics, 40*(4), 206–212.

Karp, R., & Lin, S. (2025). Olive Young: Formulating Beauty Innovation, Harvard Business School Case 725–392, January. https://www.hbs.edu/faculty/Pages/item.aspx?num=66762

Kim, K. T. (2025, March 25). K-beauty ODM two-top production capacity increases, SEDaily. https://v.daum.net/v/20250324174107945

Lee, K., Song, J., & Kwak, J. (2015). An exploratory study on the transition from OEM to OBM: Case studies of SMEs in Korea. *Industry and Innovation, 22*(5), 423–442.

Lin, Y. Y., & Chen, Y. C. (2007). Does innovation lead to performance? An empirical study of SMEs in Taiwan. *Management Research News, 30*(2), 115–132.

Lin, M. C. Y., & Wong, P. (2016, June 1–11). Recapturing the Taiwan miracle diversifying the economy through innovation and collaboration. Milken Institute Asia Center. https://milkeninstitute.org/sites/default/files/reports-pdf/Recapturing-the-Taiwan-Miracle_0.pdf

Liu, C. L. E., & Zhang, Y. (2014). Learning process and capability formation in cross-border buyer–supplier relationships: A qualitative case study of Taiwanese technological firms. *International Business Review, 23*(4), 718–730.

Ng, S. C. H., Zhao, X., Fan, X., & Rungtusanatham, J. M. (2014). TQM and brand-building by Chinese original brand manufacturers: Impact on business performance. *International Journal of Production Research, 52*, 825–846.

Park, H., Hong, S., & Shin, H. (2023). Rising and thriving in the post COVID-19 era: A case study of COSMAX, a leader of the Korean cosmetic industry. *Asia Pacific Business Review, 29*(4), 1105–1124.

Slama, D. (2023). Digital OEM. *The digital playbook: A practitioner's guide to smart, connected products and solutions with AIoT* (pp. 71–82). Springer International Publishing.

Sun, H., & Zhao, Y. (2010). The empirical relationship between quality management and the speed of new product development. *Total Quality Management & Business Excellence, 21*, 351–361.

Sun, H., Zhao, Y., & Yau, K. (2009). The relationship between quality management and the speed of new product development. *The TQM Journal, 21*(6), 576–588.

Teece, D. J. (2007). Explicating dynamic capabilities: The nature and microfoundations of (sustainable) enterprise performance. *Strategic Management Journal, 28*(13), 1319–1350.

Yap, X. S., & Rasiah, R. (2017). Catching up and leapfrogging in a high-tech manufacturing industry: Towards a firm-level taxonomy of knowledge accumulation. *Knowledge Management Research & Practice, 15*(1), 114–129.

Chapter 3
Crafting a Global Vision: Purpose Management for OBM

1 Introduction: The Meaning of Purpose in the OBM Era

As the cosmetics industry transitions from Original Equipment Manufacturing (OEM) and Original Design Manufacturing (ODM) to Original Brand Manufacturing (OBM), the question of purpose becomes central to leadership. While digital technologies and data analytics have fueled this evolution, the true differentiator lies in whether firms can build lasting purpose—grounded in social value, global impact, and stakeholder trust. For OBM firms to move beyond short-term product innovation, they must adopt purpose-driven leadership that integrates long-term vision with agile strategy.

Purpose in the OBM context goes beyond brand storytelling or corporate social responsibility (CSR). It requires an integrated strategic framework that links innovation, ethics, collaboration, and long-term stakeholder engagement. With the rise of global beauty culture and cross-border commerce, purpose has become a strategic necessity—shaping everything from sourcing and packaging to digital retail experiences and regulatory alignment. OBM firms are no longer just makers of beauty products; they are curators of meaning, agents of sustainability, and platforms of cultural transmission.

This transformation is particularly relevant in the context of K-beauty, where consumer expectations increasingly prioritize transparency, inclusivity, and localized resonance. In this environment, the success of OBM firms hinges on their ability to craft not only appealing products but also compelling value systems. The global rise of K-beauty is not merely the result of aesthetic appeal—it is rooted in a deeper narrative that combines innovation, heritage, and purpose. For OBM firms, aligning with this narrative requires leadership that sees beyond profit and competition.

Purpose management in OBM involves several layers. First, it entails a shift from transactional business models to ecosystem thinking. This includes partnerships with suppliers, contract manufacturers, retailers, and digital platforms that share a commitment to quality and ethical standards. Second, purpose requires internal

Y. W. Park et al., *Original Brand Manufacturing Business Model*,
https://doi.org/10.1007/978-981-95-0253-0_3

coherence. Companies must align employee values, operational policies, and brand identity with a shared mission. This alignment enhances organizational agility and builds trust both internally and externally. Third, purpose must be future-oriented. It calls for investments in sustainable practices, inclusive innovation, and digital transformation that anticipate the evolving needs of global consumers.

The shift toward purpose is also shaped by broader macroeconomic and sociocultural trends. Increasingly, consumers expect brands to take stands on environmental, social, and governance (ESG) issues. Regulators demand transparency and compliance. Investors seek long-term value creation over short-term returns. In this landscape, purpose is not just a moral imperative—it is a competitive one. Companies that fail to articulate and operationalize purpose risk being left behind in a market defined by meaning-driven consumption.

Against this backdrop, the leadership of Lee Kyung-soo, founder and chairman of COSMAX, stands out as a compelling case. Rather than launching a consumer-facing brand, Chairman Lee envisioned COSMAX as an enabler of other OBM brands—a platform that provides R&D expertise, manufacturing excellence, regulatory support, and global scale. This choice reflects a different kind of ambition—one that prioritizes collective success over individual visibility. COSMAX's business model is purpose-driven not because of marketing slogans, but because of structural decisions that embed purpose into every layer of the organization.

Chairman Lee's leadership reflects a deep understanding of what it means to build an OBM ecosystem rather than a singular brand. COSMAX does not compete with its clients. Instead, it empowers them—supporting indie startups and multinational corporations alike with tools, technologies, and expertise tailored to their growth. This model reflects what some scholars call a "silent leadership" approach, where influence is measured not by public recognition but by impact within ecosystems. COSMAX's low public profile contrasts sharply with its high strategic importance to the global beauty industry.

Furthermore, Chairman Lee's vision demonstrates how purpose can be scaled without dilution. COSMAX operates across over 20 countries, with R&D centers and manufacturing hubs in Korea, China, the United States, and Southeast Asia. Each site is locally responsive but globally integrated, reflecting a philosophy of glocalization—think globally, act locally. This operational design aligns with the values of diversity, adaptability, and inclusivity that are central to OBM success.

The COSMAX case also illustrates how purpose can drive innovation. By investing in AI-powered trend analysis, digital quality management systems, and modular manufacturing infrastructure, COSMAX has created a flexible and future-ready platform. These capabilities allow clients to reduce time-to-market, ensure compliance with evolving regulations (such as the US MoCRA), and deliver personalized beauty experiences to consumers worldwide. Innovation, in this model, is not an end in itself but a means of fulfilling a broader mission: to democratize access to high-quality beauty solutions.

Importantly, COSMAX's purpose is not static—it evolves in response to new challenges and opportunities. During the COVID-19 pandemic, the company accelerated its digital transformation, expanded automation, and opened new international offices to support client resilience. It also deepened its commitment to sustainability, launching initiatives in green chemistry, water stewardship, and biodegradable packaging. These actions show that purpose, when taken seriously, becomes a strategic compass that guides decision-making in both crisis and growth.

This chapter explores how COSMAX, under Chairman Lee Kyung-soo's leadership, operationalizes purpose across its global ecosystem. It draws on existing research in OBM, leadership theory, and purpose management to contextualize this case within broader academic and industry debates. By examining COSMAX not as a brand but as a purpose-driven enabler of brands, we can better understand the evolving role of leadership in the OBM era.

The story of COSMAX is not just about scaling operations or launching new products—it is about redefining what it means to lead in a connected, competitive, and conscience-driven world. In an industry where trends change rapidly and visibility often trumps substance, COSMAX offers a powerful counter-narrative that the most enduring impact comes from helping others succeed. Through this lens, purpose is not a statement—it is a system. And leadership, at its best, is the architecture of that system.

2 Previous Research on Purpose, Leadership, and OBM Transformation

The integration of purpose into strategic leadership has become a defining theme in contemporary management research. Especially in contexts where Original Brand Manufacturing (OBM) plays a central role, scholars increasingly emphasize the significance of leadership models that prioritize long-term societal value, inter-organizational collaboration, and cultural responsiveness. For OBM firms operating in dynamic, consumer-centric markets like beauty, purpose-driven leadership is not simply a moral aspiration—it is a competitive necessity.

George et al. (2007) articulate the concept of "authentic leadership," which stresses the importance of self-awareness, transparency, ethical grounding, and consistency between values and actions. Their framework posits that when leaders act in alignment with their deeply held beliefs, they foster resilient and engaged organizations. In the OBM context, where firms must navigate global value chains, manage diverse teams, and respond to shifting consumer expectations, this form of leadership enhances internal coherence and external trust.

Porter and Kramer (2011) introduce the idea of "creating shared value" (CSV), arguing that the alignment of profit-making with social good is not only possible but essential for sustainable competitive advantage. In OBM, this model encourages firms to develop products and services that address environmental and social needs—such as clean beauty innovations, inclusive skincare, and sustainable packaging—while generating economic value. Shared value reinforces the notion that purpose must be embedded in business models, not appended as afterthoughts.

Equally critical is the concept of inter-organizational learning, as presented by Liu and Zhang (2014). Their research highlights that OBM success often arises not from isolated innovation but from dynamic collaboration among OEMs, OBMs, and retail partners. Through shared R&D efforts, capability transfers, and co-branding strategies, firms co-create value and adapt to rapidly evolving market demands. These learning networks thrive when built on trust and aligned purpose—elements exemplified by companies like COSMAX that choose to support, rather than compete with, their clients.

The dynamic capabilities framework proposed by Teece (2007) offers another lens through which to understand OBM transformation. Teece identifies three core capabilities—sensing, seizing, and reconfiguring—that organizations must master to remain competitive in uncertain environments. In the beauty industry, where regulatory landscapes shift quickly and consumer trends can be unpredictable, dynamic capabilities enable OBM firms to respond with agility. When infused with purpose, these capabilities guide not just rapid response, but mission-aligned transformation.

The literature on OBM transformation has also been enriched by region-specific insights. Higo et al. (2020) focus on how Japanese and Korean manufacturing firms are evolving from mass production toward brand-centered innovation. They argue that in East Asia, OBM success is increasingly driven by narratives—stories of craftsmanship, heritage, and authenticity. Such narratives rely on leadership that understands brand not as a logo, but as a vessel of meaning. Senoo (2019) adds further nuance by examining the conceptual shift from the traditional 3R model (Reduce, Reuse, Recycle) to a more proactive form of sustainability aligned with the circular economy. He emphasizes the value of long-term product lifecycles, reinvention, and localized customization—all of which demand strategic foresight and purpose-driven leadership.

As OBM firms enter the digital age, new paradigms emerge. Slama (2023) introduces the concept of the "Digital OEM"—a manufacturer that no longer limits itself to production but evolves into a full-service platform. These firms integrate AI, machine learning, trend analytics, and regulatory technologies to empower brands from ideation to market. This evolution is particularly salient in beauty, where product cycles are short, and consumer preferences are hyper-fragmented. Digital OBM enablers like COSMAX exemplify how firms can remain invisible to end consumers yet indispensable to their success.

Leadership psychology research further affirms the organizational value of purpose. Sinek's (2009) proposition to "start with why" underscores the psychological pull of purpose for both employees and customers. Gartenberg et al. (2019) provide empirical validation, showing a positive correlation between purpose clarity and firm performance. Their findings suggest that when purpose is not just stated but lived—when it pervades hiring practices, R&D investments, and client relationships—it becomes a source of competitive strength.

These conceptual frameworks are not abstract in the OBM domain. The beauty industry itself provides fertile ground for their practical application. Imschloss et al. (2024) report that post-pandemic beauty consumers increasingly seek transparency, ethical sourcing, and cultural authenticity. Brands that fail to meet these expectations are swiftly marginalized. For OBM firms, this means that the ability to support brand clients in areas such as ESG compliance, clean formulation, and inclusive design is no longer optional. It is integral to value creation.

Ambidextrous leadership, as theorized by O'Reilly and Tushman (2013), also has particular relevance to OBM transformation. Their model advocates for leaders who can simultaneously exploit existing capabilities and explore new opportunities. This balancing act is evident in the leadership style of COSMAX's Chairman Lee Kyung-soo, who has strengthened operational excellence while continuously investing in digital infrastructure and global expansion. His ability to move seamlessly between stability and innovation reflects the ambidextrous traits needed in the modern OBM environment.

Trust is another recurring theme in OBM transformation literature. Ng et al. (2014) argue that Total Quality Management (TQM) principles underpin brand building in OBM settings. These principles include rigorous quality control, traceability, and cross-functional accountability—all of which build consumer trust over time. In a B2B2C model, where OBMs sell to brands who in turn serve end users, maintaining trust at every level of the value chain is critical. COSMAX's commitment to transparency and reliability—reflected in its robust compliance systems and client-first philosophy—offers a real-world case of TQM principles in action.

Importantly, these scholarly insights converge on several meta-themes. First, OBM transformation requires a strategic reorientation around purpose. Technical capability alone is insufficient. Purpose provides the connective tissue across functions, geographies, and stakeholder groups. Second, effective leadership must be ethically grounded and future-oriented. Leaders must navigate complexity not with control, but with clarity and conviction. Third, digitalization is both a challenge and a catalyst. It exposes organizations to new risks but also unlocks unprecedented capabilities for customization, speed, and feedback. Fourth, and perhaps most radically, the OBMs of the future may not be those that build the most recognizable brands—but those that build the most robust ecosystems.

This makes COSMAX an ideal case study. Under Chairman Lee Kyung-soo's leadership, the company exemplifies a form of "silent leadership"—influential not through brand dominance, but through ecosystem orchestration. COSMAX has helped shape the trajectory of Korean and global beauty by embedding purpose into the architecture of its operations. It does not just manufacture products; it curates processes, relationships, and capabilities that allow other brands to thrive.

By integrating insights from authentic leadership, dynamic capabilities, shared value, ambidexterity, and trust-based management, COSMAX illustrates how purpose becomes not just a guiding philosophy, but a performance-enhancing system. In a world where OBM firms must navigate consumer activism, geopolitical flux, and technological disruption, such systems will define who leads and who lags.

In conclusion, the body of academic and empirical research provides a rich foundation for understanding purpose-driven OBM transformation. From leadership theory to supply chain innovation, the consensus is clear: purpose matters. It shapes culture, drives innovation, builds trust, and ensures longevity. As digital and cultural shifts continue to redefine what consumers expect and what firms must deliver, OBM leaders will increasingly be called upon to lead not just their companies, but the ecosystems they inhabit. COSMAX's journey demonstrates that when purpose is embedded in every decision, the result is not only business success—but also strategic and societal relevance.

3 Leadership of an OBM Firm: Building COSMAX as a Purpose-Driven OBM Enabler

The rise of Original Brand Manufacturing (OBM) in the global beauty industry marks a fundamental shift from traditional manufacturing paradigms toward value creation through brand, purpose, and cultural relevance. Within this transformative context, the leadership of Lee Kyung-soo, Chairman and Founder of COSMAX, presents a compelling blueprint for how OBM firms can be reimagined not merely as brand owners, but as ecosystem builders. COSMAX's evolution under Chairman Lee's stewardship exemplifies a model of leadership rooted in strategic humility, long-term vision, and a deeply embedded philosophy of purpose.

3.1 The Three Apples Philosophy: Barum, Darum, Arum

Chairman Lee's leadership philosophy is distilled into what he calls the "Three Apples Philosophy": Barum (the Apple of Integrity), Darum (the Apple of Invention), and Arum (the Apple of Beauty). These symbolic anchors represent more than guiding principles—they serve as COSMAX's organizational DNA (Fig. 1).

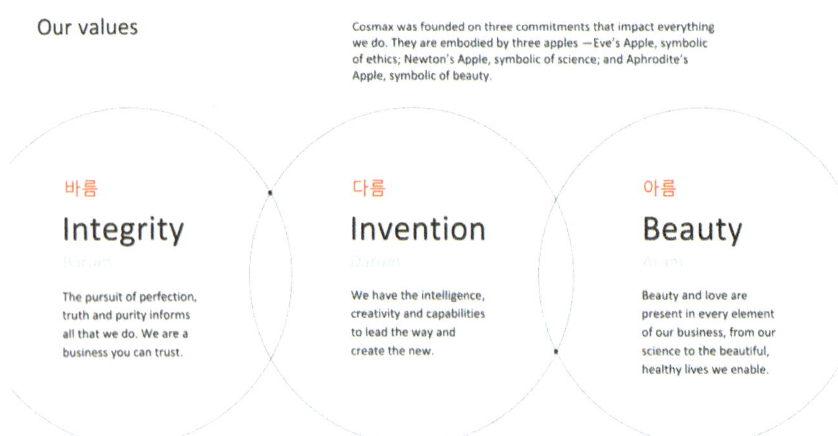

Fig. 1 COSMAX's three apples philosophy

Barum (Integrity) emphasizes ethical behavior and honesty, including respecting customers and diligently fulfilling entrusted responsibilities. For Chairman Lee, honesty means showing respect to customers, faithfully carrying out one's duties, and instilling trust in every interaction. Darum (Invention) gains its value when driven by professionalism and creative innovation. It reflects a corporate spirit that pursues scientific rigor, innovation, and evidence-based development. Arum (Beauty) embodies the spirit of sharing and aims for environmental management. It captures the aesthetic and emotional dimensions of beauty, grounded in cultural inclusiveness and ethical production. Together, these three apples form the ethical and operational foundation of COSMAX, allowing the company to scale while remaining purpose-centered.

3.2 Founding Vision: Purpose Before Profit

Chairman Lee's journey into entrepreneurship did not begin with a clear plan for domination in cosmetics. After two decades in corporate life—including executive positions at major pharmaceutical firms—he realized that consistent values such as honesty, customer respect, and collaborative spirit were the real bedrock of success. His decision to found COSMAX was not driven by a pursuit of wealth or fame, but by a belief in building a company grounded in enduring principles.

Influenced by both personal experience and the advice of peers, Chairman Lee chose to focus on ODM and later OBM enablement, inspired by similar models in Japan and Europe. Rather than establishing a brand that would compete with others, COSMAX would serve as a platform for innovation and support, empowering both indie startups and multinational corporations. This model of facilitative leadership allowed COSMAX to occupy a central but invisible role in global beauty.

3.3 Barum: The Apple of Honesty

At the heart of Chairman Lee's leadership lies the value of integrity. From its founding, COSMAX embraced a policy of non-competition with clients. As Chairman Lee famously said, "We are not here to steal the spotlight. We are here to build the stage." By refusing to launch its own brand, COSMAX created a culture of trust with its customers. This approach ensured clients felt comfortable sharing proprietary information, confident that COSMAX would act as an enabler, not a rival.

This trust is operationalized through robust systems: blockchain-based ingredient tracking, strict intellectual property safeguards, and compliance infrastructure tailored to regional regulations. During crises such as COVID-19, COSMAX proactively shared updates, extended delivery timelines, and digitized operations to help clients survive disruptions.

Chairman Lee's notion of honesty also manifests in the company's internal culture. He believes leadership must be accountable and transparent—not only with partners but also with employees. Honesty, to Chairman Lee, is not a tactic but a way of being.

3.4 *Darum: The Apple of Science*

Science is not a support function at COSMAX—it is a strategic driver. From its early days, Chairman Lee invested in R&D even when resources were scarce. The decision to prioritize internal scientific capability, including resisting pressure from early Japanese partners to forgo a research lab, marked a critical turning point. Chairman Lee, a pharmacy graduate, insisted on having an internal research team, believing that true differentiation would come from proprietary science.

Today, COSMAX allocates over 5% of annual revenue to R&I, with more than 1100 researchers across Korea, China, the United States, and Southeast Asia. The company's Pangyo headquarters hosts a convergence R&D model that integrates skincare and makeup development.

While most research institutes separate laboratories and office desks into different areas, COSMAX places laboratory benches and office desks together to emphasize "speed"—so that ideas can be immediately tested at the lab bench. COSMAX, the world's No.1 cushion manufacturer with a cumulative sales volume of about 800 million units, was able to pioneer such an innovative category thanks to its research system that fosters integration and communication, enabling the professional expertise of researchers to flourish. COSMAX has pioneered hybrid formulations that combine skincare benefits with makeup functionality, achieving remarkable global success with products such as cushion foundations, gel eyeliners, sun sprays, multi-balms, and multi-lip and cheek items (Fig. 2).

Specifically, COSMAX assigns both basic skincare researchers and color cosmetics researchers to the same lab. For example, in the CF Lab, a cream researcher

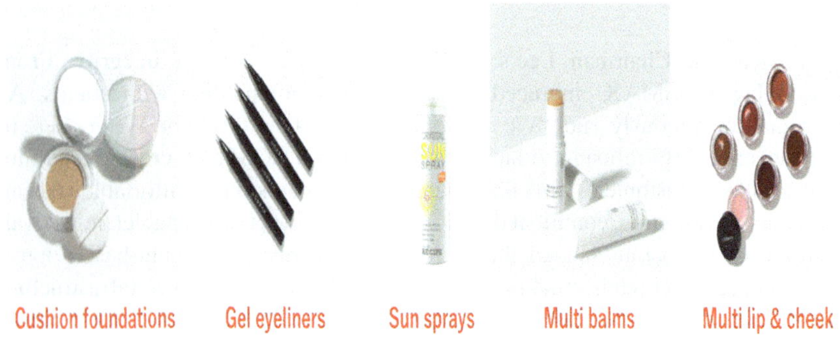

Fig. 2 COSMAX's hybrid formulations

studies the color aspects of foundation, while a foundation researcher explores the functional aspects of cream—leading to the creation of convergent products.

COSMAX's scientific credibility is reinforced through international collaborations and participation in global forums like IFSCC and the World Congress of Dermatology. It was also the first Korean ODM to secure US FDA OTC drug certification and Health Canada approval, along with Halal, ISO, and Ecocert certifications. Scientific integrity, for Chairman Lee, is both a duty and a differentiator.

3.5 *Arum: The Apple of Beauty*

Chairman Lee's aesthetic philosophy is shaped by a deep appreciation for culture, artistry, and emotional resonance. COSMAX does not produce branded goods, but its creative fingerprints are everywhere—from minimalist designs by Anua to high-tech offerings by Medicube. Through AI-driven trend analysis and consumer insight mining, COSMAX helps OBMs tailor offerings to regional preferences.

The company's aesthetic sensibility extends to sustainability. From biodegradable packaging to clean formulation development, COSMAX ensures that beauty does not come at the planet's expense. For Chairman Lee, Arum is about more than appearance—it is about harmony, empathy, and cultural relevance.

3.6 *Leadership Through Slogans: Organizational Cohesion*

Chairman Lee believes that slogans are powerful tools to align teams and focus collective energy. From "Dream to be the Best Partner" in the early days to "Be Innovative, Be Simple, Be Number One" during global expansion, COSMAX's slogans reflect its evolving strategic priorities. These rallying cries serve not only as communication tools but as cultural rituals that reinforce purpose.

Slogans like "Flexibility and Speed" underscored the importance of responsiveness as the company transitioned from OEM to ODM. More recently, slogans such as "Global is Our Front Yard" and "One COSMAX" signal a commitment to integration, localization, and global collaboration. These internal campaigns have helped unify a growing global workforce around shared ideals.

3.7 *Strategic Humility: Choosing to Empower*

One of the most striking features of Chairman Lee's leadership is his refusal to pursue COSMAX's own consumer-facing brand. In an industry where visibility often defines success, Chairman Lee chose strategic humility. COSMAX would serve, not compete. This ethos enables deep, long-term partnerships and eliminates the trust deficit that plagues many B2B relationships.

This humility is not passive—it is purposeful. It allows COSMAX to support clients without bias or agenda. As Chairman Lee puts it, "We thrive when our partners shine." By avoiding the limelight, COSMAX has become a silent architect behind some of the world's most successful beauty products.

3.8 Resilience and Crisis Leadership

The 1997 Asian financial crisis (IMF crisis) tested the resilience of many Korean firms. For COSMAX, this moment revealed the strength of its leadership. Chairman Lee adopted three crisis policies: stabilize prices despite currency volatility, reduce minimum order quantities to ease customer burdens, and ensure timely deliveries through a weekend production system.

This proactive stance won COSMAX a reputation for reliability and care. These decisions were not about short-term gains—they were about protecting long-term relationships. This ethos would become critical again during the COVID-19 pandemic, when COSMAX ramped up automation, opened new global offices, and invested in remote collaboration tools to ensure continuity.

3.9 Global Expansion with Local Sensitivity

COSMAX's global journey began with early entry into China in the early 2000s. Unlike competitors who sought cheap labor, Chairman Lee focused on market proximity, choosing Shanghai despite higher costs. This decision reflected an understanding that prestige and quality matter more than short-term savings.

Chairman Lee's strategy was to partner with local companies and build from within China—an approach that paid off handsomely. COSMAX became the top ODM in China by working with Chinese firms that needed quality and compliance to compete with global brands. The company's reputation for transparency and reliability attracted both local and multinational clients.

Expansion into Southeast Asia and the United States followed. In each case, COSMAX adapted to local regulatory and cultural contexts. COSMAX has pursued market diversification by establishing subsidiaries in the United States, its largest market, as well as in key ASEAN countries such as Indonesia and Thailand. The current annual production capacity (CAPA) of its global manufacturing bases reaches 3.2 billion cosmetic units (Fig. 3). Its exports have expanded to over 100 countries, serving as a strategic foothold for K-beauty across Asia, North America, and Europe. In 2024, the company's industry leadership was recognized with the "200 Million Dollar Export Tower" award.

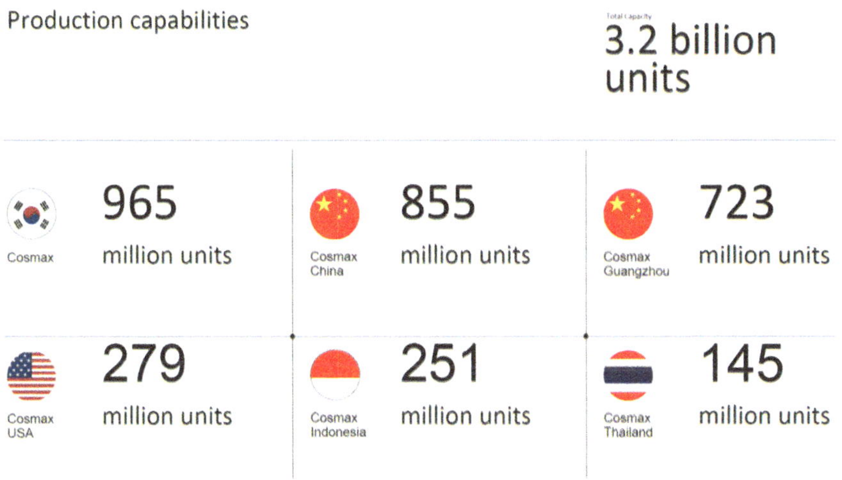

Fig. 3 COSMAX's annual production capacity

3.10 *Ecosystem Thinking and the Digital OBM Model*

Chairman Lee's leadership aligns closely with the emerging "Digital OEM/OBM" paradigm, where manufacturing firms serve as full-service platforms. COSMAX integrates AI-driven trend analytics, global regulatory advisory, modular formulation libraries, and digital commerce support into a seamless offering.

This ecosystem model accelerates time-to-market for clients while reducing risk. It also transforms COSMAX from a supplier into a strategic partner. By embedding itself into every phase of the OBM lifecycle—from ideation to international distribution—COSMAX redefines what it means to be a manufacturer.

Chairman Lee's approach goes beyond transactional logic. It is about shared growth. By supporting clients' long-term aspirations, COSMAX creates a resilient network of mutual benefit. It is this network—not individual products—that forms the real source of COSMAX's power.

3.11 *Investing in People and Trust*

Trust is not only extended to clients, but also to employees. Chairman Lee believes in empowering trusted individuals, even during uncertain times. One notable example is COSMAX's entry into the Chinese market. During a difficult period, a young local manager faced criticism from both Chinese and Korean sides. Despite this, the company made the strategic decision to keep only that young manager in China while bringing all other expatriate staff back to Korea, and instead dispatched more capable personnel. As a result, the team rallied around the young manager, overcame the initial challenges, and ultimately achieved success. This executive played a crucial role in COSMAX's success in the Chinese market.

This trust-based approach also extends to talent development. COSMAX invests in employee education, global rotations, and interdisciplinary collaboration. It fosters a culture where professional excellence is balanced with personal growth and ethical responsibility.

3.12 *Toward an OBM-Centered Ecosystem*

Chairman Lee's vision positions COSMAX not just as a company, but as a platform for building the future of OBM. The firm connects raw material suppliers, packaging vendors, regulatory experts, and distribution platforms into a coherent whole. This integrated ecosystem allows even small OBM brands to compete on a global scale.

COSMAX's approach shows that OBM does not need to mean owning a brand. It can mean owning the capability to create, enable, and scale brands. In this sense, COSMAX represents a new archetype: the OBM enabler as ecosystem architect.

3.13 *Leadership as Architecture of Purpose*

Chairman Lee Kyung-soo's leadership embodies a distinctive model of purpose-driven OBM enablement. Through the Three Apples Philosophy—Barum (integrity), Darum (invention), and Arum (beauty)—he has built a company that is simultaneously ethical, innovative, and culturally resonant.

His strategic humility, global foresight, and deep commitment to enabling others challenge conventional definitions of success. COSMAX does not seek the spotlight, yet it shapes the very stage upon which beauty brands perform. It does not dominate, yet it leads through service. It does not advertise its purpose—it lives it.

In an era defined by transparency, cultural nuance, and stakeholder capitalism, COSMAX offers a model for how manufacturing firms can thrive by becoming ecosystems of purpose. And in Chairman Lee's vision, we find a leadership paradigm that sees purpose not as a marketing angle, but as the architecture of the future OBM world.

4 Conclusion: Toward a Purpose-Centered OBM Paradigm

COSMAX's evolution under the leadership of Chairman Lee Kyung-soo offers a compelling model for OBM firms navigating the complexities of a globalized, digitally accelerated beauty industry. In this context, purpose is not merely a philosophical stance or a brand narrative—it is a structural and strategic foundation. It shapes decisions across all dimensions of the firm: from where to build factories and how to engage with clients, to how R&D is prioritized and what kind of organizational culture is cultivated. For COSMAX, purpose is a system—anchored in ethics, driven by innovation, and attuned to beauty as a cultural and emotional experience.

What distinguishes COSMAX is not just its scale or success, but its role as an enabler in the OBM value chain. While many firms in the industry seek market dominance through branding and visibility, COSMAX has chosen a path of strategic humility. It does not compete with the very brands it supports. Instead, it uplifts them—providing cutting-edge formulation, rigorous regulatory expertise, and trend-driven innovation infrastructure. This quiet but powerful position has made COSMAX an indispensable partner to thousands of OBM firms worldwide. In doing so, it has redefined what leadership means in the OBM age: less about controlling outcomes, more about cultivating ecosystems of mutual growth.

Chairman Lee's leadership philosophy—epitomized by the "Three Apples" framework of Barum (integrity), Darum (invention), and Arum (beauty)—illustrates how values can be operationalized. These pillars are not static slogans but dynamic principles woven into every aspect of the company. Barum informs COSMAX's commitment to trust, transparency, and partnership. Darum drives its unwavering focus on scientific excellence and continuous R&D investment. Arum reflects an understanding that beauty must resonate emotionally, ethically, and culturally. Taken together, these values create a cohesive identity that allows COSMAX to remain adaptable while maintaining its core integrity.

The impact of such purpose-driven leadership becomes particularly clear in times of crisis. During both the 1997 Asian Financial Crisis and the COVID-19 pandemic, COSMAX took bold yet compassionate steps to protect its partners, maintain supply chain integrity, and invest in future-readiness. Rather than retreat or default to short-term cost-cutting, the company upheld its commitments—safeguarding client relationships and reinforcing its reputation as a reliable, values-oriented partner. These responses demonstrate how purpose, when deeply embedded, acts as a compass during uncertainty. It enables consistency in decision-making and builds the kind of trust that transactional strategies can never replicate.

Equally significant is COSMAX's approach to globalization. Unlike firms that pursue international expansion solely for cost advantages, COSMAX integrates local responsiveness with global coherence—a strategy Chairman Lee refers to as "thinking globally, acting locally." COSMAX has established R&D and production facilities in key markets such as China, the United States, and Southeast Asia, and achieves localized operations tailored to each region's consumer preferences, regulations, and cultural aesthetic standards. To this end, COSMAX defines three principles of localization—complying with local laws, supporting local business partners, and fostering a sense of loyalty among local employees—and through these, ensures both local relevance and resilience. Its model demonstrates that globalization does not necessarily mean homogenization, but that inclusive localization can serve as a pathway to growth.

The lessons from COSMAX's journey point to a broader shift in OBM leadership logic. In an era where speed, aesthetics, compliance, and digital fluency define competitive advantage, purpose provides strategic clarity. It unites disparate functions—innovation, marketing, manufacturing, compliance—under a common mission. It inspires employees, reassures investors, and builds enduring brand trust. Most importantly, it positions OBM firms not merely as product creators, but as stewards of value, identity, and sustainability.

Chairman Lee Kyung-soo's leadership is not flashy, but it is transformative. By resisting the urge to dominate or self-promote, he has built a company that empowers others to lead. COSMAX's choice to remain behind the scenes—enabling indie startups and multinational giants alike—demonstrates the power of service-based leadership. In doing so, it challenges traditional assumptions about what success looks like in the OBM world. Sometimes, the most influential players are those who create the infrastructure for others to thrive.

As the OBM model continues to evolve—shaped by digital disruption, ESG imperatives, and increasingly discerning consumers—firms will need more than operational efficiency or trend alignment. They will need a deep, durable sense of why. Purpose will not just differentiate brands—it will define ecosystems. Those who lead with clarity, humility, and systems thinking—as COSMAX has—will be best positioned to build futures, not just products.

In sum, COSMAX stands as a living case study in purpose-centered leadership. It reminds us that influence does not always come from visibility, and that true innovation often lies in enabling others. In an increasingly complex and interconnected OBM landscape, Chairman Lee Kyung-soo's approach remains deeply relevant, demonstrating that true leadership lies in purposeful service, and that such service is the foundation of a lasting legacy.

References

Gartenberg, C., Prat, A., & Serafeim, G. (2019). Corporate purpose and financial performance. *Organization Science, 30*(1), 1–18.

George, B., Sims, P., McLean, A. N., & Mayer, D. (2007). Discovering your authentic leadership. *Harvard Business Review, 85*(2), 129.

Higo, M., Tsunoo, S., & Tanaka, J. (2020). The impact of the circular economy and the direction of Japanese companies: Transition from a mass consumption society to a circular society in the manufacturing industry. *Knowledge Creation and Integration, 28*(12), 20–33.

Imschloss, M., & Schwemmle, M. (2024). Value creation in post-pandemic retailing: A conceptual framework and implications. *Journal of Business Economics, 94*(6), 851–889.

Liu, C. L. E., & Zhang, Y. (2014). Learning process and capability formation in cross-border buyer–supplier relationships: A qualitative case study of Taiwanese technological firms. *International Business Review, 23*(4), 718–730.

Ng, S. C. H., Zhao, X., Fan, X., & Rungtusanatham, J. M. (2014). TQM and brand-building by Chinese original brand manufacturers: Impact on business performance. *International Journal of Production Research, 52*, 825–846.

O'Reilly, C. A., III., & Tushman, M. L. (2013). Organizational ambidexterity: Past, present, and future. *Academy of Management Perspectives, 27*(4), 324–338.

Porter, M. E., & Kramer, M. R. (2011). How to reinvent capitalism—And unleash a wave of innovation and growth. *Journal of Management and Sustainability Business, 323.*

Senoo, K. (2019). From new production and sales doctrine to existing product continued use doctrine: A consideration on the deconstruction of the 3Rs in response to the circular economy. *Proceedings of the Annual Conference of the Japan Society for Research Policy and Innovation Management, 34*, 7–10.

Sinek, S. (2009). *Start with why: How great leaders inspire everyone to take action*. Penguin.

Slama, D. (2023). Digital OEM. *The digital playbook: A Practitioner's guide to smart, connected products and solutions with AIoT* (pp. 71–82). Springer International Publishing.

Teece, D. J. (2007). Explicating dynamic capabilities: The nature and microfoundations of (sustainable) enterprise performance. *Strategic Management Journal, 28*(13), 1319–1350.

Chapter 4
Innovation at the Core: R&D Strategies for OBM

1 Introduction: R&D as a Strategic Engine in OBM

In the evolution from Original Equipment Manufacturing (OEM) and Original Design Manufacturing (ODM) to Original Brand Manufacturing (OBM), the strategic value of research and development (R&D) becomes profoundly amplified. Unlike OEMs and ODMs, which historically optimized production for efficiency and cost, OBMs must now pursue innovation, identity, and responsiveness at unprecedented levels. In this context, R&D is not a back-end support function but a core engine for market creation, product differentiation, and long-term value generation.

As Lee et al. (2015) note, the transition to OBM requires firms to reconfigure their innovation systems, particularly through the internalization of tacit knowledge and the creation of original design capabilities. These new capabilities extend beyond product engineering to include regulatory foresight, cultural adaptation, and consumer-driven formulation. For latecomer firms in Asia, such as those in South Korea and Japan, this transition has been catalyzed by external pressures to escape the low-margin manufacturing trap and enter high-value brand ecosystems (Higo et al., 2020).

R&D becomes the linchpin of this strategic shift. In OBM, innovation must be continuous, consumer-centric, and culturally attuned. It must not only produce new formulations but also integrate feedback from influencers, regulatory changes, and cross-border market dynamics. Kittilaksanawong (2015) emphasizes that in such contexts, the acquisition of path-breaking capabilities depends on both technological upgrading and organizational learning across networks of suppliers, customers, and regulators.

This section argues that OBM success depends on embedding R&D into the very DNA of brand management. It will explore how firms like COSMAX, a leading K-beauty contract manufacturer turned OBM enabler, have built globally integrated R&D platforms that support both indie and multinational brands. Through COSMAX, we observe a convergence of technology, science, regulation, and design

Y. W. Park et al., *Original Brand Manufacturing Business Model*,
https://doi.org/10.1007/978-981-95-0253-0_4

into a unified system that supports agility and innovation at scale. The sections that follow detail this transformation through theoretical frameworks and practical case analysis.

Moreover, as K-beauty transitions into a new premium-oriented phase, the role of R&D is being elevated even further. The Korean cosmetics industry, once known for "affordable innovation" or "value-for-money," has now shifted toward creating high-value, luxurious beauty products driven by proprietary technology and unique materials. According to recent reports, South Korea's cosmetics exports surpassed $10 billion in 2024, achieving record highs. In key advanced markets such as the United States and Japan, Korea has now overtaken France in import market share.

This transformation is being driven by firms like COSMAX, which enable the shift from mass-market appeal to premiumization. COSMAX has moved beyond its original ODM/OEM model and emerged as a strategic partner to OBM firms through its comprehensive R&D infrastructure. This includes global research hubs, AI-powered formulation engines, and region-specific compliance capabilities (such as for MoCRA in the United States and Halal certifications in Southeast Asia). The firm has pioneered innovations in formulation science, such as stable stick-type skincare products with enhanced usability and absorption—products now gaining global attention.

COSMAX's recent R&D achievements include securing patents related to an oil-dispersed stick-type cosmetic composition containing plant-based butter. This innovation improves upon traditional stick products that often fail to retain consistency or hydration in changing climates. In doing so, COSMAX not only addresses a rising consumer demand for hygienic and portable skincare but also creates a new category of high-function, high-convenience beauty products. These advances are now being applied to both indie and established brand portfolios seeking global expansion.

Such R&D-based differentiation reflects the broader shift in K-beauty from volume to value. As consumer tastes evolve toward sustainability, efficacy, and personalization, brands must align with suppliers who can offer next-generation scientific capabilities. COSMAX's model supports rapid co-development cycles with client firms, reducing time-to-market and fostering data-driven decision-making across the product lifecycle.

For instance, during the COVID-19 pandemic, COSMAX accelerated its investment in digital tools for trend forecasting and remote formulation collaboration. This enabled clients like Anua and Medicube to pivot quickly and maintain global sales momentum. By combining AI-enabled insight generation with cross-border production agility, COSMAX has established itself as the backbone of OBM success—not by building its own brand, but by enabling others to build differentiated, scalable, and compliant beauty platforms.

In short, the future of OBM is not in copying legacy products—it lies in mastering originality. The shift toward premium and science-backed skincare aligns perfectly with the OBM logic of brand equity, authenticity, and sustained consumer relationships. As stakeholders increasingly demand transparency, sustainability, and efficacy, R&D must evolve from a support role to a strategic leadership function. Korean firms, with their flexible innovation networks and rising global presence, are uniquely positioned to lead this transformation—and COSMAX is at the center of that evolution.

2 From Contract Manufacturing to Innovation Ownership

The transformation of COSMAX's R&D into a global OBM platform has been years in the making. According to the head of COSMAX's R&I center, the company's research organization started modestly in 1994 and underwent a major expansion after relocating to Pangyo in 2011. The previous research team was composed of around 50 members, but it has since grown into a global research institute with approximately 1,100 members, reflecting the company's scaling ambitions and its evolving innovation mandate.

This growth trajectory was guided in part by a leadership vision committed to purpose-driven innovation. The current research head, who joined COSMAX in 2010 after a tenure at Amorepacific, has played a pivotal role in shaping this evolution. Initially focused on ODM product development, COSMAX gradually built its capabilities in upstream innovation—covering everything from novel ingredient development and efficacy testing to global regulatory compliance. COSMAX's move into full-fledged OBM enablement was not incidental but the result of intentional investments in talent, infrastructure, and cross-functional integration.

The R&I Center (based on COSMAX, excluding BTI) has restructured its previously integrated formulation-based organization into a more specialized system and is now operating 23 labs to enhance global competitiveness (Fig. 1). It has newly established the PM Lab to strengthen expertise in mask sheets and pack formulations, the PS Lab to enhance capabilities in eco-friendly packaging, and has expanded and made the SC (Sun Care) Lab independent to drive innovation in sunscreen products. Among them, approximately 240 researchers are dedicated to formulation development. In addition to formulation, the analytics and materials divisions support specialized functions such as efficacy evaluation, stability testing, and regulatory alignment.

COSMAX operates on a matrix organizational structure introduced in 2015, combining domain expertise with interdisciplinary collaboration. For example, makeup and skincare researchers are housed in the same lab, fostering the development of hybrid products such as BB and CC creams.

This reorganization enables product development from multiple perspectives, encouraging novel combinations and category innovation. Experienced researchers (5+ years) focus on ideation and long-term innovation, while junior researchers specialize in rapid response product development aligned with market feedback.

Innovation at COSMAX is driven by a culture of proactive suggestion-making—an approach that founder Lee Kyung-soo encourages in order to differentiate from passive OEM models. Rather than waiting for customer requests, COSMAX formulates and pitches new textures, materials, and packaging formats. The successful development of jelly-type cosmetics (for shadow, blush, lip color, etc.)—a global

Fig. 1 Exterior view of COSMAX Pangyo headquarters

first—is a case in point. COSMAX's ability to propose innovations has led to deeper relationships with global giants like L'Oréal, who now entrust COSMAX with R&D for premium lines like Lancôme, Yves Saint Laurent, Kiehl's, and Shu Uemura.

Importantly, COSMAX's innovation function is both decentralized and globally responsive. In addition to its Pangyo R&I center, it operates regional research labs in the United States, China, and Southeast Asia. These centers address specific market preferences—for example, lightweight, humidity-resistant formulations for Southeast Asia—and feed into a centralized data ecosystem. The AI Lab within the R&I Center monitors trends, digital reviews, and emerging consumer behaviors, translating them into product opportunities.

COSMAX also conducts joint research with Seoul National University, Harvard University in the United States, Jiangnan and Fudan Universities in China, and the National University of Singapore, allocating significant funding to next-generation materials and biotechnology platforms. This proactive stance enables the company to address complex market expectations such as transparency, ingredient safety, and inclusivity.

The integration of AI and IoT into R&D processes is underway. COSMAX has begun collecting structured data on past product development, customer feedback, and formulation outcomes. The goal is to create a system that can simulate how specific consumer demands—such as texture, function, or fragrance—can be met through predictive formulation design. This digital transformation aligns with CEO Lee's vision to build a responsive, data-augmented innovation engine that is not limited by traditional development cycles.

Furthermore, COSMAX's innovation leadership is intertwined with its organizational philosophy. The research department is divided into agile teams responsible for exploring new categories and formats. Monthly benchmarking exercises and quarterly ideation sessions ensure a continuous inflow of new concepts. Among the numerous formulations developed each year, approximately 35% are ultimately selected through rigorous screening and testing, resulting in the launch of around 8,000 new products annually. This high trial-to-launch ratio ensures that only the most viable and competitive products reach the market.

Ultimately, the COSMAX R&D organization is structured for both depth and agility. It supports thousands of OBM clients by absorbing complex market signals, transforming them into technical opportunities, and operationalizing them into scalable product platforms. As retail models shift from mono-brand stores to multi-brand H&B formats and online-first experiences, COSMAX's responsive and suggestive R&D model becomes even more essential.

By integrating open innovation, digital governance, and ESG priorities into the very core of its R&D, COSMAX has repositioned itself from a manufacturer into a global innovation partner. Its Pangyo R&I center now symbolizes more than just a research hub—it is the nerve center of a distributed, forward-looking OBM ecosystem.

3 Knowledge Integration and Open Innovation Models

Another defining feature of OBM R&D strategies is the embrace of open innovation. Unlike traditional models of in-house R&D, which focus on internal resource optimization, open innovation emphasizes collaboration across organizational boundaries. As Liu and Zhang (2014) point out, OBMs can significantly enhance innovation by engaging in inter-organizational learning and alliance-based R&D. Such engagement allows access to diverse perspectives, faster knowledge transfer, and shared risk in experimentation.

This approach is particularly crucial in the cosmetics sector, where trends evolve rapidly and consumer trust hinges on transparency and efficacy. COSMAX exemplifies this paradigm with a hybrid open innovation strategy that draws on partnerships with academic institutions, dermatological research centers, material suppliers, and industry regulators. COSMAX's global research ecosystem enables continuous engagement with regional market dynamics and emerging scientific knowledge.

The firm's innovation model is underpinned by a matrix organizational structure implemented in 2015. Within COSMAX's 23 R&I labs (based on COSMAX, excluding BTI), cross-functional teams integrate skills in formulation, marketing, data analytics, and consumer insights. These interdisciplinary teams include experts from biology, chemistry, design, and the humanities—ensuring that product development accounts for both technical feasibility and cultural relevance.

COSMAX's open innovation framework encompasses both upstream and downstream collaboration. At the upstream end, COSMAX maintains long-standing research alliances with Seoul National University and other institutions to co-develop advanced materials, evaluate ingredient efficacy, and investigate biofunctional compounds. At the downstream end, it collaborates with OBM clients, digital influencers, and dermatological experts to co-develop formulations informed by real-time consumer feedback.

Internal interviews reveal that this structure fosters daily knowledge sharing across boundaries. For instance, global research teams stationed in China, Southeast Asia, and the US feed local trend data into COSMAX's centralized planning system. This system combines qualitative observations—such as changing consumer attitudes toward sustainability or skin inclusivity—with quantitative metrics derived from digital sentiment analysis and e-commerce reviews.

COSMAX's ideation model is particularly noteworthy. On a monthly basis, each lab conducts competitor benchmarking to evaluate emerging market innovations. Additionally, quarterly "ideation workshops" invite employees across departments to submit blue-sky product ideas—some of which combine unexpected elements like hybrid beauty/skincare categories or cross-functional textures.

The inclusion of junior and senior researchers in these workshops fosters a culture of democratized creativity. Junior scientists, often with less than five years' experience, are encouraged to focus on tactical responsiveness and trend mirroring. Senior researchers, on the other hand, engage in cross-category fusion and long-term pipeline planning. This dual-pronged structure—balancing speed and depth—enables COSMAX to support both incremental improvements and breakthrough innovations.

The interview with COSMAX's R&D leader underscores how the firm institutionalized "propositional R&D." Rather than passively responding to client briefs, COSMAX proactively suggests novel textures, formulations, and packaging concepts. These are often based on proprietary research or new patent filings. COSMAX's development of jelly-type color cosmetics, for example, set a global precedent and opened new categories for both color and base makeup.

A key enabler of this innovation culture is the firm's data-centric design system. COSMAX is in the process of building an AI-driven simulation environment that leverages past formulation data, consumer feedback, and environmental conditions to generate predictive models. These simulations guide R&D teams in assessing the feasibility, market fit, and regulatory viability of prospective products before physical prototyping.

Knowledge integration also extends to regulatory science. COSMAX's regulatory teams work in tandem with R&D personnel to interpret international guidelines—such as MoCRA, REACH, and halal regulations—and ensure that ingredient lists, packaging materials, and clinical claims align with local standards. This early-stage compliance integration minimizes costly reformulations and accelerates time-to-market.

COSMAX's open innovation model is not limited to large clients. The firm provides modular innovation services to indie and SME OBM brands. These include private label strategy kits and regulatory consulting. Through its R&I center and global sales offices, COSMAX facilitates rapid testing of these offerings in pilot markets such as Japan, Thailand, and the United States.

The organizational design supports real-time responsiveness to shifting retail environments. As the market has moved from single-brand storefronts to multi-brand

and online-first models, COSMAX's labs have developed products tailored to these formats. Teams now prototype formulations that cater to social media aesthetics (e.g., high-contrast finishes for TikTok), refillable packaging for H&B stores, and clean beauty certifications for online wellness platforms.

Moreover, COSMAX's digital transformation strategy includes creating a data repository for ingredient efficacy, consumer demographics, and formulation performance. This resource supports knowledge reuse and accelerates R&D cycles across regions. Since approximately 8,000 new products—about 35% of all newly developed items—are produced after going through a screening process, the ability to mine historical data for patterns and best practices is critical.

In summary, COSMAX's approach to knowledge integration and open innovation reflects a maturity well beyond traditional OEM or ODM frameworks. The firm has reimagined R&D not as a siloed function but as a porous, participatory, and scalable ecosystem. Through strategic partnerships, internal ideation frameworks, and digital augmentation, COSMAX offers a compelling model of how OBM firms can embed open innovation at the core of their strategy.

In doing so, COSMAX not only enhances its own agility but also acts as an enabler for hundreds of emerging OBM brands—especially those without access to high-end labs or regulatory expertise. It allows these clients to leapfrog from concept to market with confidence, speed, and technical sophistication.

The COSMAX model demonstrates that in the era of OBM, knowledge is not only power—it is the platform. The ability to integrate and circulate knowledge across borders, functions, and organizations distinguishes market leaders from mere participants. In that light, COSMAX's transformation is not simply about scaling innovation—it is about scaling trust, capability, and collaborative intelligence.

4 Regulatory-Driven Innovation and ESG Integration

In the current global beauty landscape, regulatory compliance and ESG (Environmental, Social, and Governance) considerations are no longer supplementary concerns—they are core to innovation itself. For OBM firms seeking to lead, regulatory awareness and sustainable design must be integrated at the earliest stages of R&D. As COSMAX has demonstrated, responding to complex compliance frameworks while simultaneously building ethical, future-ready products requires not only technical expertise but also organizational foresight.

As Park et al. (2023) emphasize in their case study on COSMAX, regulatory segmentation is now a foundational innovation strategy. COSMAX has strategically established specialized teams for distinct compliance areas—such as MoCRA (Modernization of Cosmetics Regulation Act) in the United States, OTC (Over-The-Counter) drug standards, halal certification for Muslim-majority markets, and EU's REACH regulations. These teams do not operate in isolation; they are embedded in the early R&D pipeline and co-develop products with formulators and packaging designers to ensure that regulatory alignment is a design feature, not a post-development fix.

The significance of this structure was reinforced in our interview with COSMAX's R&D leader, who described how the company's compliance teams are positioned as innovation catalysts. By collaborating with regulatory consultants and global watchdog organizations, COSMAX stays ahead of shifting standards. This proactive engagement minimizes reformulation risk and enables faster time-to-market in high-barrier jurisdictions like the United States, European Union, and Middle East.

In addition to regulatory foresight, COSMAX's ESG integration is exemplary. The company has committed to embedding sustainability principles across its innovation value chain. Since 2015, COSMAX has developed waterless formulations, refillable packaging designs, and natural ingredient portfolios. More recently, it has implemented traceability systems that allow brand partners and end consumers to verify the origin and ethicality of key raw materials.

Higo et al. (2020) describe such transitions as part of a broader shift toward the circular economy. COSMAX has internalized this shift by repurposing waste streams from its manufacturing processes, investing in biodegradable packaging materials, and launching pilot programs for carbon–neutral products. These practices are not only aligned with ESG goals but also reflect a new understanding of R&D as a conduit for public good.

Interview insights further support this trajectory. According to COSMAX's research head, the company has reorganized its R&I teams to include environmental scientists and ESG analysts. These professionals work closely with cosmetic chemists and packaging engineers to co-develop products that meet both market and regulatory expectations for sustainability. One example is the development of high-viscosity creams that use less plastic in packaging without compromising shelf life or user experience.

Moreover, COSMAX's regulatory innovation is underpinned by digital transformation. The company is investing in AI-based compliance monitoring tools that can automatically cross-reference formulations against evolving legal databases. This reduces human error and supports dynamic reformulation where needed. These systems also assist in tracking consumer feedback on issues like skin sensitivity or allergen content, enabling a closed-loop feedback cycle between compliance, product development, and consumer safety.

This digital approach aligns with Senoo's (2019) argument that sustainable innovation requires dismantling traditional 3R (Reduce, Reuse, Recycle) frameworks in favor of co-creative, data-driven ecosystems. COSMAX's IoT-integrated manufacturing system, which tracks carbon emissions, energy use, and water consumption in real time, is an example of how digital and sustainable priorities can be harmonized.

COSMAX also prioritizes social inclusion through its innovation agenda. It develops products tailored for a wide spectrum of consumers across geographies, skin types, and cultural norms. For instance, foundation products such as COSMAX's Cushion Foundation are representative examples (Fig. 2). Through an inclusive formulation protocol, COSMAX reflects the skin tones of diverse ethnic backgrounds

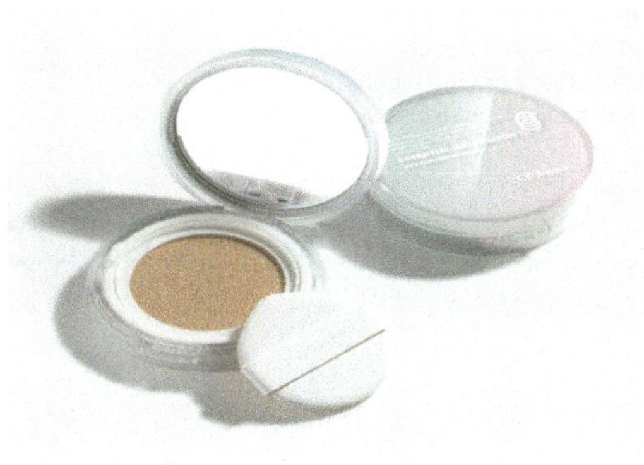

Fig. 2 COSMAX's cushion foundation product

in pigment design, while its safety and efficacy research team tracks regional climate conditions to ensure product performance across various usage scenarios. COSMAX developed a cushion foundation for the indie brand TIRTIR, which became the first Korean product to rank No. 1 in sales in Amazon's US beauty category. TIRTIR approached COSMAX in late 2023 with a request to create a cushion suitable for Black skin tones. Within just two months, by January of the following year, COSMAX began producing cushion foundations in 30 shades targeting multiethnic consumers. In the second half of that year, the number of shades increased to 40. The TIRTIR product manufactured by COSMAX quickly went viral on social media, praised for matching Black skin tones perfectly. The secret to launching a multi-shade cushion within two months of receiving the request lies in COSMAX's strong R&D capabilities. Having long produced liquid foundations for global companies like L'Oréal, COSMAX already possessed the technical expertise to develop cushions for multiethnic markets.

The firm's commitment to regulatory-driven ESG innovation is further evidenced by its training and talent development programs. COSMAX invests in upskilling researchers in sustainability. Workshops are held regularly on new cosmetic directives, ingredient safety thresholds, and eco-certification procedures. Figure 3 shows a researcher at the COSMAX R&I Center conducting a product safety assessment. This culture of continuous learning supports long-term resilience and aligns with Teece's (2007) emphasis on reconfigurable organizational capabilities.

One of the most compelling illustrations of this approach is COSMAX's early move to secure halal certification for its production facilities in Indonesia and Thailand. Unlike other firms that treat halal compliance as a marketing add-on, COSMAX embeds these requirements at the formulation stage, ensuring ingredient sourcing, water handling, and equipment sanitization conform to Islamic principles. This enables clients to export to Muslim-majority countries without additional verification steps.

Additionally, COSMAX's partnerships with universities and green-tech startups support the co-development of future-ready products. Projects underway include biodegradable glitter for eco-friendly makeup, marine-safe sunscreens, and

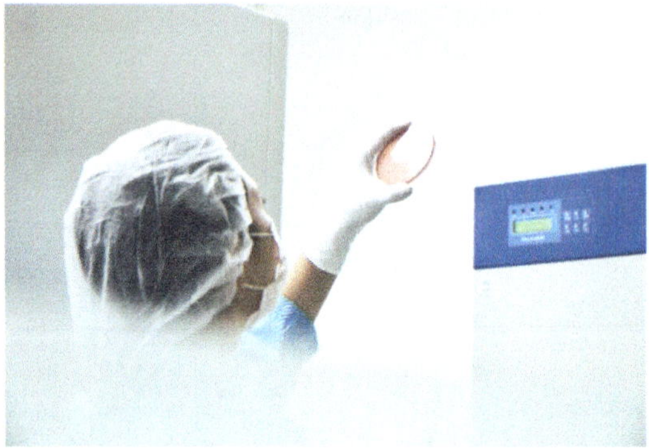

Fig. 3 A researcher at the COSMAX R&I center conducting a product safety assessment

probiotic-infused skincare. These innovations reflect the expanding scope of ESG in the beauty sector—from environmental impact to human microbiome safety.

Internally, COSMAX's matrix organizational structure facilitates ESG integration. R&D teams are cross-pollinated with compliance specialists, materials scientists, and consumer insight analysts. The goal is to ensure that every formulation or packaging design considers toxicity, recyclability, and user health as baseline criteria—not afterthoughts.

Even the firm's ideation process is structured to prioritize ESG. During quarterly ideation workshops, teams are encouraged to propose innovations that reduce plastic use, minimize carbon footprint, or meet new ethical sourcing guidelines. Approved ideas are fast-tracked into prototyping and tested in small markets to validate demand before large-scale rollout.

COSMAX's open innovation model complements this strategy. The firm collaborates with indie brands focused on sustainability, offering them access to proprietary clean beauty formulations and low carbon manufacturing lines. It also shares ESG-related consumer data and co-markets these attributes through customized brand storytelling support. This approach enables smaller brands to compete in premium sustainability segments without building in-house capabilities.

From a governance perspective, COSMAX reports ESG performance through third-party audited disclosures and aligns its R&D goals with the UN's Sustainable Development Goals (SDGs). These include SDG 12 (Responsible Consumption and Production), SDG 13 (Climate Action), and SDG 3 (Good Health and Well-Being). The company has also joined global initiatives like the Global Reporting Initiative (GRI) and CDP (Carbon Disclosure Project).

In conclusion, COSMAX's approach to regulatory-driven innovation and ESG integration reveals a new R&D paradigm—one that transcends compliance and actively reshapes value creation. Its organizational design, digital augmentation, and ecosystem partnerships illustrate how R&D can become a transformative force within the OBM model. Rather than seeing regulation and ESG as constraints, COSMAX has turned them into catalysts for brand differentiation, consumer trust, and long-term sustainability.

For OBM firms globally, this model offers a clear lesson: innovation must not only satisfy the consumer but also anticipate the future. That future is increasingly governed by ethical, environmental, and legal imperatives—and those who embed them into their core strategies today will define the industry tomorrow.

5 R&D as a Platform for Global OBM Enablement

COSMAX's research and development functions serve as a strategic platform for enabling global OBM transformation. Rather than following the conventional OEM approach of passively responding to client requests, COSMAX operates on a proactive innovation model cultivated under the leadership of founder Lee Kyung-soo. This model encourages continuous proposal-making across the product development pipeline—ranging from novel textures and active ingredients to packaging formats—positioning COSMAX as a co-creator rather than a subcontractor. The successful development of jelly-type cosmetics—across eye shadow, blush, and lip color—illustrates this philosophy in action. Figure 4 shows COSMAX's representative hybrid products, which are multi-lip & cheek and multi-balm products.

As the first company to commercialize such a formulation globally, COSMAX demonstrated its ability to lead innovation and shape new market segments. This capacity for initiative-driven R&D has deepened collaborative relationships with major global OBM firms such as L'Oréal, who now entrust COSMAX with R&D responsibilities for their premium lines, including Shu Uemura.

Structurally, the COSMAX R&D organization is designed for both depth in technical expertise and agility in responding to market shifts. It supports thousands of OBM clients worldwide by capturing fragmented consumer signals across geographies and channels, translating them into formulation strategies, and operationalizing them into scalable product platforms. As distribution models shift from mono-brand stores to multi-brand H&B formats and e-commerce-first strategies, COSMAX's responsive R&D infrastructure becomes increasingly essential for supporting brand differentiation and speed-to-market.

Furthermore, COSMAX has embedded open innovation principles, digital governance systems, and ESG-oriented design into the core of its R&D operations. This integration transforms its R&D function into more than a technical capability—it becomes a systemic enabler for sustainable, high-impact OBM growth. The Pangyo R&I Center, serving as the nucleus of this global innovation architecture, acts as a knowledge-sharing hub and platform for cross-border collaboration, thereby reinforcing COSMAX's position as a strategic partner in global OBM ecosystems. Through this multifaceted R&D platform, COSMAX not only delivers product innovation but also empowers OBM clients with the speed, flexibility, and insight required to compete in diverse and rapidly evolving markets.

Fig. 4 COSMAX's representative hybrid products

6 Conclusion: Reframing R&D as the Strategic Core of OBM Success

In the dynamic, consumer-driven world of Original Brand Manufacturing (OBM), research and development (R&D) is no longer a behind-the-scenes function—it is the strategic nucleus of value creation, brand differentiation, and sustainable growth. The preceding sections of this chapter have examined how leading firms, particularly COSMAX, have redefined R&D from a linear, internalized process into a collaborative, platform-based innovation ecosystem that empowers brands across the global beauty industry.

What becomes evident is that the transition from OEM/ODM to OBM is not merely a matter of branding or marketing. It requires a fundamental reconfiguration of organizational strategy, knowledge flows, and technological capabilities. In this context, COSMAX serves as a global benchmark—demonstrating how a manufacturer can evolve into a purpose-driven enabler of OBM success through world-class innovation infrastructure.

From the outset, the journey from contract manufacturing to innovation ownership establishes a crucial foundation. For decades, firms in the beauty sector succeeded by optimizing production costs and supply chains. However, OBM demands a different mindset—one that prioritizes originality, consumer experience, and brand authenticity. COSMAX's investment in global R&I centers, automation, and AI analytics signals a clear departure from transactional production toward proactive, knowledge-driven innovation. Its capability to localize innovation while maintaining global consistency is a testament to the maturity of its innovation engine.

The shift toward open innovation models reflects another crucial turning point in OBM strategy. No longer is R&D confined within the boundaries of the firm. COSMAX's approach to co-developing products with ingredient suppliers, dermatological researchers, and digital content creators reveals the power of ecosystem collaboration. This aligns with the principles articulated by scholars like Chesbrough (2003) and Liu and Zhang (2014), who emphasize the strategic advantage of external knowledge integration. In the OBM landscape, where speed, trust, and consumer insight are paramount, open innovation is not optional—it is imperative.

Yet, innovation in the OBM era is not only about novelty and speed—it must also be ethical, sustainable, and compliant. This chapter also underscored the increasing centrality of regulation and ESG mandates in R&D strategy. COSMAX's regulatory segmentation model—featuring dedicated teams for MoCRA, halal, and OTC compliance—is illustrative of a new kind of integrated innovation logic. Rather than treating compliance as a barrier, COSMAX embeds it into the design phase, ensuring that all products are market-ready from inception. Its use of AI technology for ingredient traceability, investment in waterless formulations, and commitment to inclusive dermatological testing demonstrate how ESG and innovation can operate in tandem to future-proof OBM offerings.

Perhaps the most transformative dimension is the platformization of R&D, as discussed before. COSMAX's innovation-as-a-service model dismantles the traditional silo between manufacturer and brand. Instead, it offers a scalable infrastructure that provides indie and multinational brands alike with rapid access to product libraries, regulatory intelligence, consumer analytics, and content creation. This is not merely a support function—it is a strategic enabler that empowers brands to focus on storytelling, customer connection, and market expansion. Through this platform, COSMAX becomes more than a supplier; it is a co-author of brand success and a curator of innovation culture across markets.

The broader implication is that R&D, when reimagined through the lens of OBM, becomes a unifying capability—integrating technology, creativity, compliance, and sustainability. It becomes the connective tissue that aligns a firm's internal assets with the dynamic conditions of global beauty markets. It enables agility without chaos, personalization without complexity, and compliance without delay.

Moreover, the COSMAX case challenges the industry to think beyond the traditional dichotomies of scale versus creativity, standardization versus localization, and ownership versus partnership. In its model, innovation is distributed yet coordinated, customized yet compliant, and data-driven yet deeply human. It represents the next frontier of OBM R&D: one where firms operate not as isolated innovators, but as orchestrators of global, inclusive, and ethically grounded innovation networks.

As the OBM sector continues to evolve—shaped by AI, consumer empowerment, and cross-cultural exchange—the ability to operationalize innovation at scale while maintaining flexibility and values alignment will determine long-term leadership. R&D, therefore, is not just about better products—it is about building better systems for value delivery, trust creation, and purpose-driven growth.

In closing, this chapter has shown that innovation is not the domain of laboratories alone; it is a firm-wide, ecosystem-enabled, and socially accountable practice. For OBM firms navigating the complexities of global competition, regulatory scrutiny, and consumer activism, COSMAX offers a compelling vision: a future where R&D is not just an internal advantage, but a shared asset that accelerates excellence for all.

References

Chesbrough, H. (2003). The logic of open innovation: Managing intellectual property. *California Management Review, 45*(3), 33–58.

Higo, M., Tsunoo, S., & Tanaka, J. (2020). The impact of the circular economy and the direction of Japanese companies: Transition from a mass consumption society to a circular society in the manufacturing industry. *Knowledge Creation and Integration, 28*(12), 20–33.

Kittilaksanawong, W. (2015). How do emerging economy firms learn to evolve from contract manufacturing to own brand management? *Global Enterprise Management, 2*, 1–17.

Lee, K., Song, J., & Kwak, J. (2015). An exploratory study on the transition from OEM to OBM: Case studies of SMEs in Korea. *Industry and Innovation, 22*(5), 423–442.

Liu, C. L. E., & Zhang, Y. (2014). Learning process and capability formation in cross-border buyer–supplier relationships: A qualitative case study of Taiwanese technological firms. *International Business Review, 23*(4), 718–730.

Park, H., Hong, S., & Shin, H. (2023). Rising and thriving in the post COVID-19 era: A case study of COSMAX, a leader of the Korean cosmetic industry. *Asia Pacific Business Review, 29*(4), 1105–1124.

Senoo, K. (2019). From new production and sales doctrine to existing product continued use doctrine: A consideration on the deconstruction of the 3Rs in response to the circular economy. *Proceedings of the Annual Conference of the Japan Society for Research Policy and Innovation Management, 34*, 7–10.

Teece, D. J. (2007). Explicating dynamic capabilities: The nature and microfoundations of (sustainable) enterprise performance. *Strategic Management Journal, 28*(13), 1319–1350.

Chapter 5
Building Brand Power: Marketing Strategies for OBM

1 Introduction

The journey from Original Equipment Manufacturing (OEM) to Original Brand Manufacturing (OBM) marks a pivotal transformation in the strategic orientation of firms, especially in emerging economies. While OEM firms primarily compete on cost-efficiency, OBM firms are value creators, embedding their identity, vision, and values into products that resonate with consumers. At the heart of this transformation lies a critical lever: branding.

Branding is no longer a superficial concern relegated to logos and taglines; it has evolved into a complex, strategic process that defines how a firm is perceived and experienced in the marketplace. In a hypercompetitive, globalized environment, where commoditization can rapidly erode margins, branding allows OBM firms to carve out distinct market positions, command premium pricing, and build enduring customer relationships. It is through branding that OBM firms articulate their purpose, cultivate emotional bonds with consumers, and tell stories that connect across cultures.

Marketing in the OBM context shifts from promoting products to managing perceptions, experiences, and values. This requires a rethinking of traditional marketing roles and the development of capabilities in market intelligence, storytelling, digital engagement, and customer co-creation. It also demands organizational alignment—from product development to sales to after-service—around a unified brand vision. For many firms transitioning from OEM to OBM, this shift entails not only external repositioning but also deep internal transformation.

In Asia, where manufacturing prowess has historically been prioritized over brand building, the move toward OBM represents a significant strategic leap. Countries like Korea, Taiwan, and China have seen a surge in firms aspiring to launch their own brands on the global stage. Yet, while the manufacturing infrastructure is often mature, the branding and marketing ecosystems are still evolving. OBM firms in these regions face the dual challenge of developing globally resonant brands while

Y. W. Park et al., *Original Brand Manufacturing Business Model*,
https://doi.org/10.1007/978-981-95-0253-0_5

navigating domestic institutional gaps, talent shortages, and legacy mindsets rooted in OEM paradigms.

Amid these challenges, success stories have begun to emerge. Korean firms such as Samsung, LG, and Hyundai have become household names worldwide, demonstrating the potential for Asian firms to compete not just in production, but in brand equity. In the cosmetics sector, OBM-oriented ODMs like COSMAX are enabling a new wave of brand innovation by integrating marketing and R&D functions, leveraging digital platforms, and cultivating deep customer insights.

The rise of digital technologies has further altered the branding landscape. Social media, influencer marketing, AI-driven personalization, and e-commerce have revolutionized how consumers discover, evaluate, and engage with brands. For OBM firms, digital tools offer powerful means to reach global audiences, test product concepts rapidly, and build communities around shared values. However, they also demand speed, agility, and a data-savvy mindset—qualities that may be underdeveloped in firms with OEM legacies.

Furthermore, OBM branding today must be grounded in authenticity and purpose. Consumers increasingly seek brands that align with their values, stand for more than profit, and contribute positively to society and the environment. Purpose-driven branding, therefore, is not just a trend but a strategic imperative. OBM firms must not only differentiate on function and form but also convey a larger mission—whether related to sustainability, inclusivity, or cultural relevance.

This chapter delves into the core marketing strategies that OBM firms deploy to build brand power. Drawing on interdisciplinary research and rich field data across Asian firms, particularly in Korea, China, and Taiwan, we explore the evolution of marketing capabilities, the rise of digital ecosystems, and the strategic dilemmas encountered during the branding journey. Anchored by the case of COSMAX, we examine how technology, creativity, and customer-centricity converge in the OBM paradigm. By unpacking both the triumphs and tensions of branding in OBM transitions, we aim to provide a roadmap for firms seeking to craft resilient, resonant, and globally competitive brands.

2 Strategic Shifts: From Cost-Based Competition to Brand Value

The shift from Original Equipment Manufacturing (OEM) to Original Brand Manufacturing (OBM) is more than a change in business model—it represents a fundamental redefinition of what it means to create and capture value in a globalized economy. In the OEM paradigm, firms are positioned at the back-end of the value chain, tasked with executing the designs, specifications, and production plans of brand-owning clients. Their primary competitive levers are cost efficiency, process optimization, and delivery reliability. Margins are thin, differentiation is low, and customer loyalty is transactional.

By contrast, OBM places the firm at the forefront of the value chain. OBM firms must conceive, create, and communicate a unique value proposition that is embodied in their brand. This includes defining a brand vision, establishing a distinctive voice, and building trust with consumers across channels and borders. The transition from OEM to OBM requires a shift in organizational mindset—from manufacturing to marketing, from inputs to outcomes, and from cost-cutting to value creation.

2.1 From Commodities to Experiences

In OEM, products are often undifferentiated and fungible—one component is easily substituted for another. OBM demands the opposite: products must be imbued with meaning, identity, and emotional resonance. This means OBM firms must shift their strategic focus from producing commodities to delivering experiences. A smartphone is not just a device; it is a lifestyle symbol. A skincare product is not merely a formulation; it is a promise of beauty, wellness, or self-care.

Such experiential branding requires investments in design, customer insight, storytelling, and brand positioning. It also calls for a deeper understanding of culture, psychology, and societal trends. Firms must ask: What do we stand for? Who do we serve? Why do our products matter in the lives of consumers?

2.2 Customer Ownership and Relationship Building

One of the most significant shifts in OBM is the firm's ownership of the customer relationship. OEM firms typically operate behind the scenes, with little to no direct engagement with end users. OBM firms, by contrast, must develop, manage, and nurture customer relationships through marketing campaigns, customer service, loyalty programs, and direct sales channels.

This requires new capabilities in customer data management, omnichannel engagement, and community-building. It also introduces new risks—brand visibility brings reputational exposure, and customer expectations become more demanding. But it also offers the opportunity to build brand equity that drives repeat purchases, word-of-mouth referrals, and long-term value.

2.3 Strategic Autonomy and Global Positioning

Another major transformation is the pursuit of strategic autonomy. OEM firms are often dependent on a few major clients and subject to their terms and timelines. OBM firms, by creating their own brands, gain control over pricing, product development, and market entry strategies. This autonomy enables them to pursue differentiated positioning and long-term growth.

Global positioning becomes a key concern. OBM firms must decide how to present their brand in international markets—whether to adopt a standardized global image or tailor offerings to local tastes. This involves brand architecture decisions (e.g., umbrella branding vs. sub-branding), cultural adaptation, and partnerships with local distributors or digital platforms.

2.4 Organizational Transformation and Capability Building

Internally, the shift to OBM necessitates the restructuring of teams, processes, and performance metrics. Marketing becomes a strategic function, not merely a support service. R&D must align with brand vision and consumer trends. Human resources must recruit and retain creative talent, brand strategists, and digital marketers.

Leadership must also evolve. OEM leaders often have engineering or operations backgrounds. OBM leaders need to be brand storytellers, market shapers, and customer advocates. The shift from back-end execution to front-end innovation changes the firm's identity and the competencies it must develop.

2.5 Branding as a Strategic Resource

In the OBM landscape, brand is more than a logo or a name; it is a strategic asset that encapsulates firm identity, consumer trust, and long-term competitiveness. According to Yan et al. (2011), successful OBM transformations in Taiwan involved strategic leadership that could navigate this shift, balancing legacy OEM operations with new brand-building imperatives.

A brand acts as a signal of quality, a repository of trust, and a vehicle for storytelling. It differentiates a firm's offerings in crowded markets and provides a psychological shortcut for consumer decision-making. Strong brands enable price premiums, reduce marketing costs over time, and provide resilience during downturns.

2.6 The Economics of Branding: Value Capture vs. Value Creation

OEM firms are typically value creators—they add technical and operational value to a product. OBM firms, however, are positioned to capture more value. By owning the brand, they control the customer relationship, determine pricing, and shape perceptions.

Consider a beauty product manufactured for an international brand: the OEM may receive a few dollars per unit, while the brand captures tenfold that amount through its control of retail pricing, marketing, and positioning. OBM transforms firms from being subcontractors to market makers.

2.7 Brand Equity as a Competitive Moat

Brand equity is the accumulated value of customer perceptions, experiences, and expectations. It functions as a competitive moat by making customers more likely to choose the brand over alternatives, even when price or features are comparable.

Developing brand equity requires consistent delivery on the brand promise, emotional resonance, and active engagement with audiences. It is not a static asset—it must be nurtured through innovation, relevance, and responsiveness. In dynamic markets, the ability to renew and reinforce brand equity is a key determinant of sustained success.

2.8 Case Examples from Asia

In Korea, companies like LG and Amorepacific have made the leap from domestic brands to global brands. LG, once known primarily as a manufacturing powerhouse, now commands respect for its innovation-led, design-forward brand positioning. Amorepacific has built strong beauty brands with global appeal, combining traditional Korean ingredients with modern marketing.

Taiwanese firms such as Giant Bicycles and ASUS have also successfully branded themselves as leaders in their categories. Their global transitions were marked by strategic investments in design, global branding campaigns, and distribution networks. They also engaged in partnerships with influencers, athletes, and media to amplify brand narratives.

In China, firms like Huawei and Haier have moved from contract manufacturing to OBM, though often facing geopolitical and branding challenges. Their strategies highlight the importance of intellectual property protection, local adaptation, and global branding efforts that go beyond price and function.

2.9 Digital Shift and Its Strategic Implications

The digital revolution has transformed the strategic logic of branding. Digital platforms allow even small OBM firms to access global markets, build direct-to-consumer channels, and gather real-time customer feedback. At the same time, the pace of competition has accelerated, requiring rapid adaptation and innovation.

In this context, digital brand presence—through websites, social media, e-commerce, and content platforms—is critical. Brand reputation can be made or broken online. Thus, OBM firms must invest in digital storytelling, search engine optimization (SEO), social listening, and performance marketing.

Furthermore, data analytics enables firms to understand consumer behavior, personalize offerings, and optimize marketing spend. Digital transformation is not optional—it is central to the OBM value proposition.

2.10 From Supplier to Brand Owner

The strategic shift from OEM to OBM is not merely a marketing upgrade—it is a fundamental change in how value is created, delivered, and captured. It requires a rethinking of the firm's mission, structure, capabilities, and leadership. Branding becomes the linchpin of this transformation.

By owning the brand, OBM firms gain control over their destiny. They move from being invisible suppliers to visible creators, from cost-driven subcontractors to experience-driven innovators. This shift is complex and challenging, but it also opens the door to long-term resilience, global recognition, and sustainable growth.

In the OBM landscape, brand is more than a logo or a name; it is a strategic asset that encapsulates firm identity, consumer trust, and long-term competitiveness. Moreover, a strong brand enables price premiums, resilience against market shocks, and enhanced bargaining power in global value chains. It becomes a key source of competitive advantage, especially when aligned with marketing, design, and innovation functions.

3 Core Branding Capabilities for OBM Firms

Transitioning to OBM entails the cultivation of new capabilities, particularly within the marketing domain. Research highlights several core areas where OBM firms must excel, each of which plays a vital role in establishing brand identity, communicating value, and fostering customer loyalty.

3.1 *Brand Identity and Storytelling*

Developing a coherent and compelling brand identity is foundational to any OBM strategy. A brand is not simply a name or a logo; it embodies a firm's ethos, personality, and promise to the consumer. Effective branding connects at an emotional level, creating a sense of familiarity, aspiration, and trust.

Storytelling is a crucial tool in this process. Through narratives that reflect the brand's origin, mission, and values, OBM firms can differentiate themselves in saturated markets. A compelling story humanizes the brand, makes it relatable, and inspires customer loyalty. For instance, Japanese cosmetic brands often leverage traditional narratives or craftsmanship to create a sense of heritage and authenticity.

In the OBM context, storytelling must be adapted to multiple cultural contexts. Global brands often tailor their stories to reflect local values while maintaining a consistent core identity. This glocalization of brand storytelling requires deep cultural sensitivity and narrative agility.

3.2 *Market Intelligence and Customer Proximity*

Customer-centricity is at the heart of successful branding. OBM firms must go beyond demographics to understand psychographics—the values, aspirations, and lifestyles that influence purchase decisions. This involves continuous engagement with customers through surveys, social listening, in-depth interviews, ethnographic research, and digital analytics.

Market intelligence also includes trend forecasting and competitive analysis. OBM firms must be able to sense emerging trends in fashion, technology, and society, and align their product offerings accordingly. For example, the growing demand for clean beauty or gender-neutral products requires brands to adapt quickly or risk becoming obsolete.

Customer proximity is not just about understanding but about participation. Leading OBM firms involve consumers in product development, allowing for co-creation and rapid iteration. This participatory approach fosters a sense of ownership and loyalty among customers, turning them into brand advocates.

3.3 *Design Management and Aesthetic Strategy*

Design plays a dual role in OBM: functional innovation and symbolic differentiation. Product design influences usability, desirability, and brand perception. Strong design management ensures that aesthetic and functional aspects align with brand identity and consumer expectations.

Leading OBM firms integrate design thinking into all stages of product development, from ideation to prototyping to market launch. Design teams work closely with R&D, marketing, and branding departments to ensure coherence and relevance. Companies like Apple and Dyson have shown how superior design can become a core part of the brand's competitive advantage.

In the beauty and fashion sectors, packaging design is particularly important. It not only protects the product but also conveys brand value, sustainability commitments, and lifestyle positioning. Innovative packaging, sustainable materials, and tactile appeal all contribute to consumer perception.

3.4 Innovation and Product-Market Fit

OBM success hinges on innovation that aligns with consumer needs and brand positioning. Innovation can take the form of technological advancement, new business models, or reimagined customer experiences. The key is not innovation for its own sake but innovation that resonates with consumers and reinforces the brand.

For example, in the skincare industry, firms are increasingly adopting AI and biotech to offer personalized solutions. OBM firms that embed innovation into their branding narrative are better positioned to capture early adopters and thought leaders.

Product-market fit is not static. OBM firms must continuously refine their offerings based on feedback, reviews, and evolving trends. Agile development processes, iterative design, and MVP (minimum viable product) testing can help ensure that products meet market needs while reinforcing the brand's image.

3.5 Channel Strategy and Brand Experience

How and where consumers experience a brand is as important as the product itself. OBM firms must curate end-to-end brand experiences across multiple touchpoints—retail, online, events, and customer service.

Channel strategy should reflect the brand's positioning. Premium brands may focus on exclusive boutiques and high-end department stores, while mass-market brands might prioritize online marketplaces and discount retailers. The rise of D2C (direct-to-consumer) channels offers OBM firms a chance to control the narrative, pricing, and customer relationship more directly.

Brand experience includes the aesthetics of the retail space, the tone of customer interactions, the usability of the website, and the packaging of the product. OBM firms must ensure that these elements are harmonized to deliver a seamless and memorable customer journey.

3.6 Internal Brand Alignment and Organizational Culture

A brand is not only what a company says externally; it is also what it believes and practices internally. OBM firms must cultivate internal brand alignment by ensuring that employees understand, believe in, and live the brand values. This requires effective internal communication, training, and leadership.

Organizational culture is a key enabler of brand consistency. Employees across departments should be encouraged to see themselves as brand ambassadors. Customer service representatives, salespeople, and product designers should all be aligned in delivering the brand promise.

Some firms use internal storytelling, rituals, and recognition programs to reinforce brand values. For example, employee onboarding programs often include brand immersion sessions that introduce new hires to the brand's history, mission, and customer expectations.

3.7 Metrics and Performance Measurement

Building brand power requires rigorous performance measurement. OBM firms must track both short-term marketing metrics and long-term brand equity indicators. Key performance indicators (KPIs) might include brand awareness and recognition, net promoter score (NPS), share of voice and media impact, customer lifetime value (CLV), return on marketing investment (ROMI), and emotional connection and brand favorability.

These metrics help OBM firms assess the effectiveness of branding initiatives and guide future investments. Advanced analytics can also help firms segment customers, predict churn, and personalize offerings.

3.8 Resilience and Crisis Management

Strong brands are not immune to crises, but they are better equipped to weather them. OBM firms must develop capabilities in crisis communication, reputation management, and brand recovery. When faced with scandals, product recalls, or public backlash, a well-prepared firm can mitigate damage and even strengthen customer loyalty through transparency and accountability.

Proactive brand governance—including social media monitoring, scenario planning, and stakeholder engagement—is essential. OBM firms must also consider brand risks related to supply chain ethics, labor practices, and environmental sustainability, which are increasingly scrutinized by consumers and investors alike.

3.9 *Purpose-Driven Branding*

In the contemporary marketplace, brands are increasingly expected to take stands on social and environmental issues. Purpose-driven branding aligns business goals with broader societal values. OBM firms that articulate a clear purpose—such as environmental stewardship, inclusivity, or community empowerment—can build deeper emotional connections with consumers.

Purpose must be authentic and embedded across the organization. It cannot be reduced to one-off campaigns or superficial claims. Brands like Patagonia and The Body Shop have demonstrated how purpose can drive loyalty, attract talent, and create a resilient brand community.

For OBM firms in Asia, purpose-driven branding also involves engaging with local communities, honoring cultural heritage, and contributing to national development goals. These efforts reinforce legitimacy and trust.

4 COSMAX Case Study: Digital Transformation in OBM Marketing

The case of COSMAX offers a nuanced view into how a firm that began as a contract manufacturer evolved into a global innovation hub, seamlessly integrating digital transformation, global market responsiveness, and customer-centric marketing to empower OBM growth. Drawing from interviews with COSMAX executives and an extensive review of recent industry developments, this section explores COSMAX's transformation and its far-reaching impact on the OBM ecosystem.

4.1 *COSMAX's Rise: From ODM to OBM Enabler*

COSMAX's journey from a behind-the-scenes producer to a front-line innovator encapsulates the shifting dynamics of the global cosmetics industry. As one of Korea's two dominant ODM firms—alongside Kolmar—COSMAX has shaped not just product pipelines but also brand trajectories. According to internal data, COSMAX's revenue surpassed that of its long-time Italian competitor Intercos in 2015. COSMAX's rise as the global No.1 leader in the ODM sector demonstrates its ability to harmoniously combine outstanding formulation capabilities with a customer-centric marketing strategy. Figure 1 illustrates COSMAX's extraordinary growth over a 30-year period (1994–2024), during which the company achieved a compound annual growth rate (CAGR) exceeding 30%. Starting with annual revenue of ₩10 billion in the first decade, COSMAX expanded to ₩100 billion in the second decade, and reached ₩1 trillion in the third—demonstrating a consistent tenfold growth every 10 years. Growth milestones segmented by intervals of 5, 11, 8, 3,

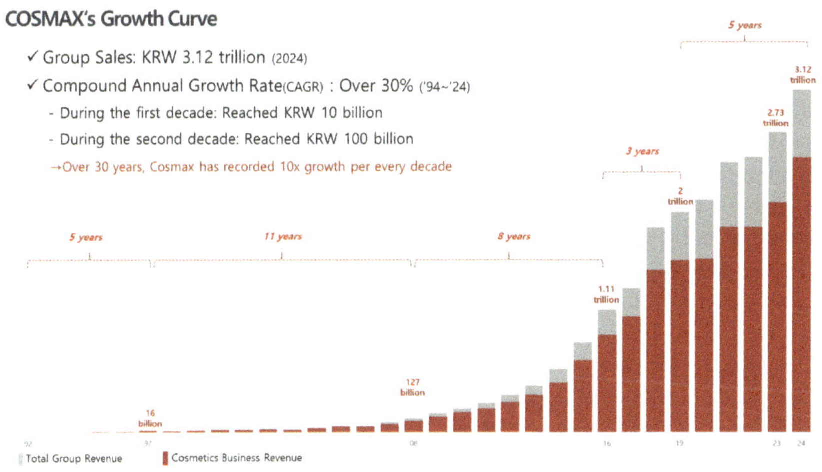

Fig. 1 COSMAX's growth curve

and 5 years, showing accelerated scaling in recent years. This remarkable trajectory reflects COSMAX's transformation from a behind-the-scenes manufacturer to a global OBM (Original Brand Manufacturing) leader. The company's commitment to R&I, design innovation, and customer-centric branding has enabled its evolution into a data-driven, sustainability-conscious brand partner—empowering both indie and multinational brands worldwide.

COSMAX's formula library spans every category of cosmetic products, enabling rapid response to market needs. Its breadth allows it to serve multinational OBMs and agile startups alike. COSMAX highlights that COSMAX's rise has hinged on three interlocking pillars: speed, quality, and trust. Product life cycles are now as short as 12 months, necessitating rapid development cycles. COSMAX has reduced global time-to-market from 18 months to as little as 6 months in key markets like China.

This acceleration is enabled by trust. COSMAX's lab infrastructure is so advanced that global clients like L'Oréal now accept its data without requiring external validation. Such confidence has allowed COSMAX to operate as a partner rather than just a vendor.

4.2 *A New Era of Flexibility and Digital Integration*

At the core of COSMAX's operational model is its "One COSMAX" strategy—an integrated system that links headquarters with semi-autonomous regional branches through shared protocols, trend analysis, and compliance frameworks. This coordination allows COSMAX to deliver regionally tailored products while maintaining global consistency.

Digital integration plays a pivotal role. Rather than investing blindly in AI hype, COSMAX has focused on digital tools with demonstrable impact. Influencer mapping, real-time trend analytics, and integrated digital planning dashboards are now part of its day-to-day operations. Robotics and AI are increasingly used in production and testing phases, boosting small-batch capabilities and enabling agile experimentation.

This system ensures that when a digital-first OBM or influencer brand initiates a product, COSMAX can manage the concept-to-shelf lifecycle quickly and with design precision. These capabilities are critical in an environment where visual identity and speed-to-market are decisive factors for brand success.

4.3 Supporting the Indie and Influencer Ecosystem

Perhaps COSMAX's most transformative contribution lies in its role as a launchpad for indie and influencer brands. Recent years have seen a wave of influencers and creators entering the cosmetics industry—often without the capital or infrastructure traditionally required. COSMAX has become the engine behind this democratization.

One high-profile example is the launch of "reii reii" by Park Mak-Rye, a content creator who transitioned into beauty entrepreneurship. COSMAX supported this launch from ideation to delivery, providing packaging design, formulation customization, and compliance guidance. This is emblematic of a broader shift: micro-entrepreneurs have become brand owners, and COSMAX has become their steadfast partner.

COSMAX's domestic marketing department has built a team that supports approximately 10,000 SKUs annually. The online sales division—founded to respond to the rise of D2C and social commerce—includes a dedicated unit that assists influencers and startups with packaging, regulatory paperwork, and even promotional strategy. With MOQs as low as 1,000 units and an R&D structure that allows for rapid prototyping, COSMAX levels the playing field for newcomers.

4.4 Global Expansion, Local Sensitivity

COSMAX's global strategy hinges on tailoring solutions for specific markets. In the UAE, where K-beauty exports nearly doubled between 2023 and 2024, COSMAX launched climate-specific products with light, non-greasy formulations and suncare integration. Its Middle East task force explores not just product ingredients but packaging and cultural resonance.

Meanwhile, in Japan, COSMAX has invested heavily in localization. Through its collaboration with Qoo10 Japan—now the top K-beauty platform in the country—it has introduced lip and base products tuned to Japanese sensibilities. A new factory is scheduled for construction to support long-term growth in this highly discerning market.

In the United States, COSMAX's West Coast office in LA targets the celebrity and influencer market. The partnership with Selena Gomez's Rare Beauty exemplifies this strategy. COSMAX's ability to deliver fast, customized, high-quality products makes it attractive to indie American brands looking to scale quickly.

Emerging markets such as Indonesia and Latin America are also part of COSMAX's roadmap. A new Latin American hub is being planned, designed to service not just local demand but also act as a gateway for North American expansion.

4.5 Navigating Digital Risk and Strategic Complexity

While the rise of TikTok and Instagram has enabled OBMs to achieve viral growth, these channels are also sources of strategic uncertainty. The looming TikTok ban in the United States underscores the vulnerability of single-channel marketing. COSMAX responds by advising clients to diversify across platforms—Amazon, YouTube Shorts, local e-commerce—and by building multi-channel marketing kits. Figure 2 illustrates a top-selling product on Amazon developed in collaboration with COSMAX and shows a collection of eight cosmetic products displayed in two rows. The top row includes products labeled "Anua," "Gahi," "TIRTIR," and "Rom&nd." The bottom row features products labeled "COSRX," "Abib," "Beauty of Joseon," and "Goodal." Each product is accompanied by its respective Korean name.

Fig. 2 Amazon bestseller with COSMAX

Moreover, COSMAX closely monitors changes in digital privacy laws, AI regulation, and global logistics bottlenecks. It uses this foresight to help OBMs navigate market risks. Its RA (Regulatory Affairs) team ensures that every product meets the evolving standards of target markets—from FDA approvals in the United States. to Halal certification in Southeast Asia.

4.6 Scaling Production and Strategic Alliances

COSMAX now has an annual production capacity of over 3.2 billion units across its global factories. Its production footprint includes Korea, China, the United States, Indonesia, Thailand, and soon Japan. These locations were chosen to balance cost, talent, and proximity to high-growth regions. Automation is central to COSMAX's ability to maintain speed and quality at scale.

To support its indie brand partners, COSMAX is building modular production systems that can handle smaller orders without disrupting large-scale operations. AI is being introduced into manufacturing workflows to improve yield prediction, color matching, and inventory management.

Strategic partnerships are another growth driver. COSMAX's alliance with Qoo10 Japan targets the creation of 20 "unicorn" beauty brands with 100 billion yen (approximately 980 billion KRW) valuations. This ambitious plan, publicly announced in 2025, includes full-stack support from product development to e-commerce logistics. Similarly, COSMAX's collaborations with Amazon and TikTok influencers have yielded viral hits in the United States and Southeast Asia.

4.7 COSMAX and the OBM Future

The evolution of COSMAX from a traditional ODM to a full-spectrum OBM enabler reflects a broader transformation in the beauty industry. Where once only large corporations could build globally relevant brands, now influencers and niche entrepreneurs can do the same—with COSMAX as their infrastructure.

The firm's integration of digital marketing insight, global regulatory navigation, and production agility makes it uniquely positioned to shape the next decade of OBM. Its ability to move between roles—as formulator, designer, advisor, and manufacturer—redefines the possibilities of what an ODM can be.

As global markets continue to shift and consumer expectations evolve, COSMAX remains not just reactive but proactive. It doesn't simply follow beauty trends—it helps create them.

Through its partnerships, platform strategies, and continuous investment in technology and talent, COSMAX illustrates how OBM brand power today is as much about collaborative ecosystem building as it is about individual product innovation.

It is, in essence, the silent force behind many of the world's most visible beauty brands.

5 Institutional and Organizational Challenges

While OBM firms increasingly rely on agile marketing and innovation strategies to stand out in the global market, their ability to sustain brand power hinges significantly on how well they navigate institutional and organizational challenges. These challenges range from regulatory shifts and labor market constraints to legacy systems and internal cultural inertia. For firms like COSMAX, the transition from a production-centric to a brand-enabling model has meant confronting and recalibrating their institutional foundations.

5.1 Regulatory and Compliance Complexities

One of the most pressing institutional challenges for OBM-enabling firms lies in navigating the increasingly complex web of international regulations. Each market comes with distinct standards—be it the FDA in the United States, EMA in Europe, or Halal certification requirements in Southeast Asia. OBM firms must therefore build sophisticated compliance capabilities or rely heavily on partners like COSMAX who possess the infrastructure to adapt products to varying standards.

COSMAX's case reveals a model of anticipatory compliance. Rather than waiting for regulatory pressure to react, COSMAX has institutionalized cross-border legal foresight by maintaining compliance experts at both global and local levels. This enables early adaptation to changing ingredient regulations, labeling laws, and digital advertising policies. OBMs who fail to internalize or outsource these functions face growth barriers, especially as global scrutiny around clean beauty, environmental sustainability, and data privacy intensifies.

5.2 Organizational Silos and Cross-Functional Integration

The second major challenge is internal: how to move from siloed departmental structures to cross-functional collaboration. OBM success requires tight coordination between R&D, marketing, logistics, and sales. However, traditional organizations often separate these units, creating disconnects that delay product launches and dilute brand coherence.

COSMAX's "One COSMAX" initiative directly addresses this issue by flattening hierarchical layers and integrating project-based teams. When an OBM brand enters COSMAX's pipeline, cross-functional teams spanning design, planning, regulation, and engineering co-develop the product. This reduces lead times and ensures that brand intent aligns with execution. Yet, many OBM firms—especially those evolving from OEM roots—struggle to break down these internal silos. Institutional inertia, resistance to change, and a lack of digital tools often stall integration efforts.

5.3 Talent and Human Capital Constraints

Talent scarcity represents another organizational bottleneck. OBM marketing requires not only technical know-how but also cultural fluency, digital literacy, and creative agility. Recruiting and retaining such talent is a persistent challenge, particularly in fast-changing sectors like beauty and personal care.

Firms like COSMAX have responded by establishing internal academies for design, regulatory training, and digital marketing. They also partner with universities to build early talent pipelines. However, most OBMs—especially emerging indie brands—lack the resources for such systemic talent development. This creates dependency on external agencies and service providers, which can fragment brand messaging and dilute innovation ownership.

Furthermore, talent retention in OBM firms is undermined by the "project economy" nature of beauty product development. Teams often disband after a launch, creating knowledge discontinuities. Institutionalizing knowledge management—through CRM systems, internal wikis, and shared playbooks—remains a weak spot for many OBM firms.

5.4 Governance, Leadership, and Decision-Making Speed

Governance structures in OBM firms often lag behind their strategic ambitions. Decision-making tends to be centralized, slow, and risk-averse. This is especially true for legacy companies transitioning into the OBM space from OEM backgrounds. Their governance models, built for manufacturing stability, are ill-suited to the rapid-fire dynamics of brand-building and digital commerce.

COSMAX's governance model offers a partial counterpoint. While still hierarchical, its OBM-facing divisions operate with quasi-startup agility. Key executives at COSMAX are empowered to make real-time decisions on collaborations, product pivots, and promotional strategies. COSMAX's internal governance thus balances top-down oversight with bottom-up initiative.

For OBMs, restructuring governance to empower middle managers, introduce digital dashboards for performance tracking, and shorten feedback loops is imperative. Without such shifts, even the most visionary brand concepts can stall in bureaucratic gridlock.

5.5 Digital Transformation Resistance

Despite growing digital dependence, institutional resistance to digital transformation remains widespread. Many OBM firms still treat digital tools as add-ons rather than core infrastructure. They invest in social media advertising but lack integrated data systems. They launch e-commerce channels but fail to integrate inventory, customer support, and analytics into one platform.

Digital transformation is not just about tools—it's about rewiring organizational DNA. COSMAX illustrates this principle through its approach to digital integration. Rather than creating separate digital departments, digital capabilities are embedded into each team. Product developers use AI-assisted trend forecasting; marketing staff access real-time influencer metrics; and logistics teams use predictive modeling for demand planning.

For OBMs to catch up, institutional change must include digital upskilling, platform interoperability, and cultural buy-in from leadership. Otherwise, digital initiatives risk remaining fragmented and ineffective.

5.6 Scale vs. Agility Dilemma

One of the paradoxes OBM firms face is the tension between scale and agility. As brands grow, they require standardized processes, hierarchical structures, and robust oversight. Yet these very systems can choke the speed and experimentation that make OBMs successful.

COSMAX's solution lies in modularization. Rather than apply one-size-fits-all processes, it segments its operations by brand type—legacy vs. indie, domestic vs. global—and adjusts protocols accordingly. This allows it to preserve agility for influencer-driven launches while ensuring scalability for multinational clients.

OBMs must learn from this dual-mode operation. Establishing agile task forces, maintaining innovation sandboxes, and deploying flexible manufacturing partners are ways to resolve this dichotomy. However, many firms lack the organizational elasticity to pivot between these modes, leading to strategic misalignment.

5.7 Institutional Legacy and Cultural Inertia

Finally, deep-seated cultural assumptions often impede transformation. Many traditional firms equate brand value with advertising spend rather than community engagement or storytelling. Others view OBM simply as a channel strategy rather than a holistic identity transformation.

Cultural inertia is especially evident in firms with long histories in OEM or B2B business models. Their organizational language, incentives, and training programs remain rooted in production excellence rather than brand equity building.

COSMAX has actively worked to shift this mindset internally by redefining its mission—not merely as a manufacturer but as a brand enabler. This reframing has been critical in attracting new talent, building partnerships with digital-native firms, and expanding into emotionally resonant categories like clean beauty and wellness.

For OBMs, institutional transformation must begin with narrative change. Redefining internal success metrics, celebrating brand storytelling as much as revenue, and aligning KPIs with long-term brand equity are key steps. These institutional and organizational challenges are not peripheral—they sit at the heart of what makes OBM firms succeed or stall. As this chapter has argued, brand power today is not simply a product of marketing brilliance. It is built—or broken—by the strength and adaptability of institutional scaffolding.

6 Conclusion: Toward Resilient and Resonant OBM Branding

The transformation from OEM to OBM is not simply a business maneuver—it is a reimagination of the firm's identity, capabilities, and contribution to the marketplace. In this chapter, we have examined how OBM firms build brand power through strategic marketing, digital integration, and a customer-centric approach, while also navigating institutional and organizational hurdles. As we conclude, it is important to synthesize key insights and articulate a forward-looking vision for OBM branding in the age of digital globalization.

At its core, OBM branding is about narrative ownership. Whereas OEM firms remain invisible to end users, OBM firms step into the spotlight, crafting stories that resonate with consumer aspirations and cultural values (Holt, 2004; Kapferer, 2012). This narrative function is no longer optional—it is fundamental. As markets become more fragmented, noisy, and algorithmically mediated, the ability to define and control one's story becomes a source of differentiation and resilience.

However, owning the narrative is not a one-time task; it is a dynamic process that demands sustained attention to design, customer experience, and cultural relevance (Aaker, 1996). OBM firms must move beyond transactional marketing to create immersive brand ecosystems where consumers feel seen, valued, and emotionally engaged. In this sense, brand power stems not just from visibility, but from authenticity and participation (Safeer et al., 2021; Zhang & Han, 2025).

The COSMAX case underscores this evolution. From an ODM powerhouse, COSMAX has grown into an OBM enabler by embedding flexibility, design thinking, and digital foresight into its operations. It demonstrates how firms can leverage supply chain strength as a platform for brand empowerment, not just efficiency. COSMAX's support for indie brands, influencer entrepreneurs, and multinational giants illustrates the democratizing potential of next-generation OBM ecosystems.

Yet, even as COSMAX excels, the broader OBM landscape faces enduring constraints. Regulatory complexity, talent shortages, legacy cultures, and governance misalignment all threaten to impede OBM advancement (Choi & Johnson, 2022; Helm & Jones, 2010). As this chapter highlighted, true brand power cannot be built on marketing alone—it must be undergirded by institutional capacity. Organizational design, decision-making speed, cross-functional integration, and digital transformation are now intrinsic to brand building (Park et al., 2023).

The implications are profound. Firms must invest not only in external branding but also in internal brand alignment. They must treat design, data, and storytelling as strategic assets (Kapferer, 2012). They must empower middle managers, decentralize decision-making, and cultivate learning cultures that value experimentation and feedback.

Digital technology is a double-edged sword. It lowers entry barriers and expands reach, but it also amplifies risk and accelerates competition (Kotler et al., 2018). In this context, OBM firms must adopt digital not as a bolt-on solution but as an operating system—a way of working, thinking, and engaging. Real-time analytics, influencer mapping, AI-assisted product development, and omnichannel storytelling are no longer differentiators—they are requirements (de Amaral, 2020; Kim et al., 2025; Shipton, 2024).

Equally vital is purpose. As consumers increasingly reward brands that stand for something, OBM firms must define their purpose with clarity and conviction. Whether it is environmental sustainability, cultural authenticity, or social inclusion, brand purpose offers a north star that can guide strategic choices, shape consumer perception, and build lasting trust (Senoo, 2019).

Looking ahead, the future of OBM will be shaped by those who can marry agility with scale, technology with humanity, and purpose with profit. Firms that understand branding as a systemic capability—not a surface-level function—will be best positioned to thrive (Yan et al., 2011).

In conclusion, building brand power in OBM is not a linear process; it is an iterative, multi-dimensional journey that touches every facet of the enterprise. Success belongs to those who treat brand not as an output, but as an organizing principle. As the OBM landscape continues to evolve, the most resilient and resonant brands will be those that integrate strategy, structure, and story into a cohesive whole. These are the brands that will not only survive market disruptions but also define the future of global business.

References

Aaker, D. A. (1996). Measuring brand equity across products and markets. *California Management Review, 38*(3), 102-120.

Choi, E., & Johnson, D. A. (2022). Common antecedent strategies within organizational behavior management: The use of goal setting, task clarification, and job aids. *Journal of Organizational Behavior Management, 42*(1), 75–95.

Helm, C., & Jones, R. (2010). Brand governance: The new agenda in brand management. *Journal of Brand Management, 17*, 545–547.

Holt, D. B. (2004). *How brands become icons: The principles of cultural branding*. Harvard Business Press.

Kapferer, J. N. (2012). Abundant rarity: The key to luxury growth. *Business Horizons, 55*(5), 453–462.

Kim, G., Jin, B. E., & Jo, H. (2025). Effective video storytelling for small fashion businesses: The mediating role of brand trust. *Journal of Fashion Marketing and Management: An International Journal, 29*(2), 327–352.

Kotler, P., Kartajaya, H., & Setiawan, I. (2018). Marketing 3.0: From products to customers to the human spirit. In *Marketing wisdom* (pp. 139–156). Springer Singapore.

Park, J., Hong, E., & Park, Y. N. (2023). Toward a new business model of retail industry: The role of brand experience and brand authenticity. *Journal of Retailing and Consumer Services, 74*, Article 103426.

Safeer, A. A., He, Y., & Abrar, M. (2021). The influence of brand experience on brand authenticity and brand love: An empirical study from Asian consumers' perspective. *Asia Pacific Journal of Marketing and Logistics, 33*(5), 1123–1138.

Senoo, K. (2019). From new production and sales doctrine to existing product continued use doctrine: A consideration on the deconstruction of the 3Rs in response to the circular economy. *Proceedings of the Annual Conference of the Japan Society for Research Policy and Innovation Management, 34*, 7–10.

Shipton, N. J. (2024). Application of storytelling for marketing purposes: A study with Korean tourism students. *Culinary Science & Hospitality Research, 30*(9), 58–67.

Yan, H. D., Chiang, C., & Chien, C. S. (2011). From original equipment manufacturing to branding: Entrepreneurship, strategic leadership, and Taiwan's firm transformation. *International Entrepreneurship and Management Journal, 10*, 81–102.

Zhang, C., & Han, B. (2025). How perceived brand localness affects purchase intentions: Examining the role of brand authenticity. *Journal of Global Scholars of Marketing Science, 35*(1), 76–97.

de Amaral, I. G. (2020). How Chanel adapted its storytelling to the digital age, within its masstige segment: A Case Study of the Perfume Chanel Number 5 (Master's thesis, Universidade Catolica Portuguesa (Portugal)).

Chapter 6
Efficiency and Value Creation: Production Strategies in OBM

1 Introduction: From Manufacturing Backbone to Strategic Value Creation

The transformation from Original Equipment Manufacturing (OEM) to Original Brand Manufacturing (OBM) signifies a fundamental reorientation in how firms view their production functions—not merely as operational necessities but as strategic assets. In the OBM paradigm, production is no longer confined to executing tasks dictated by client specifications; rather, it is an integral component of value creation, brand storytelling, and market differentiation. As firms evolve from being anonymous manufacturers to global brand-builders, production strategies must simultaneously uphold operational excellence and reinforce brand identity, innovation, and customer intimacy.

Historically, manufacturing firms in East Asia—particularly in South Korea, Taiwan, and China—played the role of the world's factory, delivering cost-efficient, high-volume output for Western brands. This OEM model, while profitable during the initial phases of industrialization, trapped many companies in a low-margin, low-autonomy loop. The challenge for these firms has been to break free from this loop, climb the value chain, and emerge as OBM leaders capable of influencing global trends and consumer behavior.

In this context, production becomes a critical battleground for strategic control. OBM firms must not only maintain the operational efficiencies developed during their OEM years but also invest in adaptive, agile, and innovative production systems that support brand-driven growth. The integration of production with R&D, marketing, and customer service is vital. Products must now reflect a firm's unique design language, cultural positioning, and technological edge—all of which require a close coupling of production capabilities with strategic intent.

This is particularly salient in the beauty and cosmetics industry, where product quality, customization, and speed-to-market are decisive. Here, firms like COSMAX

Y. W. Park et al., *Original Brand Manufacturing Business Model*,
https://doi.org/10.1007/978-981-95-0253-0_6

exemplify the transformation from traditional contract manufacturing to agile, brand-enabled production. COSMAX's evolution underscores a broader industry trend: production no longer plays a backstage role but becomes central to a brand's promise, agility, and global competitiveness.

In today's OBM landscape, the strategic imperatives of production encompass several dimensions:

First, responsiveness. OBM firms need production systems capable of rapid scaling and customization. Markets are increasingly volatile, with short product life cycles, viral demand surges, and fast-shifting consumer preferences. The ability to quickly prototype, test, and deliver new products provides a competitive edge.

Second, innovation. Production must enable rather than constrain creativity. This means investing in flexible technologies—robotics, AI, data-driven manufacturing, and digital twins—that allow for real-time adjustments, error detection, and tailored production runs. For OBM firms, the production line is not merely an efficiency mechanism but a laboratory for design, formulation, and user experience.

Third, sustainability. Consumers are increasingly sensitive to environmental and ethical concerns. OBM production strategies must therefore incorporate sustainable practices, from sourcing and energy use to waste management and labor conditions. Eco-friendly packaging, clean ingredients, and transparent supply chains are no longer optional—they are part of the brand value proposition.

Fourth, integration. Production must be tightly integrated with upstream and downstream functions. This means a strong interface with R&D to translate scientific innovation into manufacturable products, and with marketing to align product features with brand narratives. Cross-functional collaboration and digital integration tools—such as ERP, SCM platforms, and customer analytics—are essential.

Fifth, localization. As OBM firms expand globally, production must adapt to regional regulatory requirements, cultural preferences, and logistical constraints. Multi-site manufacturing strategies, local sourcing, and customization capabilities allow firms to maintain global consistency while achieving local relevance.

These imperatives have profound implications for organizational design, talent development, and capital investment. OBM firms must redesign their factories into smart production ecosystems, recruit engineering and design talent attuned to brand values, and deploy capital not just for capacity, but for flexibility and innovation.

The transition is not without challenges. Many OBM firms inherit legacy production systems optimized for batch processing and cost minimization. These systems must be retooled to support variety, speed, and quality. Moreover, the shift from OEM to OBM often reveals organizational misalignments—between production and marketing, between leadership and frontline operations, and between global strategy and local execution.

This chapter explores how OBM firms are addressing these challenges and turning production into a strategic lever for value creation. Drawing from interdisciplinary literature—including works by Higo et al. (2020), Senoo (2019), and Baldwin and Evenett (2015)—and empirical data from leading Asian firms, we investigate the evolving production models in OBM, their capabilities, constraints, and competitive logics (Jing et al., 2023; Manzakoğlu & Er, 2018).

We pay special attention to COSMAX, a company that epitomizes the new OBM production paradigm. COSMAX's transformation from a behind-the-scenes manufacturer to a global OBM enabler has been fueled by its advanced production capabilities, digital infrastructure, and customer-centric operations. Its case illustrates how production, when aligned with strategy and brand purpose, becomes a source of innovation, resilience, and global competitiveness.

In sum, production in the OBM era is no longer a back-office concern—it is a strategic front line. Those who master the integration of brand and manufacturing will not only build better products but create enduring value in the eyes of consumers and stakeholders alike.

2 Strategic Production Shifts: Beyond Cost Minimization

The shift from OEM to OBM entails not only a new strategic focus but also a reconfiguration of production logic. Under the OEM paradigm, production strategies are oriented toward economies of scale, cost efficiency, and standardization. Production was optimized for high-volume, low-variability manufacturing, with little attention to consumer trends, product diversity, or brand alignment. OBM, by contrast, introduces a demand for versatility, speed, customization, and brand coherence—attributes that traditional OEM production lines are ill-equipped to deliver.

This transformation is not merely operational; it is conceptual. The underlying production logic shifts from one rooted in scale and control to one centered on flexibility and responsiveness. In an OBM context, value is no longer generated solely through operational efficiency but through the ability to rapidly turn market insights into differentiated products. As Higo et al. (2020) argue, the transition to a circular economy and brand-based competition necessitates production systems that are not only efficient but also adaptive, creative, and sustainable.

2.1 From Volume to Variety: The Rise of Flexible Manufacturing

Traditional OEM systems rely on long production runs and low unit costs to maintain competitiveness. In OBM, where product lifecycles are shorter and consumer demand more segmented, production systems must accommodate frequent changeovers, limited batches, and rapid time-to-market. Flexible manufacturing systems (FMS), modular production lines, and small-batch technologies become essential.

This flexibility is especially important in industries like cosmetics and fashion, where seasonal trends, influencer-driven demand, and consumer personalization are the norm. As Senoo (2019) notes, value creation today lies in continuous usage and renewal rather than planned obsolescence, requiring production to be both agile and iterative.

In practice, this means investing in reconfigurable machinery, integrated supply chains, and digital platforms that allow real-time adjustments. Companies such as COSMAX have implemented scalable production infrastructure that allows both mass and niche product manufacturing with minimal downtime, ensuring both breadth and speed.

2.2 *Quality and Speed: The Dual Imperative*

In the OBM context, firms can no longer choose between quality and speed—they must deliver both. Consumers associate brand value with consistent quality, while also expecting rapid availability of new products. This dual imperative challenges traditional production setups, which often optimized for one at the expense of the other.

Lean manufacturing, Total Quality Management (TQM), and Six Sigma have long provided frameworks for balancing quality with efficiency. However, OBM firms must push these principles further, integrating them with real-time data analytics, predictive maintenance, and AI-powered quality control. As Jing et al. (2023) emphasize, OBM firms must transform their manufacturing from "repetitive competence" to "dynamic competence," capable of rapid learning and continuous improvement.

Moreover, quality becomes a strategic differentiator in brand-centric markets. In beauty products, for instance, tactile experience, scent consistency, and application behavior are part of the brand promise. OBM production must ensure not only technical quality but also sensory alignment with brand identity.

2.3 *From Cost Control to Value Optimization*

OEM production is predominantly cost-driven. The goal is to minimize unit costs and ensure margin through scale and sourcing efficiency. OBM production, however, must balance cost with strategic value. This involves decisions such as whether to use premium ingredients, whether to invest in sustainable packaging, or whether to allocate resources to faster delivery.

In OBM, production inputs must align with the brand's positioning. For a luxury skincare brand, cost minimization at the expense of ingredient quality may damage brand equity. Conversely, a mass-market brand must find ways to deliver perceived value at scale. Thus, the emphasis shifts from cost control to value optimization.

This requires sophisticated cost-modeling, margin forecasting, and alignment between production, marketing, and finance. It also calls for strategic supplier partnerships, wherein suppliers are engaged not only for price but for innovation, sustainability, and reliability.

2.4 Digitalization and Production Intelligence

One of the most transformative forces in OBM production strategy is digitalization. Technologies such as the Internet of Things (IoT), AI, and big data enable firms to create "smart factories" that are data-driven, responsive, and self-correcting.

Smart production systems collect real-time data across the production chain—machine performance, material flow, defect rates, and environmental conditions—and use this data to optimize output. Predictive analytics can foresee equipment failures, optimize maintenance schedules, and adjust workflows based on demand signals.

OBM firms are uniquely positioned to leverage these technologies, as their production must serve not only volume but brand-enhancing variability. For example, personalized skincare products—based on consumer data or skin diagnostics—require on-demand, highly adaptive manufacturing.

Digital twins, which create virtual models of production systems, allow simulation of different scenarios before implementation, reducing downtime and waste. Augmented reality (AR) and machine learning (ML) support operator training, quality checks, and predictive interventions. These technologies turn production into a core site of innovation.

2.5 Co-creation and Customer-Driven Production

The OBM shift is also marked by the integration of customer voice into production decisions. Customer co-creation, rapid prototyping, and feedback loops redefine the traditional separation between market research and manufacturing.

OBM firms now increasingly adopt agile product development cycles, where consumer input is gathered early and often. Limited drops, pilot batches, and beta launches—common in D2C brands—require production systems that can respond to small-batch variability and short lead times. Senoo (2019) emphasizes this convergence of production and consumption, wherein the consumer is no longer a passive recipient but an active participant. OBM firms that master co-creation unlock both product relevance and brand loyalty.

2.6 Environmental Sustainability and Compliance

Sustainability in production is no longer an optional corporate social responsibility initiative—it is a strategic requirement. Consumers, regulators, and investors increasingly expect OBM firms to reduce environmental impact, ensure ethical labor, and embrace circular economy principles. This places new demands on production strategy. Waste reduction, energy efficiency, water management, and carbon tracking become essential KPIs. Firms must adopt eco-friendly materials, biodegradable packaging, and low-impact manufacturing methods.

Moreover, compliance with international environmental and safety standards—such as REACH, RoHS, and ISO 14001—must be embedded into production workflows. The ability to produce clean, compliant, and traceable products becomes a market entry barrier and brand enabler. Higo et al. (2020) and Manzakoğlu and Er (2018) argue that circular economy principles, when integrated into production, drive not only ecological benefits but also operational innovation and brand differentiation.

2.7 *Organizational Shifts and Production Culture*

Transforming production strategy requires a corresponding transformation in organizational mindset and culture. Production teams must move from task execution to strategic engagement. Cross-functional collaboration becomes essential, as production interfaces with design, marketing, logistics, and compliance.

Leadership must promote a culture of innovation, accountability, and continuous improvement. Training and talent development are crucial—production workers must be digitally literate, brand-conscious, and agile.

OBM firms often restructure production around value streams rather than departments. Teams are organized around product lines, market segments, or brand themes, allowing greater alignment between strategic objectives and operational execution. Senoo (2019) notes that such shifts require not only new skills but new metrics—evaluating production not just by output and cost, but by brand impact, time-to-market, and innovation contribution.

2.8 *Global Production Footprints and Localization*

As OBM firms globalize, they must balance centralized control with localized agility. This involves a distributed production footprint, with regional hubs tailored to specific markets. Local production reduces lead times, aligns with local regulations, and enhances cultural relevance. At the same time, global coordination ensures brand consistency, quality standards, and strategic coherence. Firms must manage supply chain complexity, IP protection, and geopolitical risk.

Digital infrastructure plays a key role in synchronizing global production networks. Cloud-based ERP, SCM platforms, and real-time dashboards enable visibility and control across sites. COSMAX's "One COSMAX" strategy exemplifies this integration.

In sum, the strategic shift in production from OEM to OBM involves a rethinking of everything from plant layout to performance metrics. It is a shift from static optimization to dynamic capability. OBM firms that successfully navigate this transition not only gain operational efficiency but also unlock brand potential, customer intimacy, and long-term resilience.

In the following section, we explore how firms develop these dynamic capabilities and build learning-oriented production systems that support continuous innovation and brand differentiation.

3 Dynamic Capabilities and Learning in Production Transformation

The transition from OEM to OBM requires more than just operational adjustments—it necessitates the development of dynamic capabilities that allow firms to sense, seize, and transform in response to fast-changing market conditions. Dynamic capabilities are not static assets but ongoing processes of learning, coordination, and innovation. In the OBM production context, these capabilities support agility, customization, quality enhancement, and continuous alignment between production and brand identity.

3.1 The Nature of Dynamic Capabilities in Production

Teece (2007) defines dynamic capabilities as a firm's ability to integrate, build, and reconfigure internal and external competencies to address rapidly changing environments. In production, this translates into the ability to quickly retool manufacturing systems, repurpose assets, and reconfigure workflows to match strategic shifts.

For OBM firms, dynamic capabilities are especially vital due to the frequent evolution of customer preferences, technological advances, and brand repositioning. Unlike OEM firms that often operate under stable production contracts, OBM firms must be alert and responsive to their own evolving value propositions.

These include three capabilities: first, sensing market trends through close monitoring of sales, social media, and consumer insights; second, seizing opportunities through rapid product development and scalable production adjustments; and third, transforming organizational routines to align with new brand strategies or market conditions. Production teams in OBM firms become innovation partners rather than passive executors.

3.2 Learning Mechanisms and Organizational Adaptability

A key feature of dynamic capabilities is organizational learning. This involves systematic efforts to capture, disseminate, and apply knowledge gained from production activities. Learning mechanisms may include after-action reviews, quality audits, cross-functional workshops, and digital feedback loops. Jing et al. (2023) highlight the role of "learning factories" in Asia—production environments that double as training grounds for innovation. In these spaces, frontline workers, engineers, and managers collaborate to refine processes, test new materials, and document lessons learned.

In OBM firms, production learning must also be customer-facing. Feedback from returns, reviews, or customer support interactions should feed into production adjustments. For example, if a skincare product consistently receives feedback about pump malfunction, production must work with design and procurement to address the issue in the next batch. At COSMAX, the ability to produce over 8,000 new SKUs annually while maintaining quality depends on highly routinized yet adaptive learning systems. Operators are trained to recognize deviations, suggest improvements, and act on insights without bureaucratic delays.

3.3 Digitalization as a Learning Catalyst

Digital platforms enhance learning by making tacit knowledge explicit and widely accessible. Through IoT sensors, production lines can generate data on temperature, humidity, speed, pressure, and material usage. This data can be analyzed to identify patterns, flag anomalies, and optimize routines. Machine learning algorithms support predictive maintenance, automated inspections, and adaptive scheduling. Visualization tools allow operators to understand performance trends, benchmark outcomes, and test simulations. These tools accelerate the learning curve across the production organization.

Senoo (2019) emphasizes the need for circular learning—where feedback from the market, brand managers, and product development is looped back into production strategies. Digital dashboards and ERP integrations allow OBM firms to connect customer-facing and production-facing data into a single decision-making platform. At COSMAX, the central control room in the Hwaseong factory collects production metrics across hundreds of lines. This system enables traceability, quality tracking, and real-time intervention. Data is also archived to inform future formulations and capacity planning.

3.4 Human Capital and Capability Building

Dynamic capabilities depend on human capital. OBM production requires a workforce that is skilled, curious, and empowered. Training programs, rotational assignments, and internal assessment schemes help cultivate multi-skilled employees who can operate different lines, troubleshoot issues, and participate in improvement initiatives. At COSMAX, production employees are categorized into levels (L6 to L1) through a structured promotion pathway, reflecting a well-established advancement system. Training covers safety, equipment, brand understanding, and soft skills such as communication and teamwork.

Furthermore, the emphasis on "internal branding" helps align production workers with the company's mission. These are further reinforced through COSMAX's core value-based training modules—Barum (integrity), Darum (invention), and Arum (beauty)—along with posters and performance evaluations. Employees are encouraged to see themselves not just as factory workers but as contributors to global beauty brands.

3.5 Supplier Learning and Collaborative Innovation

Dynamic capabilities also extend beyond the firm's boundaries. OBM firms must coordinate learning with their suppliers, especially in areas such as materials science, packaging, and logistics. Supplier partnerships can become sources of innovation if managed with transparency and shared goals. In the OBM context, where brand identity is closely tied to aesthetics and sustainability, suppliers must be involved early in the product development process. Co-design sessions, shared digital platforms, and joint forecasting improve alignment and responsiveness.

COSMAX's global supplier network sources ingredients from Japan, Europe, the United States, and China. Learning how to adapt formulations based on changing ingredient availability—as seen during the 2017–2019 THAAD-related supply disruptions—is part of its strategic resilience. In response, COSMAX increased use of Chinese raw materials, improved storage planning, and diversified supplier portfolios. Such practices demonstrate "absorptive capacity"—the ability to recognize valuable external knowledge, assimilate it, and apply it. This capacity is essential for dynamic production in OBM firms.

3.6 Institutional Scaffolding and Dynamic Governance

Building dynamic capabilities requires supportive institutional arrangements. Governance structures, decision rights, and incentive systems must facilitate experimentation, cross-functional integration, and rapid response. Traditional production governance often prioritizes compliance, cost control, and throughput. For OBM firms, these remain important—but must be balanced with agility, creativity, and customer alignment. COSMAX's an organic collaboration system between the headquarters and overseas subsidiaries—"One COSMAX"—allows each region (e.g., South Korea, China, the United States, Indonesia, and Thailand) to adapt processes based on local demand, while sharing a unified IT, compliance, and quality framework. This decentralized autonomy enables innovation while preserving consistency.

Performance metrics also evolve. Instead of only tracking units produced or downtime, OBM factories assess time-to-market, SKU diversity, NPD (new product development) support, and customer satisfaction. These metrics reinforce a culture of learning and brand contribution.

In conclusion, dynamic capabilities and learning are at the heart of successful OBM production strategies. As market demands intensify and brand expectations rise, production must become not only a site of efficiency but of innovation and adaptation. In the next section, we turn to COSMAX as a leading example of how OBM-oriented production systems are built, scaled, and continuously reinvented.

4 Case Study: COSMAX—Agile Production and Strategic Integration

4.1 Factory Network and Production Capacity

COSMAX operates one of the most sophisticated global manufacturing networks in the cosmetics industry. Its domestic factories are located in Hwaseong and Pyeongtaek, Gyeonggi Province, including seven major plants, each with unique production roles. Figure 1 shows an exterior view of COSMAX's Hwaseong factory.

Factory 1, established in 1997, specializes in skincare products in Hwaseong. Factory 2, which started in 1994 as a leased facility and was acquired in 2001, focuses on color cosmetics such as lipstick, mascara, and eyeliner. Factory 3 expanded in 2004 for powder production, while Factory 5—acquired between 2010 and 2014—is dedicated to sheet masks. A new factory in Pyeongtaek with 9,100 square meters of space began operations recently, adjacent to a 22,000-pallet warehouse, improving logistics capacity. Pyeongtaek Factory 1 focuses on customized cosmetics, while Pyeongtaek Factory 2 specializes in makeup products, including powder formulations and lip products. Figure 2 shows an exterior view of COSMAX's Pyeongtaek factory.

COSMAX's aggressive expansion continued into 2024 and 2025, driven by surging K-beauty exports. In October 2024, COSMAX hit a record production

Fig. 1 COSMAX's Hwaseong factory

Fig. 2 COSMAX's Pyeongtaek factory

volume of 52 million units domestically, and it aims to increase monthly production volume to 70 million in 2025. To meet this target, it is expanding production lines by 30% and integrating advanced automation equipment across its Hwaseong and Pyeongtaek plants. The Pyeongtaek 2nd Factory alone, which commenced full operation in early 2024, boasts an annual capacity of 175 million units and covers a land area of over 14,000 square meters.

Internationally, COSMAX's reach includes facilities in Shanghai (where a new headquarters with production capacity is under construction), Guangzhou, the United States, Indonesia, and Thailand. Notably, Vietnam was excluded from factory expansion due to low purchasing power (GDP per capita around USD 2,400), with COSMAX preferring to serve Southeast Asia through Thai and Indonesian plants. By 2026, the Shanghai expansion is expected to include joint research facilities with external organizations and will be developed into a comprehensive hub for the cosmetics business—encompassing research, production, and marketing.

As of 2025, COSMAX's Korean factories have an annual production capacity of 960 million units, while the company's total global production capacity has surpassed approximately 3.2 billion units. Factory automation upgrades, such as robot-assisted packaging and AI-based inspection systems, are enabling further efficiency gains.

4.2 Agile Production and MTO Operations

COSMAX adopts a Make-To-Order (MTO) system, producing items only after receiving confirmed orders. This reduces inventory risks, especially since COSMAX, as an ODM/OBM partner, does not engage in consumer promotions. Exceptions are made only when forecasting is coordinated closely with clients. The firm emphasizes accurate material demand forecasting to ensure rapid response after order placement.

To handle tight deadlines, clients—especially overseas—must place orders well in advance, often up to 12 weeks before delivery. The ERP system runs daily MRP analyses, supporting 40 material and component planners. Based on material lead times, the production team collaborates with sales managers to adjust schedules as needed.

Agility is evident in COSMAX's ability to rapidly switch between large and small-batch production. For instance, while skincare lines can produce 15,000–20,000 units in eight hours, they can also handle 1,000-unit niche orders, albeit with more frequent cleaning and downtime. With 150 total lines, of which 90 are for packaging, flexibility in handling diverse container formats is a core strength. This responsiveness is essential, particularly in meeting the demands of global indie brands, many of which now constitute a significant share of COSMAX's top clients. According to SCM head, half of the company's top 20 clients are now indie brands—a sharp rise from just two or three a few years ago.

4.3 Automation, Digitalization, and Quality Monitoring

Factory operations are digitally monitored through a central control room, first implemented in 2017. This facility, with five dedicated staff, tracks machine operation, quality indicators, temperature, and quantity data. COSMAX is increasingly embedding digital tools such as robotic arms and vision inspection systems. In its Pyeongtaek Factory 2, robotic assembly lines can produce 40 color cosmetic items per minute—twice the rate of manual operations. Figure 3 depicts the automated production process of lipstick products at the COSMAX Pyeongtaek factory.

The cushion compact production lines at the Hwaseong plant can produce up to 6 million units monthly. With increasing demand, especially for diverse skin tones in international markets, COSMAX has developed up to 40 shades for specific clients such as TIRTIR, turning around initial production within just two months of receiving the brief. Figure 4 shows the interior production facilities at COSMAX's Hwaseong factory.

The automation system includes robotic handling of powders, pressing operations, liquid dispensing into sponge applicators, and robotic labeling. These technologies not only improve speed but also enable quality control through AI-driven visual inspection. While tasks with high variability or those related to packaging still require human involvement, COSMAX is aiming to further increase throughput and reduce

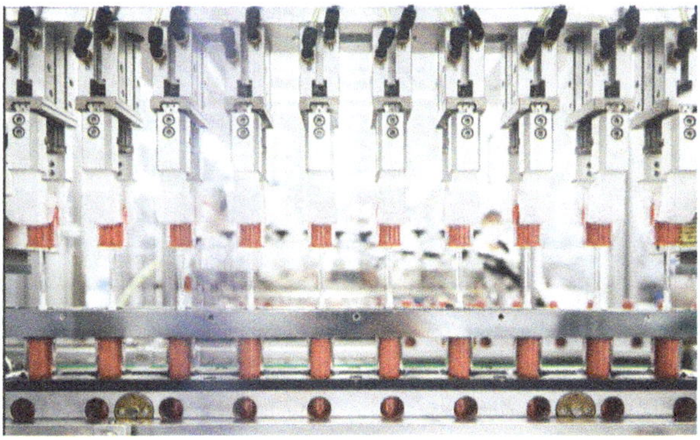

Fig. 3 The automated production of lipstick products at COSMAX's Pyeongtaek factory

Fig. 4 The interior production facilities at COSMAX's Hwaseong factory

human error by adding five additional robotic lines in Pyeongtaek. The company has introduced vision AI inspection—originally used in semiconductors and secondary batteries—for detecting cosmetic defects, and is utilizing around 100 robots for tasks such as raw material transfer and component feeding. Figure 5 depicts the manufacturing process of cushion foundation products at COSMAX's Hwaseong factory.

4.4 Global Sourcing and Raw Material Flexibility

COSMAX sources raw materials globally—Japan (10–15%), Europe (20–25%), Korea (35–40%), the Americas (5–10%), and China (5–10%). It maintains safety stock for key ingredients but faces challenges with custom packaging components,

Fig. 5 The manufacturing process of cushion foundation products at COSMAX's Hwaseong factory

which are client-specific and require 2–6 weeks for production domestically—or up to five months internationally.

Supply shocks, particularly the THAAD-induced decline in Chinese tourism to Korea and the rise of J-beauty, strained Japanese raw material supply from 2017 to 2019. COSMAX mitigated this by securing new Japanese suppliers and encouraging production expansion, while also diversifying to Chinese sources, which had improved in quality. Switching raw material suppliers can be difficult due to formulation stability, especially with emulsifiers like those from Shin-Etsu. Once a formula is set, substitutions require revalidation, adding to complexity.

Recent years have seen a gradual shift toward Chinese ingredients due to improved refinement and competitive pricing. COSMAX leverages historical data to plan procurement, working with trading firms across regions and adjusting quickly to volatility in global supply chains.

4.5 Human Capital and Organizational Design

COSMAX directly employs approximately 820 workers at its factories. Recruitment is primarily conducted through open hiring, and the company maintains an annual hiring growth rate of around 10%. Production workers are typically hired from local areas—Hwaseong, Suwon, and Pyeongtaek—and commute using 51 shuttle buses.

The job grade system consists of four levels (G4 to G1) for office staff and six levels (L6 to L1) for factory employees. The company emphasizes internal promotion and talent development. For instance, production workers typically start at L5 (staff level) and can be promoted up to L1 (Grand Master) over the course of 18 years.

Education is conducted in stages, and promotions are linked to performance evaluations and leadership assessments. COSMAX also invests in its automation workforce. Operators are trained to manage vision systems and robotic arms, supported by AI Automation Teams that continue refining machine performance. Specialist engineers are also trained to manage quality assurance, systems programming, and mechanical troubleshooting.

4.6 Strategic Alignment and Long-Term Vision

COSMAX's production strategy aligns with brand storytelling and market responsiveness. It has evolved from a traditional ODM into a flexible OBM enabler. This transition is evident in how the firm empowers smaller brands with rapid prototyping, MTO execution, and co-development platforms.

The company's responsiveness is exemplified by its role in creating culturally sensitive and skin tone-inclusive products. For example, its collaboration with TIRTIR led to the creation of 30 cushion shades within two months, now expanded to 40, tailored for multi-ethnic consumers and distributed globally—including through US platforms like Amazon, where the product reached #1 in the beauty category.

Looking ahead, COSMAX plans to further expand its cushion production capacity, invest in Shanghai's new OBM innovation hub, and strengthen its US presence via the Los Angeles sales office. It is also considering new regional hubs in Latin America. Production agility is not merely about speed—it encompasses regulatory compliance, multicultural adaptability, and design excellence. COSMAX's long-term vision integrates automation, sustainability, and global partnerships into a unified platform to empower the next generation of OBM brands.

5 Sustainable and Purpose-Driven Production

In the evolving landscape of OBM, production is no longer just about efficiency or innovation—it's also about responsibility. As consumers and regulators increasingly demand accountability in terms of environmental and social impact, OBM firms must integrate sustainability into their production systems. This shift reflects a broader transformation in the role of manufacturing: from an operational backbone to a strategic enabler of purpose-driven business models.

5.1 Embedding Sustainability in OBM Production

Sustainability in OBM goes beyond green marketing—it requires embedding ecological and ethical considerations at every stage of production, from materials sourcing to end-of-life management. Firms must rethink their supply chains, adopt cleaner technologies, reduce energy and water use, minimize waste, and ensure fair labor practices. The goal is not only compliance but the creation of shared value for all stakeholders.

As Higo et al. (2020) argue, the shift to a circular economy demands a reconfiguration of manufacturing from a linear model of "take-make-dispose" to one of resource circulation. In the OBM context, this means designing products for longevity, reusability, and recyclability—aligning production with environmental stewardship and brand purpose. At COSMAX, sustainability is treated as an innovation frontier. The company invests in sustainable packaging, biodegradable materials, and green chemistry alternatives. Through its R&D labs, COSMAX explores natural preservatives, plant-based surfactants, and waterless formulations. These innovations reduce ecological impact while aligning with consumer demand for clean beauty.

5.2 Regulatory and Stakeholder Pressures

Governments, investors, and consumers are increasing their expectations around sustainability. Regulations such as the EU Green Deal, Korea's Carbon Neutral 2050 initiative, and international agreements on plastic reduction are reshaping the manufacturing agenda. Failure to meet these expectations risks not only legal penalties but reputational damage and market exclusion.

Senoo (2019) highlights that Japanese manufacturers responding to sustainability imperatives have begun to shift from the "new production and sales doctrine" to the "continued use doctrine." This evolution calls for OBM firms to prioritize durability, repairability, and upgradability in their production designs. COSMAX responds proactively to these trends. Its factories are ISO 14001-certified for environmental management. The company conducts regular audits of energy use, carbon emissions, and waste streams. Through internal sustainability councils, it aligns its operational goals with the UN Sustainable Development Goals (SDGs).

Stakeholder engagement is also central. COSMAX collaborates with suppliers to reduce environmental impact, encourages clients to choose eco-friendly formulations and packaging, and educates employees on sustainability practices. These multi-stakeholder efforts enhance the firm's legitimacy and social capital.

5.3 Energy and Resource Efficiency

Resource efficiency is a cornerstone of sustainable production. OBM firms must minimize the environmental footprint of manufacturing by optimizing energy use, water consumption, raw material input, and waste output. This requires investments in efficient machinery, process redesign, and continuous monitoring.

At COSMAX's Hwaseong and Pyeongtaek plants, energy-efficient lighting, waste heat recovery systems, and smart HVAC controls reduce operational costs and carbon emissions. The company also uses water recirculation systems and green building designs to cut resource use. As of 2024, COSMAX reported a 30% increase in energy efficiency across its main factories. Moreover, its newly expanded Pyeongtaek Plant 2 integrates advanced automation systems that not only boost output but also reduce resource waste. The use of robotics for precise formulation and filling minimizes spillage and scrap, contributing to cleaner operations.

5.4 Supply Chain Transparency and Ethical Sourcing

Sustainable OBM production requires visibility into the upstream supply chain. This means knowing where materials come from, how they were produced, and under what labor conditions. Transparency helps mitigate risks related to human rights violations, environmental damage, and regulatory non-compliance.

COSMAX maintains a global supplier database categorized by country of origin, material type, and sustainability credentials. Japanese ingredients account for 15–20% of COSMAX's total material usage. Following the supply chain disruptions caused by Japan's export restrictions and the COVID-19 pandemic, COSMAX has diversified its supply sources to enhance both quality and cost competitiveness. In addition, COSMAX mandates documentation on the ethical sourcing of key ingredients, such as mica, palm oil, and natural extracts. It collaborates with trading companies and ingredient producers to ensure transparency and compliance. These efforts are part of its broader ESG (Environmental, Social, and Governance) strategy. Thanks to these initiatives, COSMAX was awarded a "Gold" rating by the global sustainability assessment agency EcoVadis in 2024.

5.5 Green Chemistry and Circular Product Design

Green chemistry aims to design chemical products and processes that reduce or eliminate hazardous substances. For OBM firms, this involves developing formulations that are safe, non-toxic, and biodegradable. It also includes packaging strategies that minimize environmental impact. At COSMAX, researchers are exploring solvent-free formulations, natural emulsifiers, and biodegradable polymers. The company's green chemistry program collaborates with universities and research institutes to develop next-generation eco-friendly ingredients.

Circular design principles are also being adopted. COSMAX's packaging team works with clients to create refillable, recyclable, and compostable packaging. For instance, mono-material tubes and jars that facilitate post-consumer recycling are increasingly favored. Clients are offered design templates and material choices aligned with their brand's sustainability goals. According to Jing et al. (2023), integrating circularity into OBM production requires redesigning both products and business models. Subscription services, take-back programs, and modular products can support circular flows. While such models are still emerging in cosmetics, COSMAX's experimentation in these areas positions it as a leader.

5.6 Workforce Engagement and Sustainable Culture

Sustainable production depends not only on systems but also on people. Building a culture of sustainability requires training, incentives, and values alignment. Employees must understand their role in achieving environmental and social goals. COSMAX's workforce engagement strategy includes sustainability onboarding, internal campaigns, and recognition programs. Production employees are trained on waste segregation, energy saving, and sustainable handling of materials. The company celebrates "Green Month" with factory-wide initiatives and competitions to promote sustainable practices.

In interviews, managers at COSMAX emphasized that sustainability is integrated into performance metrics and team objectives. Internal storytelling—through videos, newsletters, and events—reinforces the message that every role contributes to the company's larger mission.

5.7 Challenges and Trade-Offs

Despite progress, sustainable production in OBM faces significant challenges. These include cost pressures, technological limitations, supply chain fragmentation, and consumer price sensitivity. Eco-friendly materials may be more expensive or less stable, complicating product development. For COSMAX, various customer requirements are taken into consideration in the transition to sustainable packaging. Clients often prioritize aesthetics and brand identity over recyclability. Moreover, some markets have yet to develop infrastructure for post-consumer recycling, limiting the impact of packaging innovations. The firm also struggles with balancing flexibility and efficiency. Producing a wide variety of SKUs—each with different sustainability profiles—requires complex inventory and logistics management. Still, COSMAX continues to invest in automation and AI to manage this complexity.

5.8 Toward Purpose-Driven Production

Ultimately, sustainable production is part of a broader movement toward purpose-driven business. OBM firms must define and live out a purpose that resonates with consumers, employees, and society. This purpose becomes a guiding star for decision-making, innovation, and stakeholder engagement. COSMAX articulates its purpose as "Empowering beauty through science and care." This ethos informs its investments in sustainability, its support for indie and inclusive brands, and its commitment to ethical growth. By aligning production strategies with this purpose, COSMAX strengthens its position as a trusted partner for OBM firms. Purpose-driven manufacturing can bridge the gap between profitability and social responsibility. When sustainability becomes a source of innovation and identity, it transcends compliance and becomes a strategic asset.

6 Conclusion: Production as a Strategic Lever in OBM

The evolution of production strategies in Original Brand Manufacturing (OBM) reflects a broader transformation in how firms create, capture, and deliver value in a globalized, digital, and purpose-driven economy. No longer confined to back-end efficiency or cost containment, production today is a strategic frontier—a space where innovation, branding, customer engagement, and sustainability intersect. As OBM firms strive for global competitiveness, their production strategies must evolve in tandem with these shifts.

First and foremost, OBM production must be understood as a holistic value creation system. This system encompasses not only the physical act of manufacturing but also the strategic alignment of supply chains, technological infrastructures, and human capital. It is where the firm's purpose, brand promise, and innovation capability become materially embodied. Whether through speed to market, customization, or environmental stewardship, production is now a frontline activity in delivering brand value.

COSMAX's journey offers an instructive example. Emerging from a background as an ODM supplier, COSMAX has redefined the boundaries of production by fusing agility, customer-centricity, and digital intelligence into its operations. It has shown how a firm can become a platform for OBM partners, enabling indie brands and global players alike to realize their market ambitions. Through investments in automation, supply chain integration, and sustainable R&D, COSMAX has moved from a reactive manufacturer to a proactive innovator.

Importantly, COSMAX's strategy reveals the benefits of balancing scale with flexibility. Its ability to manage both high-volume production and small-batch innovation demonstrates that operational excellence and creative responsiveness are not mutually exclusive. Rather, they are complementary capabilities that define next-generation OBM leadership. As the company prepares to scale further through its expanded facilities and digital systems, it positions itself as a central infrastructure for global beauty brands—especially those that prioritize speed, customization, and purpose.

Moreover, the case of COSMAX illustrates how production can serve as a foundation for ecosystem building. In today's interconnected markets, no firm operates in isolation. OBM brands depend on networks of collaborators—designers, ingredient suppliers, tech platforms, logistics providers. By becoming a collaborative hub, COSMAX enables rapid experimentation, co-creation, and shared learning across the value chain. Its proactive support for indie and influencer brands exemplifies how production can empower entrepreneurship and democratize innovation.

The sustainability dimension adds further depth to this transformation. As discussed before, responsible production is not a peripheral concern but a central strategic imperative. Consumers, investors, and regulators are demanding transparency, ethical sourcing, and circular design. OBM firms must respond by embedding sustainability into their core production logic. COSMAX's integration of green chemistry, ethical sourcing, and ESG practices demonstrates how production can align with societal values without compromising performance.

Yet, these transformations are not without challenges. OBM firms must navigate tensions between efficiency and differentiation, standardization and customization, automation and craftsmanship. They must also overcome internal silos, legacy mindsets, and fragmented digital systems. Organizational learning, cross-functional collaboration, and continuous improvement are therefore essential.

Dynamic capabilities are critical to sustained performance. In the production domain, this means developing the foresight to anticipate market shifts, the agility to retool processes quickly, and the resilience to manage uncertainty. COSMAX's adoption of predictive analytics, digital control systems, and real-time supply chain monitoring shows how dynamic capabilities can be operationalized.

Looking forward, the role of production in OBM will only grow more strategic. Digitalization will accelerate personalization, predictive planning, and performance monitoring. Sustainability will shape product design, factory investment, and stakeholder expectations. And brand differentiation will increasingly depend on how products are made, not just what they contain. Firms that invest in their production capabilities as a source of competitive advantage—not just a cost center—will be best positioned to thrive.

In conclusion, the future of OBM lies in reimagining production as a platform for value creation, innovation, and purpose. Production is no longer the end of the process—it is the beginning of brand experience. As global markets evolve and consumer expectations rise, OBM firms must ensure their manufacturing strategies are not only efficient and scalable but also intelligent, sustainable, and aligned with their brand ethos. The case of COSMAX reminds us that production is not a backdrop—it is the stage upon which the brand is performed. And in that performance lies the power to transform markets, industries, and society.

References

Baldwin, R. E., & Evenett, S. J. (2015). Value creation and trade in 21st century manufacturing. *Journal of Regional Science, 55*(1), 31–50.

Higo, M., Tsunoo, S., & Tanaka, J. (2020). The impact of the circular economy and the direction of Japanese companies: Transition from a mass consumption society to a circular society in the manufacturing industry. *Knowledge Creation and Integration, 28*(12), 20–33.

Jing, Z., Turi, J. A., Lu, S., & Rosak-Szyrocka, J. (2023). Sustainability through factory-based learning in higher education. *Sustainability, 15*(6), 5376.

Manzakoğlu, B. T., & Er, Ö. (2018). Design management capability framework in global value chains: Integrating the functional upgrading theory from OEM to ODM and OBM. *The Design Journal, 21*(1), 139–161.

Senoo, K. (2019). From new production and sales doctrine to existing product continued use doctrine: A consideration on the deconstruction of the 3Rs in response to the circular economy. *Proceedings of the Annual Conference of the Japan Society for Research Policy and Innovation Management, 34*, 7–10.

Teece, D. J. (2007). Explicating dynamic capabilities: The nature and microfoundations of (sustainable) enterprise performance. *Strategic Management Journal, 28*(13), 1319–1350.

Chapter 7
Streamlining Operations: Supply Chain Management in OBM

1 Introduction: The Strategic Role of Supply Chains in OBM

In the era of Original Brand Manufacturing (OBM), where firms strive to innovate, differentiate, and capture premium value in global markets, supply chains have evolved into a central pillar of strategic competitiveness. Gone are the days when supply chains were merely viewed as operational backbones for logistics and cost efficiency. In OBM models, supply chains must deliver on a broader spectrum of strategic priorities—from speed to market and quality assurance, to sustainability, transparency, and innovation enablement.

The OBM paradigm centers on brand ownership, customer intimacy, and continuous innovation. These characteristics fundamentally reshape the role of supply chain management (SCM). No longer just about moving materials from point A to point B, modern OBM supply chains serve as dynamic ecosystems that support brand agility, enable product customization, manage risk, and deliver value to end consumers. For OBM firms operating in fast-moving industries such as cosmetics, fashion, or electronics, the ability to orchestrate a responsive and resilient supply chain can determine market leadership.

Supply chains in OBM firms must balance a complex array of demands. On the one hand, they must retain the operational excellence traditionally associated with OEM (Original Equipment Manufacturing) and ODM (Original Design Manufacturing)—including procurement efficiency, inventory control, and manufacturing coordination. On the other, they must align with marketing strategies, customer experience expectations, and brand values. This dual requirement means that OBM supply chains are increasingly hybrid in nature: they blend physical infrastructure with digital intelligence, and efficiency metrics with brand-driven KPIs such as product availability, responsiveness to trend shifts, and ethical sourcing.

The rise of global value chains and the proliferation of digital commerce have further amplified the need for agile and strategically integrated SCM practices. In

Y. W. Park et al., *Original Brand Manufacturing Business Model*,
https://doi.org/10.1007/978-981-95-0253-0_7

today's marketplace, OBM firms must compete not just on product features or brand narratives but on their ability to deliver the right product, at the right time, through the right channel. This imperative drives SCM innovation, from real-time data analytics and demand forecasting to AI-enabled supply planning and omnichannel fulfillment.

Moreover, OBM supply chains must be culturally attuned and regionally responsive. Consumers in different markets value different attributes—speed, authenticity, sustainability, or personalization. OBM firms must therefore configure supply chains that are globally standardized yet locally adaptable. This demands decentralized operations, local supplier engagement, and regional warehousing strategies that can flex to local consumer behaviors while maintaining global brand consistency.

A key differentiator of OBM supply chains is their role in product innovation. Unlike OEM firms, which focus on execution, OBM firms leverage supply chain partnerships to co-create value. Suppliers, manufacturers, logistics providers, and even retailers become part of a collaborative innovation network. COSMAX, for example, works closely with its raw material suppliers, packaging vendors, and retail partners such as Olive Young to anticipate trends, develop prototypes, and scale product launches in record time. The supply chain becomes a conduit for both operational flow and ideation flow.

In addition, OBM supply chains are under increasing pressure to align with environmental, social, and governance (ESG) imperatives. Consumers now demand greater transparency about product origins, working conditions, and environmental impact. Regulators are mandating sustainability disclosures and circular economy initiatives. For OBM firms, the supply chain is the frontline of ESG compliance and brand integrity. Robust traceability systems, ethical sourcing protocols, and emissions monitoring are no longer optional—they are vital to competitive positioning.

Another defining feature of OBM supply chains is their digital sophistication. From blockchain-enabled traceability to AI-powered inventory optimization, digital technologies are transforming how OBM firms manage supply chain complexity. Real-time visibility into global operations, predictive analytics for demand fluctuations, and automation in logistics and fulfillment are enabling OBM firms to respond faster, reduce waste, and delight customers. The digital maturity of a firm's supply chain increasingly correlates with its agility and resilience in a volatile global environment.

Furthermore, OBM supply chains are critical to risk management and business continuity. The COVID-19 pandemic underscored how supply chain disruptions can cripple brand performance. OBM firms must develop resilient supply networks that can withstand shocks, shift production across regions, and ensure continuity of customer experience. This involves supplier diversification, regional redundancy, and scenario-based contingency planning. It also involves investment in local production capabilities and flexible logistics models that can pivot with shifting market dynamics.

In sum, supply chain management in OBM is a strategic function that intersects with brand building, product development, customer experience, and sustainability. It is no longer confined to procurement or logistics departments but extends into marketing, R&D, compliance, and C-suite strategy. OBM firms that view their supply chains as strategic assets—rather than cost centers—are better positioned to lead in the global marketplace.

This chapter explores the transformation of supply chain management in the OBM context. It traces the evolution from OEM-centered supply networks to OBM-driven ecosystems, examines strategic sourcing models, digital integration, and risk resilience, and culminates with a forward-looking vision for future-ready supply chains. Through the case of COSMAX and its partnership with Olive Young, it illustrates how integrated, agile, and sustainable supply chains underpin the success of contemporary OBM firms.

2 From OEM Supply Chains to OBM Ecosystems: An Evolution

The evolution from Original Equipment Manufacturing (OEM) to Original Brand Manufacturing (OBM) represents not only a shift in corporate identity but also a transformation in the logic and structure of supply chains. While OEM supply chains are traditionally structured around efficiency, cost minimization, and meeting the specifications of brand owners, OBM supply chains demand a more dynamic, integrated, and consumer-focused model. In this section, we explore how supply chains evolve alongside the strategic trajectory of firms as they transition from OEM to OBM.

OEM supply chains are characterized by their linear and hierarchical structure, where the OEM firm plays a supportive role in larger brand ecosystems. These firms typically have limited visibility into end-customer demand and minimal influence over product design, branding, or go-to-market strategy. Their focus lies in achieving operational efficiency, quality compliance, and timely delivery under the guidelines set by client firms. This leads to a fragmented value chain where knowledge is compartmentalized, and strategic decision-making resides with brand-owning partners.

By contrast, OBM supply chains must be orchestrated around customer demand, brand identity, and market responsiveness. This transformation requires a shift from supply chain management to value chain orchestration. The firm's supply chain evolves into a strategic asset that links internal innovation with external market impact. As OBMs seek to differentiate themselves through branding, design, and customer experience, the supply chain becomes a conduit for these strategic objectives.

Lee et al. (2015) argue that the transition from OEM to OBM in Korean SMEs involved path creation through combining existing capabilities with new strategic directions. These SMEs restructured their supply chains to gain greater control over distribution, marketing, and product development. Instead of passively fulfilling client orders, they actively shaped their supply networks to support branding initiatives, foster agility, and engage directly with end users.

Kittilaksanawong (2015) similarly points to the need for path-breaking capabilities when evolving from OEM to OBM. Firms must go beyond process optimization and invest in new forms of knowledge—particularly in product development, consumer analytics, and brand positioning. Supply chains thus become platforms for learning and capability development. In many cases, subsidiaries in advanced economies serve as channels for acquiring strategic know-how and market intelligence that are critical for OBM success.

The case of COSMAX exemplifies this evolutionary trajectory. Initially operating as a contract manufacturer, COSMAX has restructured its supply chain to become a strategic enabler of OBM clients. Its ability to produce diverse SKUs at scale while maintaining high levels of customization and speed-to-market has turned it into a cornerstone of the K-beauty ecosystem. Through its integration with logistics partners and retailers like Olive Young, COSMAX enables even small and medium OBM brands to access sophisticated production, distribution, and retail infrastructure.

Moreover, the rise of digitalization has fundamentally altered the structure and function of OBM supply chains. Real-time data analytics, predictive demand planning, and automated inventory management allow OBM firms to align supply with fast-changing consumer preferences. Digital supply chain platforms facilitate collaboration among design teams, suppliers, and logistics partners, fostering transparency and responsiveness.

A prime example is the partnership between COSMAX and CJ Olive Young. The latter's retail ecosystem, characterized by its discovery-based shopping model and omnichannel integration, offers OBMs unprecedented access to real-time sales data and customer feedback. This feedback loop allows for rapid iteration of products, adjustment of marketing strategies, and optimization of inventory. The seamless interaction between COSMAX's manufacturing system and Olive Young's distribution network exemplifies a mature OBM supply chain ecosystem.

Guo et al. (2020) provide theoretical support for such supply chain strategies, suggesting that OBMs must weigh the trade-offs between in-house production and outsourcing under conditions of technological spillover and investment risk. Their findings indicate that OBMs are more likely to internalize production when investment costs are low and the risk of technology leakage is high. In contrast, when market preferences and production complexity rise, OBMs may prefer strategic outsourcing to non-competing partners. This strategic calculus shapes how supply chains are structured and governed.

The expansion of OBM ecosystems also involves building networks of co-development and co-marketing partners. Firms increasingly adopt open innovation models where product development involves joint ventures with ingredient suppliers, packaging companies, and research institutions. This shift mirrors the insights of Ng et al. (2014), who found that the synergy between Total Quality Management (TQM) and brand-building efforts significantly boosts OBM performance. In such models, the supply chain becomes not just a means of delivery but a collaborative space for innovation.

In the case of the K-beauty industry, the evolution toward OBM ecosystems is supported by a dense web of ODMs, branding consultants, logistics providers, and digital marketing agencies. Startups can enter the market with minimal infrastructure by leveraging these shared services. This model aligns with the findings of Yan et al. (2011), who emphasize the role of strategic leadership in navigating the branding dilemma inherent in OEM-to-OBM transitions. By partnering with ecosystem players rather than building all capabilities in-house, OBM firms can accelerate growth while maintaining strategic focus.

Another dimension of the OEM to OBM evolution is supply chain localization. As firms scale globally, they must adapt their supply chains to local contexts. This involves establishing regional production hubs, tailoring packaging and formulation to local regulations and preferences, and partnering with local logistics firms. COSMAX's overseas expansion, including its factories in China and the United States, reflects this need for glocalization—combining global efficiency with local relevance.

The role of retail in OBM ecosystems also underscores the need for agile supply chain integration. Olive Young has become a pivotal player in the Korean beauty supply chain by democratizing access to shelf space for indie brands. Its category-driven merchandising strategy, half-service retail experience, and omnichannel presence make it an ideal platform for OBMs to test, scale, and refine their offerings. Harvard Business School's case study on Olive Young highlights its innovative approach to retailing and its impact on K-beauty supply chains.

Furthermore, the ability to manage supply chain complexity becomes a source of competitive advantage in OBM ecosystems. Firms must juggle multiple SKUs, seasonal demand patterns, and fluctuating raw material availability. Advanced forecasting tools, ERP integration, and agile manufacturing systems are essential to manage this complexity without sacrificing efficiency or responsiveness. As shown by the expansion of COSMAX's production capacity and automation, investing in scalable infrastructure is critical to sustaining OBM growth.

In conclusion, the journey from OEM supply chains to OBM ecosystems involves a comprehensive transformation of organizational capabilities, network structures, and strategic mindsets. Supply chains evolve from cost centers into platforms for innovation, learning, and market engagement. This transformation is not linear but iterative, requiring firms to continuously adapt their structures and partnerships in response to evolving market conditions. The success of firms like COSMAX and Olive Young illustrates how well-orchestrated supply chain ecosystems can propel OBMs into global competitiveness.

3 Strategic Sourcing, Partnerships, and Dual-Track Models

As OBM firms mature, supply chain management becomes a critical lever for competitive differentiation and sustainable growth. While the OEM model emphasized transactional sourcing based primarily on cost and efficiency, OBM supply chains prioritize flexibility, innovation, and strategic alignment. In this section, we examine how OBM firms structure sourcing decisions, manage partnerships, and implement dual-track strategies that combine in-house and outsourced capabilities.

3.1 Strategic Sourcing: From Price to Value Creation

Strategic sourcing in OBM requires a fundamental redefinition of what constitutes value. Unlike OEMs that focus on cost reduction, OBMs must prioritize speed-to-market, innovation potential, and brand alignment. The sourcing strategy must support the firm's branding goals, customer expectations, and product positioning. As Kittilaksanawong (2015) notes, OBM firms must acquire capabilities that go beyond manufacturing to include innovation management, consumer insights, and experiential design. Consequently, suppliers are selected not just for their price competitiveness but for their ability to co-develop unique value propositions.

In the beauty industry, for instance, COSMAX's strategic sourcing model integrates partnerships with specialty ingredient suppliers, packaging innovators, and testing laboratories. These partnerships allow COSMAX to respond to customer briefs with differentiated product concepts that are both technically feasible and market-ready. This sourcing model supports rapid prototyping, customization, and compliance with diverse regulatory standards across markets.

3.2 The Role of Strategic Partnerships

Partnerships are central to OBM supply chains. Firms like COSMAX have built ecosystems of collaborators that span R&D, production, logistics, and retail. These partnerships are not simply contractual but relational, emphasizing long-term co-investment, mutual learning, and risk-sharing. Strategic partnerships facilitate this integration by aligning supply chain partners with shared performance metrics and strategic goals.

The synergy between COSMAX and Olive Young exemplifies this dynamic. Olive Young provides OBM brands with a platform to pilot products, gather real-time consumer feedback, and scale successful SKUs. This feedback loop is critical for COSMAX, which uses these insights to adjust formulations, packaging, and production runs. The result is a highly responsive supply chain that supports continuous product innovation.

3.3 Dual-Track Supply Chain Models

To balance the need for control with the benefits of flexibility, many OBM firms adopt dual-track supply chain models. These models combine in-house production

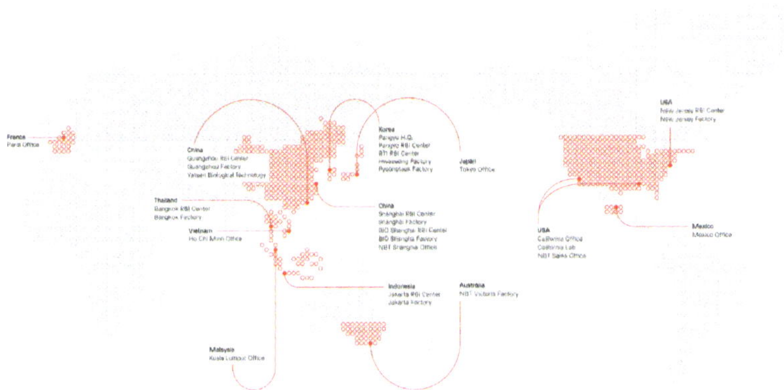

Fig. 1 COSMAX global network

capabilities with strategic outsourcing. Guo et al., (2020) demonstrate the conditions under which OBMs prefer in-house production versus outsourcing. When technology spillover risks are high and investment costs are manageable, in-house production is preferred. However, when flexibility and speed are paramount, outsourcing to trusted ODM partners becomes advantageous.

COSMAX's own operations illustrate the dual-track model in practice. While it maintains core R&D and pilot production in-house, it also relies on a network of contract manufacturers to scale production rapidly. This model allows COSMAX to respond to both high-volume and niche market demands without compromising on quality or lead times.

Moreover, COSMAX's overseas facilities—such as its plants in China and the United States—extend this dual-track model globally. These facilities provide regional capacity, reduce logistics complexity, and enable localization of products. The integration of digital tools such as ERP systems and AI-based forecasting ensures that the dual-track model operates with agility and precision. Figure 1 illustrates the COSMAX global network.

3.4 *Partnership Ecosystems: Co-Creation and Co-Innovation*

Beyond bilateral partnerships, OBM firms increasingly operate within broader partnership ecosystems. These ecosystems bring together players from academia, design studios, tech startups, and influencer communities. The aim is to co-create products that resonate with emerging consumer trends and cultural narratives. As shown by Yan et al. (2011), such ecosystems require strategic leadership capable of balancing autonomy and integration.

For example, COSMAX's investment in open innovation has led to collaborations with universities and dermatology research centers. These partnerships yield proprietary formulations and exclusive ingredients that serve as the foundation for new OBM products. At the same time, collaborations with influencers and digital platforms ensure that product launches are aligned with consumer expectations and cultural zeitgeist.

The Olive Young ecosystem amplifies this effect. By curating a wide range of indie and mid-tier OBM brands, Olive Young fosters an environment of discovery-based shopping. Harvard Business School's case study on Olive Young describes its "half-service" retail model, which empowers consumers to explore products autonomously (Karp & Lin, 2025). This model supports agile feedback loops, enabling OBMs to iterate rapidly and improve product-market fit.

3.5 *Risk Mitigation and Governance Structures*

Strategic partnerships and dual-track models come with inherent risks—intellectual property theft, quality variance, and supply disruptions. OBM firms must implement governance structures to manage these risks while preserving the agility of their supply chains. This involves setting clear contractual terms, investing in supplier development, and maintaining a robust supplier evaluation process.

In the case of COSMAX, supplier audits and shared quality standards are embedded into the partnership agreements. Through a real-time tracking system, production milestones and delivery status can be monitored. COSMAX's efficient production management system is particularly specialized in handling urgent orders. It quickly reflects such orders in the production plan, enabling appropriate control of interconnected production processes such as material procurement. By dynamically reallocating resources based on forecast updates and supplier performance, it minimizes production disruptions. Based on this data, the company is building an AI-driven production scheduling system, which enhances the potential for operating a more productive and innovative supply chain management process.

Moreover, Olive Young's platform provides data-driven insights into SKU performance, consumer reviews, and shelf turnover. OBM brands use this information to assess their supply chain partners and make informed sourcing decisions. This level of transparency is critical for maintaining brand equity and customer trust in the highly competitive beauty market.

3.6 *Long-Term Value Co-creation*

The ultimate goal of strategic sourcing and partnerships in OBM is long-term value co-creation. Rather than focusing solely on transactional efficiency, OBMs seek to build capabilities and assets that enhance their strategic positioning. As noted by Chen et al. (2016), OBM firms must invest in design and development competencies while managing potential conflicts with existing OEM clients.

COSMAX's relationship with indie beauty brands demonstrates this principle. By offering scalable yet customizable manufacturing solutions, COSMAX enables these brands to maintain their unique value propositions while growing rapidly. This model of co-creation ensures that both COSMAX and its clients benefit from market success.

Likewise, Olive Young's commitment to showcasing emerging brands allows OBMs to gain visibility and traction in a crowded market. Its decision to expand globally, including the establishment of a US subsidiary and offline stores in Los Angeles, signals its intent to bring Korean OBMs into new markets. This global reach, combined with localized consumer insights, empowers OBMs to scale sustainably.

In conclusion, strategic sourcing, partnerships, and dual-track models are indispensable components of supply chain management in OBM. They enable firms to balance innovation with efficiency, manage complexity, and create long-term strategic value. The experiences of COSMAX and Olive Young illustrate how such models can be successfully implemented, transforming supply chains from cost centers into engines of growth, resilience, and differentiation.

4 Supply Chain Digitalization and Integration in OBM

In the era of digital transformation, OBM (Original Brand Manufacturing) firms are increasingly leveraging digital technologies to streamline their supply chains, enhance responsiveness, and unlock strategic value. Unlike OEM models that prioritize cost minimization, OBM supply chains must align with branding strategies, innovation cycles, and dynamic consumer demands. This alignment requires the integration of digital tools and platforms that enable real-time visibility, predictive analytics, and collaborative decision-making. This section explores how OBM firms like COSMAX and Olive Young are harnessing digitalization and integration to create agile, resilient, and scalable supply chain systems.

4.1 *The Digital Imperative in OBM Supply Chains*

As OBM firms transition from volume-focused OEM practices to market-driven OBM models, digitalization becomes a critical enabler. The proliferation of SKUs, increased product personalization, and multi-channel distribution models demand real-time coordination across the value chain. According to Wang et al. (2022), smart ERP systems and digital twins are reshaping inventory and production management by enhancing visibility, traceability, and adaptability.

For OBM firms, the digital imperative is not limited to operational efficiency—it extends to brand value and consumer experience (Wang et al., 2018). Platforms that allow real-time monitoring of product availability, delivery tracking, and inventory levels enable brands to uphold service level agreements and reinforce customer trust. COSMAX, for example, integrates IoT-enabled sensors and AI-driven analytics to forecast demand, manage raw materials, and dynamically adjust production schedules.

4.2 Integration of PLM, ERP, SCM, and CRM Systems

Integrated systems are at the heart of digitalized OBM supply chains. By combining Product Lifecycle Management (PLM), Enterprise Resource Planning (ERP), Supply Chain Management (SCM), and Customer Relationship Management (CRM), OBM firms can synchronize internal and external processes. These systems facilitate seamless coordination across research, procurement, production, logistics, sales, and after-sales service.

COSMAX has built a fully integrated stack of PLM, ERP, SCM, and CRM systems, enabling end-to-end visibility from product development and ingredient sourcing to final delivery (Park et al., 2023). This integration reduces silos between departments, enabling faster decision-making and better alignment with market requirements. Moreover, CRM data from retail partners like Olive Young feeds directly into the supply chain planning system, enabling demand-driven production and reducing excess inventory.

4.3 Predictive Analytics and AI-Driven Forecasting

Forecasting accuracy is paramount in OBM environments characterized by rapid product life cycles and volatile demand. AI and machine learning algorithms enhance forecasting by analyzing historical data, market trends, and real-time consumer behaviors. As shown by Xiao et al. (2024), meta-inventory systems powered by digital twins allow firms to model multiple demand scenarios and optimize stock levels.

COSMAX utilizes AI-driven forecasting to support just-in-time manufacturing and personalized product lines. For example, when a new cushion foundation formula is launched, data from online pre-orders, influencer engagement, and retail interest is aggregated to inform batch sizes and production schedules. This predictive capability minimizes waste, improves lead times, and enhances responsiveness to market signals.

4.4 Real-Time Visibility and Responsive Logistics

Real-time visibility is a cornerstone of agile supply chains. GPS-enabled tracking, RFID tagging, and blockchain-based systems provide OBM firms with granular insights into the movement of goods. This transparency supports proactive risk management, faster response to disruptions, and improved coordination with partners.

COSMAX's supply chain control tower enables real-time monitoring of production and distribution activities across its global facilities. In collaboration with CJ Logistics and other partners, Olive Young ensures that inventory is strategically positioned to serve regional markets. Olive Young's integration with logistics providers enables automated replenishment and optimal shelf-stocking, ensuring high product availability and customer satisfaction.

4.5 Collaboration Platforms and Digital Marketplaces

Digital platforms also foster collaboration across the supply chain. Cloud-based collaboration tools, digital marketplaces, and integrated dashboards allow OBM brands to work closely with suppliers, designers, and retailers. These platforms facilitate co-development, reduce cycle times, and enhance transparency. For instance, COSMAX leverages a proprietary digital collaboration portal where client brands can submit product briefs, track formulation progress, and access regulatory documentation. This transparency enhances trust and shortens development timelines.

Additionally, the online platform "COSMAXPackage.com" improves client convenience through a simplified sample request process and serves as a strategic gateway for partner companies expanding overseas. The platform showcases packaging materials produced both domestically and globally in one place, categorizing them by capacity, material, and shape to enhance search efficiency. It is available in three languages: Korean, English, and Chinese. In particular, COSMAX continues to strengthen real-time collaboration and communication between its headquarters and overseas subsidiaries, while streamlining its information-sharing systems to enable more efficient cooperation. Figure 2 shows a COSMAX designer working on the packaging design for a new product.

Olive Young's B2B digital portal provides brand partners with real-time sales data, consumer feedback, and marketing analytics—enabling rapid iteration and informed decision-making. Moreover, digital marketplaces such as the Olive Young Global

Fig. 2 A COSMAX designer working on the packaging design for a new product

Mall extend these benefits to the consumer interface. By integrating OBM brands directly into global e-commerce platforms, these digital channels shorten the path from factory to consumer, increasing brand reach and responsiveness.

4.6 Automation and Smart Manufacturing

Automation is a key feature of supply chain digitalization. From robotic process automation (RPA) in administrative tasks to robotics in warehousing and production, automation reduces human error, improves speed, and ensures consistency. COSMAX's factories feature AI-enabled robotic arms for formulation and packaging, enabling production rates of up to 1.5 units per second for certain products. In 2024, COSMAX acquired the AI startup ArtLab with plans to expand the application of artificial intelligence technologies across its entire business—from research and development to production automation and personalized cosmetics. As the company develops over 8,000 new products annually, it aims to significantly accelerate the R&D process using ArtLab's AI capabilities.

In the production sector, COSMAX plans to actively incorporate not only AI but also robotics to maximize production efficiency. In response to steadily increasing client orders, the company is working toward establishing a system for high-mix, low-volume manufacturing through robotics. Ultimately, COSMAX envisions a future in which AI shortens R&D timelines by generating formulations, while robots handle production—ushering in an era of "MOQ 1" and advancing the development of hyper-personalized cosmetics.

In parallel, smart manufacturing technologies such as MES (Manufacturing Execution Systems) and APS (Advanced Planning and Scheduling) enable fine-tuned control of shop floor operations. These systems interface with upstream planning and downstream logistics, ensuring seamless flow from raw material intake to final shipment. Smart sensors embedded in machines capture performance data, supporting predictive maintenance and minimizing downtime.

4.7 Enhancing Consumer-Centricity Through Data

OBM supply chains are not just back-end operations—they are consumer-facing assets. Data collected across touchpoints can be analyzed to personalize offerings, predict trends, and inform product development. Integration with customer-facing platforms ensures that insights from reviews, social media, and purchase behavior feed into the supply chain.

Olive Young's "discovery shopping" model illustrates this approach. By analyzing consumer browsing and purchase patterns, the platform identifies emerging preferences and relays them to manufacturing partners like COSMAX. This feedback loop accelerates the development of trend-aligned products, enhancing consumer satisfaction and brand loyalty.

In addition, Olive Young's expansion into the US leverages data from its global online mall to tailor store assortments, marketing messages, and in-store experiences. Such data-driven localization is only possible through integrated supply chain systems that connect digital intelligence with physical execution.

4.8 Challenges in Digital Supply Chain Transformation

While the benefits of digital supply chains are significant, the transformation process is complex. OBM firms must navigate issues such as legacy system integration, data standardization, cybersecurity, and organizational change. According to Eng and Spickett-Jones (2009), successful digital transformation requires alignment between technological capabilities and strategic objectives.

COSMAX addresses these challenges by adopting modular, API-driven platforms that allow for incremental upgrades without disrupting core operations. Dedicated cross-functional teams manage data governance, cybersecurity protocols, and change management initiatives. Regular training ensures that staff across the organization understand and leverage digital tools effectively.

Moreover, the strategic alignment between COSMAX and its retail partners helps standardize data formats, forecast models, and performance metrics. This alignment minimizes friction and maximizes the strategic impact of digital initiatives.

4.9 *Future Directions: AI, Blockchain, and Sustainability Integration*

Looking ahead, OBM supply chains will continue to evolve toward greater automation, intelligence, and sustainability. Emerging technologies such as blockchain offer immutable traceability, enhancing consumer trust in product origins and ethical sourcing. AI will increasingly drive autonomous decision-making in procurement, inventory management, and customer service.

Sustainability metrics are also being embedded into supply chain dashboards. COSMAX tracks energy consumption, carbon emissions, and water usage across facilities, using this data to optimize operations and communicate sustainability commitments to stakeholders. Olive Young's partnerships with eco-conscious brands and packaging innovators further align supply chain performance with environmental and social governance (ESG) goals.

In conclusion, digitalization and integration are not optional for OBM supply chains—they are strategic imperatives. By embedding intelligence, connectivity, and consumer insight into every node of the value chain, OBM firms can deliver differentiated value propositions, respond rapidly to market shifts, and build resilient, future-ready operations. The digital supply chains of COSMAX and Olive Young offer compelling models for how technology can transform supply chain management from a support function into a core driver of brand success and competitive advantage.

5 Risk Management, Resilience, and Sustainability in OBM Supply Chains

In an increasingly volatile global environment, OBM (Original Brand Manufacturing) firms face multifaceted risks across their supply chains. These include geopolitical tensions, pandemics, climate change, cyber threats, and rapid market shifts—all of which demand proactive risk management and resilience strategies. Moreover, sustainability has become a non-negotiable aspect of supply chain management, driven by regulatory requirements, stakeholder expectations, and brand values. This section explores how OBM firms such as COSMAX build resilient and sustainable supply chains that mitigate risks while enhancing long-term value creation.

5.1 *The Expanding Risk Landscape in OBM Supply Chains*

OBM firms operate in globalized and highly interconnected supply chains. While this connectivity enables market reach and operational efficiency, it also exposes firms to systemic risks. Disruptions in one region—such as raw material shortages in

Southeast Asia or shipping delays through the Suez Canal—can cascade across the value chain. According to Li et al. (2021), OBM firms that outsource production to competitive manufacturers must account for technology spillover risks and intensified competition from their own suppliers.

In response, leading OBM firms adopt a proactive risk identification framework. COSMAX, for instance, conducts quarterly risk audits across its global supply network, assessing variables such as lead time variability, supplier financial health, geopolitical exposure, and regulatory changes. This data-driven approach enables the company to build contingency plans and buffer stocks where necessary, ensuring continuity of supply.

5.2 *Building Resilience Through Redundancy and Flexibility*

Supply chain resilience refers to the capacity to recover quickly from disruptions. COSMAX has invested in regional production hubs, including facilities in China, Indonesia, and the United States, to decentralize its operations and reduce dependence on a single geography. These hubs are supported by mirrored inventory strategies and parallel supplier arrangements.

Flexible manufacturing capabilities, such as modular production lines and cross-trained labor, further enhance responsiveness. For example, when pandemic-related lockdowns disrupted sourcing from China in early 2020, COSMAX quickly shifted production to its Korean and Indonesian plants without compromising delivery timelines.

Dual-sourcing strategies also play a critical role. As Guo et al. (2020) argue, employing both competitive and non-competitive manufacturers enables OBM firms to hedge against delivery uncertainty and protect proprietary technology. COSMAX follows this approach by diversifying suppliers not only across regions but also across tiers, ensuring that critical components have backups.

5.3 *Digital Risk Monitoring and Real-Time Alerts*

Digitalization enhances risk visibility and response. COSMAX's control tower platform integrates data from production sites (Production Equipment Management System), logistics partners (eBiz system), and infrastructure risk indicators (NMS: Network Management System, SMS: Server Management System).

This real-time monitoring is supported by digital twin models that simulate supply chain scenarios under various risk conditions. By running simulations, COSMAX can stress-test its networks, identify vulnerabilities, and develop mitigation strategies in advance. Such digital preparedness allows the company to pivot quickly in times of crisis, safeguarding both brand reputation and customer loyalty.

5.4 Embedding Sustainability into Supply Chain Governance

Sustainability is no longer peripheral to supply chain strategy—it is central to long-term viability and brand differentiation. OBM firms like COSMAX embed sustainability into their supply chain governance by focusing on three dimensions: environmental impact, ethical sourcing, and circularity.

Environmentally, COSMAX tracks and reports carbon emissions, energy consumption, and water usage across its facilities. This data is used to set reduction targets and implement green manufacturing practices. Renewable energy adoption, waste minimization programs, and green chemistry innovations are integral to the firm's environmental agenda.

Ethical sourcing is another pillar. COSMAX adheres to international labor standards and requires suppliers to sign codes of conduct that prohibit forced labor, child labor, and unsafe working conditions. Regular audits and third-party assessments ensure compliance. Partnerships with NGOs and certifications such as Ecocert and RSPO (Roundtable on Sustainable Palm Oil) further reinforce credibility.

Circular economy principles are increasingly integrated into OBM supply chains. COSMAX collaborates with packaging suppliers to design recyclable, biodegradable, and refillable containers. Product development teams are tasked with optimizing formulations to reduce environmental footprint without compromising efficacy.

5.5 Collaboration for Sustainable Value Chains

No single company can achieve supply chain sustainability in isolation. OBM firms must collaborate across ecosystems to drive systemic change. COSMAX partners with Olive Young, for instance, to co-develop eco-friendly product lines and promote sustainability across the retail channel.

Olive Young's procurement strategies prioritize suppliers with strong ESG credentials. The company also runs educational campaigns to raise consumer awareness about sustainable beauty, creating demand pull for greener products. This alignment between manufacturing and retail strengthens the overall sustainability of the OBM supply chain.

Furthermore, COSMAX engages in multi-stakeholder platforms, including industry associations and governmental forums, to advocate for sustainable practices. These engagements help shape industry standards, influence regulation, and foster innovation. COSMAX has strengthened its ability to swiftly establish and internalize supply chain due diligence systems by accurately understanding global regulations and client requirements. The company is building a due diligence framework to identify and assess environmental and human rights risks within the supply chain, embedding this system across its global organization. To enhance ESG management capabilities among its key suppliers, COSMAX is reinforcing ESG assessments and audits across all areas—including labor and human rights, health and safety, environment, and ethics—based on globally recognized ESG indicators.

The company also actively supports suppliers in building carbon management systems. This includes helping them establish greenhouse gas inventories, providing energy consulting, and offering environmental management training to facilitate the production of low-carbon products and materials. COSMAX has also distributed the "Carbon Neutrality Guidelines for COSMAX Suppliers" to assist partners in continuously developing and managing improvement measures for achieving greenhouse gas reduction targets.

5.6 Transparency, Traceability, and Consumer Trust

Transparency builds trust—a core asset for OBM brands. Consumers increasingly demand to know where and how products are made. COSMAX has established and adheres to a strict quality control policy to ensure the safety, efficacy, and quality of products used by end consumers. To fulfill its social and environmental responsibilities throughout the entire product lifecycle—from development to disposal—the company operates a comprehensive, systematized lifecycle management system.

At the R&D and product development stages, COSMAX conducts ingredient and raw material registration and safety assessments. It proactively identifies and manages potential risks that may arise throughout all stages of the product lifecycle, including procurement, production, distribution, usage, and disposal.

By identifying and managing potential risks in advance and implementing a rigorous raw material selection process, COSMAX ensures that consumers can trust and safely use its products. The company is also working to reduce defective products and improve process efficiency through the introduction of automation systems such as robotics. Key performance indicators (KPIs) such as material acceptance rates and customer complaints are systematically monitored and managed as part of ongoing quality improvement efforts.

This level of traceability not only meets consumer expectations but also supports internal quality assurance and regulatory compliance. It enhances agility during recalls, audits, or certification processes. Moreover, it allows COSMAX to substantiate its sustainability claims, avoiding greenwashing and fostering brand authenticity.

5.7 Preparing for Climate and Regulatory Risks

Climate change presents both physical and transitional risks. Physical risks include supply disruptions due to extreme weather events, while transitional risks involve new regulations such as carbon pricing, product bans, and mandatory disclosures. COSMAX evaluates climate-related risks through scenario analysis and aligns its operations with global frameworks such as the Task Force on Climate-related Financial Disclosures (TCFD).

Compliance with evolving regulations, including the EU's Corporate Sustainability Reporting Directive (CSRD) and Extended Producer Responsibility (EPR) laws, is a strategic priority. COSMAX's regulatory affairs teams work with supply chain and R&D units to ensure that product designs and materials meet emerging compliance requirements. Proactive adaptation minimizes legal risks and enhances first-mover advantage.

5.8 Human Capital and Organizational Resilience

Finally, resilient supply chains depend on resilient people. COSMAX invests in employee training programs focused on risk management, crisis response, and sustainable operations. Cross-functional teams are empowered to make rapid decisions, and contingency planning is embedded into organizational culture.

During the COVID-19 pandemic, COSMAX maintained operational continuity through a combination of remote work policies, health protocols, and rapid-response teams. Lessons learned from this period have been institutionalized into the company's supply chain resilience framework.

In conclusion, the supply chain strategies of OBM firms must move beyond cost and efficiency to embrace resilience, sustainability, and stakeholder value. By investing in diversified sourcing, digital risk monitoring, sustainable practices, and collaborative ecosystems, OBM enabler firms like COSMAX not only mitigate risks but also turn adversity into competitive advantage. As climate change, digital disruption, and consumer activism reshape the global landscape, resilient and responsible supply chains will be a defining feature of successful OBM enterprises.

6 Conclusion: Building the OBM Supply Chain of the Future

As Original Brand Manufacturers (OBMs) seek to scale their presence in increasingly volatile and globalized markets, the evolution of their supply chain management strategy becomes not only an operational concern but a source of long-term strategic advantage. This chapter has explored how OBM firms like COSMAX navigate the transition from transactional OEM relationships to value-driven, innovation-enabling supply chain ecosystems. As we look to the future, several core imperatives emerge for OBM firms aiming to build world-class, future-ready supply chains.

First and foremost, supply chains must be aligned with brand vision and customer promise. Unlike OEMs, OBM firms are accountable for delivering a holistic customer experience that includes not just the final product but the entire process—from sourcing and production to delivery and service. Therefore, supply chain decisions must be informed by brand positioning, customer expectations, and product differentiation strategies. This requires deeper integration between supply chain, marketing, and product development teams, creating a seamless feedback loop that enables rapid response to consumer trends.

Second, the future OBM supply chain must be inherently agile. The volatility witnessed during the COVID-19 pandemic, geopolitical conflicts, and natural disasters has demonstrated the risks of rigid, centralized supply structures. To ensure business continuity and resilience, OBM firms must embrace distributed and decentralized supply chain models. This includes developing multiple sourcing hubs, investing in nearshoring capabilities, and maintaining buffer inventories in critical nodes. Agile supply chains enable firms to pivot quickly, reallocate resources, and adapt to changing market dynamics without compromising customer satisfaction.

Third, digital transformation will be the backbone of OBM supply chains. Technologies such as AI, machine learning, IoT, and blockchain are redefining how information flows across the value chain. Predictive analytics can forecast demand and optimize inventory levels; digital twins can simulate supply chain scenarios; and blockchain can enhance traceability and transparency. OBM firms that invest in end-to-end supply chain visibility and real-time data intelligence will be able to make proactive decisions, reduce operational risks, and create highly personalized offerings.

Fourth, sustainability and ethical responsibility must be embedded into supply chain operations. As consumers demand transparency, and regulators impose stricter ESG mandates, OBM firms will need to measure, report, and improve the environmental and social impact of their supply chains. This means investing in green logistics, ethical sourcing certifications, carbon footprint tracking, and circular economy practices. Firms that champion sustainable supply chains not only meet compliance standards but also strengthen consumer trust and brand loyalty.

Fifth, collaboration and ecosystem thinking are vital. Future supply chains will not be linear or siloed; they will be networks of co-creation involving suppliers, technology providers, logistics partners, and even competitors. Open innovation models, collaborative product development, and data sharing will redefine traditional supplier relationships. Strategic partnerships, such as the one between COSMAX and Olive Young, demonstrate how integrated supply chains can enable faster innovation, better customer insights, and mutual growth. These partnerships create a shared value chain where every actor contributes to and benefits from collective success.

Lastly, talent and organizational capability will determine the success of supply chain transformation. OBM firms must invest in supply chain leadership that understands both technical complexity and strategic business goals. Cross-functional training, digital fluency, and adaptive thinking should be fostered across the supply chain workforce. Moreover, governance structures need to support integrated decision-making, innovation experimentation, and continuous improvement.

In conclusion, building the OBM supply chain of the future requires a reimagining of roles, relationships, and responsibilities. The supply chain is no longer a back-office function but a frontline enabler of brand differentiation, market agility, and sustainable growth. Firms that can design and manage supply chains as strategic ecosystems—digitally intelligent, ethically grounded, and customer-centric—will not only survive but thrive in the competitive global economy. As the COSMAX case illustrates, the integration of production agility, digital innovation, and ecosystem collaboration holds the key to OBM leadership in the twenty-first century.

References

Chen, D., Wei, W., Hu, D., & Muralidharan, E. (2016). Survival strategy of OEM companies: A case study of the Chinese toy industry. *International Journal of Operations & Production Management, 36*(9), 1065–1088.

Eng, T. Y., & Spickett-Jones, J. G. (2009). An investigation of marketing capabilities and upgrading performance of manufacturers in mainland China and Hong Kong. *Journal of World Business, 44*(4), 463–475.

Guo, J., Wu, J., & Dai, J. (2020). Production sourcing strategy for an apparel original brand manufacturer in the presence of technology spillover. *IEEE Transactions on Engineering Management, 70*(4), 1283–1294.

Karp, R., & Lin, S. (2025). Olive Young: Formulating Beauty Innovation, Harvard Business School Case 725–392, January. https://www.hbs.edu/faculty/Pages/item.aspx?num=66762

Kittilaksanawong, W. (2015). How do emerging economy firms learn to evolve from contract manufacturing to own brand management? *Global Enterprise Management, 2*, 1–17.

Lee, K., Song, J., & Kwak, J. (2015). An exploratory study on the transition from OEM to OBM: Case studies of SMEs in Korea. *Industry and Innovation, 22*(5), 423–442.

Li, G., Wu, H., & Zheng, H. (2021). Technology investment strategy for a competitive manufacturer in the presence of technology spillover. *IEEE Transactions on Engineering Management, 70*(3), 1162–1173.

Ng, S. C. H., Zhao, X., Fan, X., & Rungtusanatham, J. M. (2014). TQM and brand-building by Chinese original brand manufacturers: Impact on business performance. *International Journal of Production Research, 52*, 825–846.

Park, H., Hong, S., & Shin, H. (2023). Rising and thriving in the post COVID-19 era: A case study of COSMAX, a leader of the Korean cosmetic industry. *Asia Pacific Business Review, 29*(4), 1105–1124.

Wang, C. H., Cheng, H. Y., & Deng, Y. T. (2018). Using Bayesian belief network and time-series model to conduct prescriptive and predictive analytics for computer industries. *Computers & Industrial Engineering, 115*, 486–494.

Wang, S., Guo, M., Hu, Y. X., Chiu, Y. K., & Jing, C. (2022). Smart manufacturing business management system for network industry spin-off enterprises. *Enterprise Information Systems, 16*(2), 285–306.

Xiao, J., Ma, S., Wang, S., & Huang, G. Q. (2024). Meta-inventory management decisions: A theoretical model. *International Journal of Production Economics, 275*, Article 109339.

Yan, H. D., Chiang, C., & Chien, C. S. (2011). From original equipment manufacturing to branding: Entrepreneurship, strategic leadership, and Taiwan's firm transformation. *International Entrepreneurship and Management Journal, 10*, 81–102.

Chapter 8
Sustainability in Focus: Circular Economy Approaches for OBM

1 Rethinking Value Creation: OBM in the Circular Economy

The circular economy is rapidly emerging as a cornerstone for sustainable industrial development. As global consumers, regulators, and investors increasingly demand accountability in environmental and social governance, the traditional linear model of "Take, Make, Dispose" is becoming untenable. In its place, a circular model seeks to extend the lifecycle of products, eliminate waste, and regenerate natural systems.

Original Brand Manufacturing (OBM) firms are uniquely positioned to drive this transition. Unlike OEM (Original Equipment Manufacturing) or ODM (Original Design Manufacturing) models, OBM entails full control over the product lifecycle, including design, branding, marketing, and after-sales services. This integrated control allows OBM firms to embed sustainability into every facet of their value chain. By owning the brand, OBM firms can also influence consumer perceptions, implement long-term innovation strategies, and shape narratives around sustainability.

The opportunity to lead circular transformation is particularly significant for OBM firms in Asia, where latecomer strategies have enabled countries like Taiwan, Korea, Vietnam, and China to climb the global value chain. Yap and Rasiah (2017) argue that for latecomer firms, the transition to OBM represents a deliberate leap forward that involves building firm-level innovative capacity. By accumulating knowledge through contract manufacturing and gradually gaining autonomy over design and branding, these firms are increasingly able to integrate sustainability into their core business strategies.

Chu (2009) emphasizes the importance of overcoming path dependence in subcontracting for Taiwan's second movers. Although many firms have the capability to develop their own brands, a lack of industrial policy support has constrained their full transition to OBM and, by extension, limited their ability to fully embed circular economy principles. In contrast, Korea's national champion strategy has

Y. W. Park et al., *Original Brand Manufacturing Business Model*,
https://doi.org/10.1007/978-981-95-0253-0_8

enabled leading OBM firms to gain global market share while embedding ESG (Environmental, Social, and Governance) principles into their operations.

Bolton (2009) introduces the concept of design-led innovation, particularly within Chinese SMEs aiming to make the leap from OEM/ODM to OBM. Design becomes not just a function of aesthetic or functional value but a strategic tool to embed sustainability, navigate supply chain uncertainty, and manage creative risks. A design-led OBM firm is capable of not only innovating more effectively but also doing so in alignment with environmental goals such as minimizing resource use, maximizing reuse, and extending product life cycles.

A key advantage of OBM firms is their position at the downstream end of the value chain, where they have direct access to consumer feedback and emerging sustainability trends. This proximity allows them to align their innovation agendas with rising consumer expectations around ethical production, zero waste, and climate impact. Wang and Wu (2012) further support this argument by showing that OBM firms, when positioned strategically within the value chain, can achieve a stronger correlation between R&D investments and operating performance than OEM firms.

A powerful illustration of this transformation can be found in the Vietnamese textile and garment sector. Dinh et al. (2024) show that OBM firms transitioning from Cut-Make-Trim (CMT) models to Free on Board (FOB), ODM, and OBM are prioritizing CSR in supplier selection—a significant deviation from cost-driven sourcing models. The shift toward sustainability-driven value creation reflects not only changing regulations but also the desire to build brands that are competitive in global markets.

This rethinking of value creation also reflects broader shifts in what consumers and stakeholders expect from brands. Increasingly, value is associated not only with the physical product but with the story behind it—how it was made, who made it, and with what impact on people and the planet. OBM firms are better equipped than OEMs to engage in this kind of storytelling, which is central to circular economy branding.

The emergence of extended producer responsibility (EPR) regulations in many countries places additional pressure on OBM firms to manage end-of-life impacts. Unlike OEM firms, OBM firms cannot pass this responsibility onto brand clients. As a result, OBM firms are beginning to explore business models that prioritize reuse, take-back schemes, product-as-a-service offerings, and recyclable packaging. These models not only reduce environmental impact but also offer new revenue streams and strengthen customer loyalty.

Moreover, the integration of digital technologies—such as blockchain for supply chain transparency, IoT for product lifecycle monitoring, and AI for demand forecasting—enables OBM firms to optimize operations while embedding sustainability. These tools support the circular economy by increasing traceability, reducing overproduction, and enabling predictive maintenance and closed-loop logistics.

In short, OBM is not merely a business strategy; it is a platform for circular transformation. By leveraging brand ownership, OBM firms can shape consumer behavior, foster sustainability-focused innovation, and influence supplier and partner practices across the value chain. The rethinking of value creation in the OBM model challenges the status quo of industrial production and positions OBM firms as catalysts for regenerative economic systems.

As global competition intensifies and ESG expectations rise, OBM firms that proactively align their business models with circular economy principles will not only mitigate risks but also enhance their reputational capital and unlock long-term growth opportunities. In this new paradigm, value is measured not just in profit, but in the capacity to deliver economic, environmental, and social returns.

2 Supplier Sustainability and Strategic Sourcing in OBM Models

Sustainable supplier selection is one of the most strategic levers OBM firms can use to operationalize circular economy principles. As OBM firms take ownership of their product's brand identity and lifecycle, they are under increasing pressure to ensure that their upstream partners—particularly suppliers—meet rigorous environmental, social, and governance (ESG) criteria. In the global shift from cost-driven to value-driven sourcing, OBM firms are leading the way by integrating sustainability into their procurement and partnership decisions.

The study by Dinh et al. (2024) offers a powerful case from the Vietnamese textile and garment sector, revealing how CSR has become the top priority in supplier selection. The use of association rule mining (ARM) to assess selection behavior across multiple firms identified CSR as the most frequently occurring factor, ahead of price, quality, and delivery. This shift in sourcing logic illustrates a broader transformation: suppliers are no longer chosen only for their efficiency but also for their alignment with environmental stewardship and social responsibility.

This transition is particularly significant for OBM firms in emerging markets, such as Vietnam and Bangladesh, where suppliers traditionally competed on low labor costs and short lead times. Fouji and Hoque (2021) demonstrate that supplier firms aiming to upgrade within global value chains are increasingly investing in their own ESG capabilities to meet OBM client expectations. These include transparent labor practices, environmental certifications, waste management systems, and participation in fair-trade or ethical sourcing schemes. For OBM firms, aligning with such suppliers enables them to build more resilient and compliant global supply networks.

Furthermore, supplier sustainability is not just a reputational issue—it's a matter of risk mitigation. Environmental non-compliance or labor violations in a supplier facility can quickly escalate into brand-damaging headlines for OBM firms. By proactively sourcing from suppliers that comply with international sustainability standards (such as ISO 14001, SA8000, or Ecovadis ratings), OBM companies reduce the risk of regulatory penalties, boycotts, and disruptions.

The Belt and Road Initiative (Le et al., 2019) has also catalyzed changes in sourcing behaviors. As infrastructure expands across Asia, OBM firms gain access to a broader array of suppliers. However, market access and preferential treatment increasingly hinge on sustainability performance. For example, tax incentives and trade benefits may be granted only to those who can demonstrate compliance with environmental impact assessments and social audit protocols.

Moreover, the competitive advantage of CSR-aligned suppliers is reinforced by consumer expectations. Particularly in markets such as the EU and North America, there is growing demand for brands to disclose their supply chain practices and guarantee ethical sourcing. OBM firms—unlike OEMs—must publicly own the consequences of supply chain failures, making transparent and values-aligned supplier relationships not just preferable but essential.

Tuntariyanond et al. (2017) expand on the value creation logic in buyer–supplier relationships, identifying that sustained value emerges when both parties engage in interactive learning. For OBM firms, this means working collaboratively with suppliers to develop more sustainable materials, reduce carbon footprints, and co-invest in cleaner production technologies. This also involves moving beyond transactional relationships to longer-term partnerships based on mutual capacity-building.

One innovative mechanism through which OBM firms are driving supplier sustainability is the supplier scorecard system. This tool allows firms to regularly assess and benchmark supplier performance not only in traditional areas like cost and delivery but also in sustainability metrics such as water usage, energy intensity, emissions, labor rights, and diversity. Such systems are integrated into supplier relationship management platforms and can be used to reward top performers with preferred supplier status or future business opportunities.

The case of COSMAX offers a notable example. As a global leader in ODM and OBM for cosmetics, COSMAX has embedded ESG criteria into its supplier contracts. These include obligations for carbon management, social responsibility audits, and even joint training programs on sustainability practices. Suppliers that fail to comply may be delisted, while those that show innovation in sustainability are publicly recognized and prioritized.

Yi et al. (2011) identify four supply chain flexibility strategies—laggard, conservative, agile, and aggressive. OBM firms striving for sustainability often combine agile and aggressive strategies: they maintain supplier flexibility to respond to market shifts (e.g., demand for low-carbon packaging) while aggressively managing compliance, quality, and sustainability performance. This hybrid approach allows OBM firms to manage the risks of environmental and social disruption while seizing opportunities to innovate with sustainable inputs.

Another dimension is the geographic sourcing strategy. OBM firms face decisions between global sourcing, nearshoring, and local sourcing. Each model has different sustainability implications. While global sourcing may offer cost savings, it increases the carbon footprint due to transportation and complicates traceability. In contrast, nearshoring or local sourcing supports shorter supply chains, easier audits, and alignment with local environmental regulations. Many OBM firms now pursue a blended model: core strategic suppliers located closer to the point of production, complemented by global specialists who meet specific sustainability criteria.

There is also growing interest in circular sourcing models. These include closed-loop systems where post-consumer materials are recovered, recycled, and reintegrated into the production process. For example, OBM firms in fashion and cosmetics are sourcing fibers or packaging made from recycled materials, working with suppliers who collect and process used products. This practice contributes directly to circular economy goals by reducing the reliance on virgin resources and minimizing waste.

Regulatory trends also push OBM firms to enhance supplier sustainability. In the EU, for instance, the proposed Corporate Sustainability Due Diligence Directive (CSDDD) will require companies to conduct thorough environmental and human rights due diligence across their entire value chains. Non-compliance could result in legal liability and reputational harm. OBM firms must, therefore, build internal systems to trace, audit, and report on supplier sustainability practices. Digital tools—such as blockchain, supply chain mapping platforms, and AI-powered monitoring—are increasingly adopted to support this process.

Educational initiatives are also important. OBM firms are investing in supplier capacity-building programs, providing training in green manufacturing, waste management, and responsible labor practices. These programs help smaller or emerging suppliers meet rising ESG standards and align with the buyer's sustainability vision. In turn, they foster loyalty and improve overall value chain resilience.

The case of COSMAX further highlights how OBM leaders are shaping supplier ecosystems. Through its ESG committee and sustainability department, COSMAX evaluates and collaborates with over a thousand suppliers to ensure alignment with global sustainability goals. It conducts regular audits, provides support for certification, and engages in joint research for developing biodegradable materials and carbon-reduced processes.

Ultimately, the shift toward supplier sustainability is not simply a moral or regulatory obligation—it is a strategic necessity. OBM firms that embed ESG into their sourcing strategies enjoy multiple benefits: stronger brand equity, compliance readiness, operational resilience, and innovation capability. They also position themselves as global leaders in the transition to a circular economy.

In conclusion, supplier sustainability and strategic sourcing are central to the OBM circular transformation. By redefining supplier relationships from transactional to transformative, OBM firms can construct responsible, transparent, and future-proof supply networks. The integration of advanced digital tools, coupled with proactive governance, education, and partnership, will be critical in enabling this shift and achieving meaningful sustainability outcomes at scale.

3 Circular Innovation and Design-Led Strategy for Sustainability

Circular innovation and design-led strategies serve as powerful tools for Original Brand Manufacturers (OBMs) in their transition toward sustainable and circular business models. Product design plays a pivotal role in shaping the sustainability outcomes of OBM firms. As studies have shown, approximately 80% of a product's environmental impact is determined during the design phase. Consequently, design decisions around materials, functionality, durability, reparability, and end-of-life treatment are critical to advancing a circular economy.

For OBM firms, which have full control over product development and branding, this creates an opportunity to integrate circularity at the source. Bolton (2009), in his study of Chinese SMEs transitioning to OBM, emphasized the centrality of design-led innovation. As these firms evolve beyond OEM and ODM roles, design ceases to be a mere aesthetic function and instead becomes a vehicle for sustainable differentiation, risk management, and customer value creation. Design-led OBMs can anticipate regulatory shifts, respond rapidly to consumer demand for green products, and align their innovation agendas with ESG principles.

Design-led innovation goes beyond product form—it encompasses the entire value proposition. For instance, designing for product modularity enables easier repair, upgrade, and reuse. This extends product life, reduces waste, and supports the transition from linear consumption models to circular systems. Similarly, design for disassembly facilitates the separation of materials for recycling and remanufacturing. These principles are increasingly being adopted by OBM firms in electronics, fashion, cosmetics, and personal care industries.

Kuo et al. (2018), in their analysis of Acer's transformation, highlight the concept of innovation ambidexterity—balancing exploitation (incremental innovation to optimize existing products) and exploration (radical innovation to create new products or models). For OBMs in a circular economy, this duality is essential. Firms must continue to refine their current offerings while also investing in disruptive innovations such as biodegradable packaging, zero-waste production, and new circular business models like leasing or product-as-a-service.

Circular innovation also involves rethinking material selection. Increasingly, OBM firms are shifting toward renewable, biodegradable, and recyclable materials. In fashion, this includes organic cotton, recycled polyester, and closed-loop textiles. In cosmetics, firms are adopting plant-based ingredients and biodegradable polymers. These material choices must be made early in the product development process and require collaboration with R&D, procurement, and suppliers.

The COSMAX case as an OBM enabler is illustrative. As a global leader in cosmetics manufacturing, COSMAX has institutionalized a design-led innovation model that prioritizes sustainability. Their CCB (COSMAX Conscious Beauty) system categorizes materials and ingredients based on their environmental and human health impact. This framework guides R&D and design teams in selecting safe, sustainable components from the outset. COSMAX's design strategies also include developing refillable packaging, metal-free pumps for easier recycling, and biodegradable containers—all based on close collaboration with packaging suppliers and global customers.

Another key aspect of circular design is digital integration. OBM firms are increasingly using digital twins, life cycle assessment (LCA) tools, and AI-powered simulations to model the environmental impact of design choices. These tools help identify hotspots in emissions, water usage, and material waste, enabling designers to optimize product configurations before manufacturing begins. This proactive approach not only reduces resource consumption but also aligns with rising stakeholder demands for environmental transparency.

The integration of design and branding is another strength of OBM firms. Unlike OEMs or ODMs, OBMs own the customer relationship and are responsible for shaping consumer perceptions. This positions them to embed sustainability into their brand storytelling and marketing strategies. Products designed with circular principles can be marketed as premium, responsible, and future-ready—attributes that increasingly resonate with consumers.

Lin and Chen (2007) observed that in Taiwanese SMEs, administrative and marketing innovations had a greater effect on firm performance than technological innovations alone. For OBMs, this underscores the value of coupling eco-design with compelling narratives. Design-led firms that effectively communicate their sustainability efforts can build stronger emotional connections with customers and command brand loyalty.

In terms of innovation structure, OBM firms benefit from cross-functional collaboration between R&D, design, marketing, and operations. Circular innovation requires breaking down silos and encouraging systems thinking. For instance, product designers need to assess how material and finish selections influence manufacturing complexity, end-of-life recyclability, and user experience. Cross-functional teams can collaboratively ensure that design aesthetics are harmonized with sustainability considerations throughout the product life cycle.

Collaboration extends beyond internal teams. OBM firms are increasingly forming design partnerships with academic institutions, startups, NGOs, and even competitors. These partnerships foster open innovation and knowledge sharing in areas such as biomimicry, material science, and sustainable packaging. Yap and Rasiah (2017) argue that interfirm collaboration and open innovation are essential for latecomer firms seeking to leapfrog into circular leadership. Intellectual property (IP) also plays a role. OBM firms that pioneer circular design features—such as proprietary refill systems, bio-based composites, or zero-waste manufacturing methods—can protect and monetize these innovations. Strategic IP management can offer competitive advantages while enabling responsible licensing models that spread circular practices across the industry.

Furthermore, circular innovation involves rethinking business models. Rather than focusing solely on volume-based sales, OBM firms can explore models that decouple revenue from resource use. Examples of circular business models include Product-as-a-Service (PaaS), in which customers lease or subscribe to products rather than purchasing them outright, enabling extended product use and easier maintenance. Buy-back and refurbishment schemes are another approach, whereby companies reclaim used products for repair, resale, or recycling, thus minimizing waste and promoting resource efficiency. Additionally, modular upgrade systems allow consumers to replace or enhance specific components—such as batteries, screens, or processors—without discarding the entire product, supporting longevity and reducing environmental impact. These models create longer customer relationships, improve product traceability, and reduce environmental impacts. They also generate valuable data on product usage, which can be used to inform future design iterations.

Policy and regulation are further drivers. OBM firms operating globally must navigate an increasingly complex landscape of product stewardship laws, eco-labeling requirements, and circular economy targets. The EU's Ecodesign Directive, for example, mandates energy efficiency, reparability, and recyclability in certain products. OBM firms that proactively design for compliance can avoid penalties and gain early-mover advantages.

The financial implications of circular design are also worth noting. While sustainable design may involve upfront investment in R&D, testing, and new materials, it can lead to long-term cost savings through material efficiency, reduced waste, and brand differentiation. Investors are increasingly assessing companies on ESG criteria, and OBM firms with circular innovation strategies are better positioned to access green financing, impact investing, and sustainability-linked loans.

Education and organizational learning play a critical role in fostering design-led sustainability. OBM firms are investing in training programs for designers, engineers, and marketers to understand circular principles. Internal knowledge platforms, design guidelines, and sustainability toolkits help embed circularity into daily practices. Design awards and innovation challenges further incentivize teams to prioritize sustainability.

Cultural transformation is necessary as well. OBM firms must cultivate a culture of experimentation, systems thinking, and long-term vision. Leadership must champion sustainability as a core strategic goal, not a peripheral initiative. Celebrating successes in circular innovation, setting clear KPIs, and integrating design goals into performance evaluations can accelerate progress.

In conclusion, circular innovation and design-led strategy represent not only a pathway to environmental responsibility but also a driver of competitive advantage for OBM firms. By embedding sustainability into the heart of design processes, OBMs can create products that meet consumer demand, comply with regulation, minimize ecological impact, and build resilient business models. The next generation of successful OBM firms will be those that see design not as a finishing touch, but as the foundation for a sustainable future.

4 Case Study: COSMAX and Sustainable Circular Transformation

COSMAX, a global OBM enabler in the cosmetics industry, offers a pioneering example of how an OBM firm can embrace the circular economy through a comprehensive and strategic ESG approach. With over 4,500 clients—including global giants such as L'Oréal and LVMH, as well as over 1,000 indie brands—COSMAX has firmly maintained its position as the world's No.1 cosmetics ODM/OBM company since 2015. Not only is it a manufacturing powerhouse, but its sustainability vision positions it as a transformative agent in Korea's broader push toward a circular economy.

In 2024, Korea's cosmetics exports exceeded 14 trillion KRW (10 billion USD). In the same year, COSMAX became the first company in the domestic ODM sector to receive the 'USD 200 Million Export Tower' award. This recognition was driven by the fact that 60% of the company's total production volume was exported abroad. Notably, COSMAX contributed to approximately 26% of the nation's total cosmetics export value.

Figure 1 illustrates COSMAX's integrated approach to sustainable circular transformation, combining corporate responsibility with material innovation. On the left, the figure highlights the company's accomplishments in ESG and ethical management. These include receiving the Gold Medal from EcoVadis in 2024, placing COSMAX within the top 5% of global companies for sustainability performance, as well as achieving the highest domestic ESG rating (AA) from SUSTINVEST. In 2023, COSMAX also earned notable scores of A—for climate change and B for water security from CDP, reflecting its proactive stance on environmental risk management. The company is a signatory to the UN Global Compact and adheres to the Women's Empowerment Principles (WEPs), underscoring its commitment to gender equality. It joined the Roundtable on Sustainable Palm Oil (RSPO) in 2021 to support responsible sourcing, and was also designated a family-friendly company by the Ministry of Gender Equality and Family in Korea, reinforcing its dedication to inclusive and supportive workplace practices.

The right side of the figure presents COSMAX's sustainable solutions, which directly contribute to circular economy objectives. These include the use of renewable energy through solar power generation and the implementation of the COSMAX ECO Project, which focuses on developing recyclable, recycled, and biodegradable packaging materials while managing packaging processes more efficiently. The company also champions ingredient transparency initiatives to ensure safety, traceability, and consumer trust. Furthermore, COSMAX is striving to eliminate microplastics from its product formulations by 2030 and is actively employing biotechnology to replace conventional chemical ingredients with greener alternatives.

Together, these initiatives reflect COSMAX's strategic vision to align product innovation with global sustainability standards. The company not only meets regulatory and social expectations but also advances toward a business model that embraces environmental stewardship, social responsibility, and long-term resilience—placing

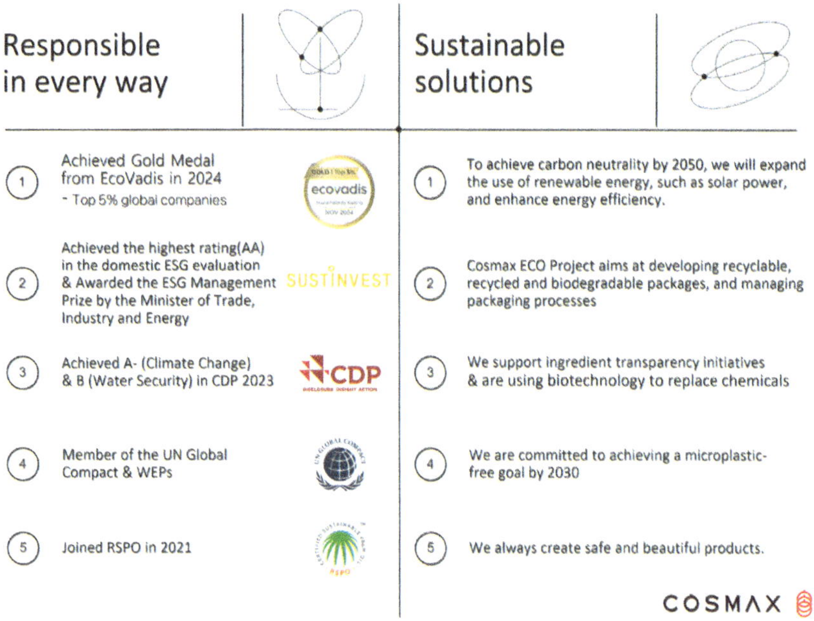

Fig. 1 COSMAX's integrated approach to sustainable circular transformation

it at the forefront of circular transformation in the global cosmetics manufacturing industry.

4.1 *Background and Vision of ESG at COSMAX*

COSMAX's ESG approach is underpinned by its recognition that global customers—especially multinational corporations—are demanding sustainable, transparent, and ethical practices throughout the value chain. ESG expectations are no longer optional or peripheral but are integrated into the procurement criteria, brand positioning, and long-term partnerships. In response, COSMAX has developed a five-pillar ESG strategy centered around eco-friendly products, carbon neutrality, customer value, social responsibility, and ethical and human rights-based governance.

The company's ESG vision states: "We strive for sustainable change and innovation so that all of humanity can enjoy a beautiful and healthy life." This statement anchors COSMAX's alignment with the United Nations Sustainable Development Goals (UNSDGs) and its positioning as a sustainability leader in the beauty and health sectors.

To execute this vision, COSMAX established a dedicated Sustainability Management Division directly under the CEO and launched an ESG Committee to oversee critical decisions. This high-level commitment ensures that ESG is not an afterthought but a board-level strategic priority.

4.2 *Circular Economy in Product Design and Innovation*

COSMAX's commitment to sustainable design is exemplified by its development of the COSMAX Conscious Beauty (CCB) system. This system rigorously screens ingredients and raw materials to assess their human and environmental safety. Products that meet the CCB standards receive certification, allowing COSMAX to guide its clients toward formulations that align with rising consumer expectations around sustainability.

A cornerstone of COSMAX's circular innovation strategy is its focus on sustainable packaging. COSMAX has developed and implemented metal-free pumps to enhance recyclability, refillable cream and stick containers, uncoated cardboard boxes, and puffs made from corn-based biodegradable materials. Additionally, it has collaborated with local firms to develop 100% recycled pulp paper for use in packaging.

COSMAX's R&I Center has also pioneered a groundbreaking microbe-based emulsion system that replaces chemical surfactants with human-friendly microbes, transforming traditional cosmetic emulsification methods. This bioconversion technology not only eliminates harmful chemicals but enables the production of completely natural cosmetics, ushering in a new paradigm in clean beauty.

4.3 *Renewable Energy and Carbon Neutrality Goals*

COSMAX has set a clear target to achieve carbon neutrality by 2050. Recognizing that its rising production volumes make absolute emissions reductions challenging, COSMAX conducted comprehensive GHG audits across all business sites and established specific reduction goals.

To support this target, COSMAX has installed solar energy systems in its domestic (Hwaseong, Pyeongtaek) and international (United States, Indonesia) manufacturing sites. The Pyeongtaek Plant 2 became operational with solar generation in 2023, further expanding the company's renewable energy portfolio.

Beyond Scope 1 and 2 emissions (direct and purchased energy), COSMAX is also addressing Scope 3 emissions—including supply chain-related emissions such as raw material production and logistics—by developing strategies across 15 emission categories. This holistic approach underscores COSMAX's leadership in applying science-based targets to reduce total carbon impact. In 2025, COSMAX will also actively support its partners in establishing carbon management systems. This includes helping them build greenhouse gas inventories, providing energy consulting, and offering environmental management training to facilitate the production of low-carbon products and materials. COSMAX has also distributed the "COSMAX Partner Carbon Neutrality Guidelines" to help suppliers continuously identify and manage improvement measures for setting greenhouse gas reduction targets.

In addition, COSMAX has adopted an internationally recognized methodology for measuring Product Carbon Footprint (PCF), initiating carbon footprint assessments throughout the entire product life cycle—from the selection of raw materials and packaging to final disposal. Through this initiative, COSMAX aims to identify and implement carbon reduction measures at the design and production stages, thereby responding to climate change and advancing its environmental management practices.

4.4 Certification and Global ESG Standards

In 2023, COSMAX received Gold-level certification from Ecovadis, placing it among the top 5% of companies globally in terms of ESG performance. The company has also obtained four key ISO certifications, including ISO 37001 for Anti-Bribery Management, ISO 37301 for Compliance Management, ISO 14001 for Environmental Management, and ISO 45001 for Occupational Health and Safety. These certifications span its operations in Korea, the United States, China, Indonesia, and Thailand—demonstrating a globally integrated ESG management framework. These standards provide formal recognition of COSMAX's internal systems for ethical governance, environmental safety, and workplace health.

The certifications are not symbolic; they reflect operational practices embedded into daily decision-making. For example, COSMAX obtained ISO certifications to reinforce COSMAX's identity as a values-driven firm. Through ISO 14001 certification, COSMAX has established a system that minimizes environmental impact and ensures compliance with environmental laws and regulations. In addition, ISO 45001 certification recognizes the company's efforts to identify workplace risk factors and to build a comprehensive safety culture, including compliance with worker safety standards in countries across the global supply chain. Furthermore, with ISO 37301 certification, COSMAX has implemented a system to proactively identify and manage compliance-related risks throughout its operations. The acquisition of ISO 37001 also demonstrates its commitment to meeting international standards for anti-bribery management systems. Altogether, these certifications reflect COSMAX's establishment of a global-standard management environment aimed at expanding its influence in the global market.

4.5 Plastic Initiative and Packaging Strategy

Recognizing the environmental damage caused by microplastics, COSMAX launched its "Plastic Initiative," aiming to halt the production of rinse-off products containing microplastics by 2025 and phase them out completely across all product lines by 2030. This strategy is supported by a long-term roadmap that involves replacing problematic ingredients with biodegradable alternatives, scaling refillable packaging for high-consumption items, eliminating hard-to-recycle components from product lines, and collaborating with suppliers to establish sustainable material supply chains.

COSMAX is also investing in sustainable packaging innovation, collaborating with automotive, food, and consumer goods industries to explore high-performance, eco-friendly materials. Through these efforts, the company is shifting the cosmetics industry from a linear packaging model to one that is regenerative and sustainable.

4.6 Human Rights, Compliance, and Supply Chain Governance

COSMAX has adopted a comprehensive code of conduct for its suppliers, incorporating clauses on human rights, environmental protection, labor practices, and business ethics. As part of its onboarding process, new suppliers must undergo ESG audits and sign compliance agreements. High-risk suppliers are subject to enhanced due diligence.

In addition, COSMAX offers education and training programs to its partners, particularly SMEs, on carbon inventory management and environmental compliance. This capacity-building initiative extends ESG benefits across the value chain and helps elevate the overall sustainability profile of its supplier network.

COSMAX has also expanded its commitment to international human rights standards by joining the United Nations Global Compact (UNGC). The firm integrates the UNGC's 10 principles across the categories of human rights, labor, environment, and anti-corruption into its ESG management.

4.7 Global Expansion of ESG and Local Responsiveness

COSMAX has successfully extended its ESG strategy across international operations. In Indonesia, for example, it obtained halal certification from the MUI, enhancing trust in Islamic markets. Its US operations obtained ISO 14001 and ISO 45001 certifications, reflecting its dedication to local regulatory alignment and safety.

COSMAX adapts its ESG strategy to local market conditions while maintaining global ESG coherence. This dual approach allows the company to maintain high global standards while engaging authentically with local communities, governments, and customers.

4.8 Future Outlook: ESG as a Growth Driver

As ESG becomes a core pillar of corporate valuation, COSMAX is positioning itself to leverage its sustainability practices for future growth. The company's ESG goals align with global industry trends, including the growing demand for vegan and clean-label cosmetics, rising investor expectations for ESG disclosure and green finance, and the tightening of regulations related to extended producer responsibility and carbon reporting.

COSMAX's proactive stance allows it to serve as a model for other OBM firms in both emerging and developed markets. Its ability to institutionalize ESG across business functions, engage in continuous innovation, and align with global sustainability benchmarks positions it as a first mover in the sustainable beauty and personal care sector.

In summary, COSMAX exemplifies how an OBM firm can move beyond compliance and become a genuine leader in circular economy transformation. Through visionary leadership, technical innovation, robust governance, and a deep commitment to stakeholder engagement, COSMAX has redefined the standards for ESG performance in its industry. Its journey offers invaluable insights for other OBM firms seeking to build resilient, responsible, and regenerative business models for the future.

5 Policy, Ecosystems, and the Path Ahead for Sustainable OBMs

For Original Brand Manufacturing (OBM) firms to successfully embed sustainability and circular economy principles, they must not only act internally but also align with evolving policy environments and participate actively in broader industry ecosystems. This final section explores the crucial role of government policy, institutional support, cross-sector partnerships, and ecosystem-level coordination in enabling OBMs to accelerate their transition toward circularity.

5.1 *The Role of Public Policy in Supporting Circular OBM Models*

Policy frameworks significantly shape the incentives and constraints under which OBM firms operate. Governments can either be catalysts for circular transformation or obstacles, depending on the coherence and ambition of their regulations. In East Asia, the experiences of Taiwan and South Korea offer instructive contrasts. Chu (2009) argues that Taiwan's absence of a national champion policy has constrained OBM firms from investing in brand-led innovation and ESG-driven upgrading. In contrast, Korea's strategic support of chaebol and OBM firms, like LG and Samsung, demonstrates the power of state-backed industrial policy.

Key policy levers to support circular OBMs include tax incentives for R&D in eco-design and sustainable packaging, public subsidies for renewable energy adoption, Extended Producer Responsibility (EPR) regulations, preferential procurement criteria for green-certified products, and mandatory sustainability disclosures aligned with global standards such as GRI and TCFD. These policies serve both as carrots and sticks, nudging OBMs toward more responsible practices while leveling the playing field against less sustainable competitors. Countries such as Germany, Sweden, and the Netherlands have embedded circularity in their national strategies, offering models that East Asian countries can learn from and adapt.

5.2 *National and Regional Ecosystems for Circular Transition*

No OBM firm operates in isolation. Their success is embedded within national and regional ecosystems involving suppliers, logistics providers, certification bodies, universities, financial institutions, and civil society. For circular economy strategies to scale, these ecosystems must be coordinated.

An example of ecosystem-wide coordination can be found in Taiwan's information technology sector. Poon (2004) describes how public research institutes, industry associations, and trade promotion agencies supported OBMs in upgrading from OEM to own-brand strategies. These institutional actors helped build R&D capacity, expand international networks, and diffuse sustainability standards.

Similarly, COSMAX's ability to lead in sustainable cosmetics is reinforced by its collaboration with Korean universities, materials innovators, and international standards bodies. Its participation in global ESG ratings platforms (e.g., Ecovadis) connects it with international best practices, while its cooperation with packaging suppliers and other industries (automotive, food, etc.) facilitates the development of eco-friendly solutions.

Regional clusters also play a role. Industrial districts that foster proximity, trust, and shared knowledge—such as those discussed by De Marchi et al. (2017)—can serve as incubators for circular innovation. OBMs in these environments benefit from shared infrastructure (e.g., recycling facilities), pooled R&D efforts, and labor mobility that accelerates skill diffusion.

5.3 Financing the Circular Transition

One of the major barriers for OBM firms, especially small and medium-sized enterprises (SMEs), is the capital required to invest in ESG systems, product redesign, supplier training, and clean technologies. Governments and financial institutions must collaborate to expand access to green financing, sustainability-linked loans, and ESG-oriented venture capital. For example, in 2022, the Korean Development Bank launched a sustainability bond program aimed at supporting SMEs in achieving carbon neutrality. Firms like COSMAX can serve as anchor borrowers in such schemes, cascading benefits to their supply networks. Private investors, too, are increasingly integrating ESG into their decision-making, rewarding OBMs that have clear sustainability metrics and transparent reporting.

Financial innovation is essential. Tools such as blended finance (combining public and private capital), ESG credit scoring, and impact investing vehicles can unlock funding for OBMs aiming to build circular capacity. These tools should be coupled with technical assistance programs to ensure funds are used effectively.

5.4 Digital Infrastructure for Circular Supply Chains

To manage the complexity of circular economy models, OBM firms require robust digital infrastructure. This includes blockchain for traceability, AI for demand forecasting, IoT for lifecycle monitoring, and cloud-based platforms for supplier engagement. Governments and ecosystem actors should invest in digital literacy, standards interoperability, and data governance to support these transitions. For instance, in the European Union, the Digital Product Passport initiative aims to enable product-level traceability of environmental and social data. OBMs participating in global markets must be ready to comply with such frameworks. Shared platforms and open data ecosystems can reduce compliance costs and create collective value.

5.5 Education, Culture, and Talent Development

Circular transformation also hinges on a skilled and sustainability-conscious workforce. OBM firms need designers who understand circular design, engineers who can optimize resource use, marketers who can communicate sustainability, and managers who can integrate ESG into business strategy.

Governments and educational institutions must develop curricula that embed circular economy principles into business, engineering, and design programs. Public–private partnerships can offer apprenticeships, co-designed courses, and research initiatives to bridge the skills gap. In East Asia, Singapore's SkillsFuture initiative offers a model for upskilling in emerging fields. Similar programs in Korea, Taiwan, and Vietnam could support OBM firms in building the human capital needed for a green transition.

5.6 International Standards and Trade Alignment

As OBM firms scale globally, they face a complex landscape of ESG-related trade barriers, standards, and certifications. Harmonizing national regulations with global frameworks is critical for reducing friction and enabling sustainable exports. OBM firms that anticipate these requirements and design for compliance gain a first-mover advantage. For example, the EU's Carbon Border Adjustment Mechanism (CBAM) and EcoDesign regulations will significantly impact Asian exporters. OBM firms that have embedded life cycle assessment, carbon tracking, and third-party certifications (e.g., ISO 14001, B Corp, FSC) will be better positioned to maintain market access. Multilateral cooperation—via the WTO, ASEAN, and APEC—can facilitate mutual recognition of standards, green trade finance mechanisms, and regional ESG knowledge hubs.

5.7 The Path Forward: Policy Recommendations

To support the circular transition of OBM firms, it is essential for policymakers, educators, and ecosystem leaders to take coordinated action across multiple fronts. First, creating incentives for circular R&D—such as tax credits, grants, and innovation prizes—can effectively stimulate investment in eco-design, packaging innovation, and the development of circular materials. Strengthening extended producer responsibility (EPR) frameworks and green procurement laws can further ensure that regulations incentivize responsible production and reward firms adopting circular product models. Targeted ESG support for small and medium-sized OBM enterprises is also critical; by providing technical assistance, funding, and capacity-building programs, governments can help smaller firms contribute meaningfully to systemic sustainability transitions.

In addition, public–private ESG alliances should be facilitated to establish collaborative platforms where governments, companies, and academic institutions can co-develop sustainability standards, tools, and transition roadmaps. Investment in robust data infrastructure is also vital, especially in building national platforms for ESG data sharing, life cycle assessment (LCA) benchmarking, and regulatory compliance reporting. Enhancing ESG transparency and reporting through standardized requirements can further strengthen consumer trust and accountability, particularly when disclosures are independently verified. Moreover, internationalizing circular innovation ecosystems is crucial. OBM firms should be encouraged to actively participate in global circular hubs, engage in cross-border R&D collaborations, and advocate for inclusive and fair-trade standards that support sustainable practices worldwide.

In conclusion, the journey toward sustainable OBM practices cannot rely solely on firm-level innovation. It demands systemic alignment with supportive policies, financial mechanisms, educational programs, digital infrastructure, and global institutional cooperation. By designing future-ready ecosystems and policy environments, we can accelerate the transformation of OBM firms into global champions of the circular economy.

6 Conclusion

The transition to a circular economy represents a transformative opportunity for OBM firms to reimagine their value creation processes, reposition themselves in global markets, and lead the shift toward sustainability-driven growth. As this chapter has illustrated, OBM firms are uniquely positioned to embed circular economy principles throughout their operations—not only because they control product development and branding, but also because they maintain direct relationships with both end consumers and upstream suppliers. This dual connectivity enables OBM firms to act as powerful change agents across the value chain.

Three key enablers have emerged as central to this transformation: supplier sustainability and strategic sourcing, design-led circular innovation, and supportive ecosystems grounded in governance, finance, and policy. Together, these elements form the foundation of a regenerative OBM model—one that goes beyond incremental improvements and aspires to systemic impact.

Supplier sustainability has become a strategic imperative. As seen in the case studies of the Vietnamese textile sector and COSMAX, OBM firms are shifting from transactional procurement to long-term partnerships aligned with environmental, social, and governance (ESG) values. Investing in supplier development not only mitigates risks but also drives innovation and strengthens brand integrity. Transparent, traceable, and circular supply chains are emerging as a new source of competitive advantage.

Design-led innovation empowers OBM firms to embed circularity from the outset. Rather than treating sustainability as an afterthought, leading firms are adopting lifecycle thinking to enhance durability, reparability, and recyclability. From biodegradable ingredients and refillable containers to digital product lifecycle management tools, OBM firms are aligning environmental goals with shifting consumer preferences. COSMAX's CCB framework and packaging innovations illustrate how design can become a catalyst for circular transformation.

This transition, however, cannot be achieved by firms in isolation. As emphasized by Park and Tamaki (2025), systemic progress toward circularity requires the integration of new system techniques and institutional frameworks. Their five-pronged model—including CE value chain management (CE-VCM), resource circulation, lifecycle IoT design, and shared CE platforms—offers a blueprint for embedding CE principles into industrial and digital strategies. Moreover, as Japan faces delays in aligning its industrial systems with international CE standards such as ISO 59000, the need for rapid institutional adaptation becomes clear. Without addressing these gaps in policy, data infrastructure, and strategic direction, Japanese OBM firms risk falling behind in the global CE race.

Supportive ecosystems play a vital role. Policy tools like tax incentives, green procurement mandates, and sustainability-linked finance can catalyze circular innovation among OBM firms. Furthermore, education, workforce upskilling, and cross-sectoral partnerships are necessary to foster a culture of circularity. The shift toward a circular economy is not just a technical transformation—it is a social and institutional one. Park and Tamaki (2025) highlight that success in CE management demands alignment with SDGs, particularly Goal 12 (Responsible Consumption and Production), and the creation of a governance structure that can bridge gaps between firms, regulators, and citizens.

Digitalization acts as a powerful enabler across all stages of the circular transition. Technologies such as IoT, blockchain, and AI help OBM firms gather real-time lifecycle data, enhance traceability, and meet global compliance standards. They also support more intelligent, responsive business models that prioritize circular performance alongside traditional metrics. In the CE era, digital systems are no longer optional—they are foundational to sustainable innovation.

The case of COSMAX illustrates what a future-ready OBM firm can look like. With its integrated ESG strategy—spanning ethical audits, green chemistry, renewable energy, and global certification—COSMAX demonstrates how OBM firms can thrive at the intersection of purpose, innovation, and performance. Its ability to operationalize circularity across business units and borders reflects the kind of systemic integration advocated by Park and Tamaki (2025).

In conclusion, circular economy approaches are redefining what it means to be an OBM firm. Long-term success will be measured not merely by profitability but by the ability to create shared value—economic, environmental, and social. As the world moves beyond the linear economy, OBM firms stand at the threshold of becoming global catalysts for sustainable industrial transformation. By harnessing the power of circular design, supplier engagement, ecosystem partnerships, and digital technologies, they can lead the way toward regenerative business models that deliver resilience, purpose, and inclusive prosperity in the decades ahead.

References

Bolton, S. (2009). The value of design-led innovation in Chinese SMEs. In *Proceedings of the 19th CIRP Design Conference – Competitive Design* (30–31, p. 369).

Chu, W. W. (2009). Can Taiwan's second movers upgrade via branding? *Research Policy, 38*(6), 1054–1065.

De Marchi, V., Gereffi, G., & Grandinetti, R. (2017). Evolutionary trajectories of industrial districts in global value chains. In *Local clusters in global value chains* (pp. 33–50). Routledge.

Dinh, T. H., Nguyen, T. T. T., Do, T. T. T., Nguyen, T. V. T., & Nguyen, H. L. (2024). Selection supplier for textile and garment enterprises in Vietnam using association rules. *The Asian Journal of Shipping and Logistics, 40*(4), 206–212.

Fouji, M. H., & Hoque, I. (2021). Supplier internationalization through upgrading in global supply chain: Evidence from the garments industry of Bangladesh. *International Journal of Global Business and Competitiveness, 16*(2), 116–129.

Kuo, T. K., Lim, S. S., & Sonko, L. K. (2018). Catch-up strategy of latecomer firms in Asia: A case study of innovation ambidexterity in PC industry. *Technology Analysis & Strategic Management, 30*(12), 1483–1497.

Le, Q. A., Tran, V. A., & Duc, B. L. N. (2019). The belt and road initiative and its perceived impacts on the textile and garment industry of Vietnam. *Journal of Open Innovation: Technology, Market, and Complexity, 5*(3), 59.

Lin, Y. Y., & Chen, Y. C. (2007). Does innovation lead to performance? An empirical study of SMEs in Taiwan. *Management Research News, 30*(2), 115–132.

Park, Y. W., & Tamaki, K. Y. (2025). *Circular economy strategy for SDG business management.* Springer Books.

Poon, T. S. C. (2004). Beyond the global production networks: A case of further upgrading of Taiwan's information technology industry. *International Journal of Technology and Globalisation, 1*(1), 130–144.

Tuntariyanond, P., Anuntavoranich, P., Mokkhamakkul, T., & Wichian, S. N. (2017). Value creation logic in buyer-seller relationships in garment industry in Thailand. *International Journal of Economic Policy in Emerging Economies, 10*(1), 31–46.

Wang, H. W., & Wu, M. C. (2012). Business type, industry value chain, and R&D performance: Evidence from high-tech firms in an emerging market. *Technological Forecasting and Social Change, 79*(2), 326–340.

Yap, X. S., & Rasiah, R. (2017). Catching up and leapfrogging in a high-tech manufacturing industry: Towards a firm-level taxonomy of knowledge accumulation. *Knowledge Management Research & Practice, 15*(1), 114–129.

Yi, C. Y., Ngai, E. W. T., & Moon, K. L. (2011). Supply chain flexibility in an uncertain environment: Exploratory findings from five case studies. *Supply Chain Management: An International Journal, 16*(4), 271–283.

Chapter 9
Shaping the Future: Trends and Prospects for OBM Evolution

1 Introduction

The evolution of Original Brand Manufacturing (OBM) represents a fundamental shift in the global industrial landscape. Once relegated to the role of anonymous producers for multinational corporations, firms in emerging markets have increasingly sought to assert themselves on the world stage through brand ownership, design innovation, and market differentiation. The transition from Original Equipment Manufacturing (OEM) to OBM has become a hallmark of industrial upgrading, especially in East Asia. This transformation underscores a broader narrative of latecomer innovation, where firms in developing economies leap beyond traditional trajectories to establish their own value in global markets.

This chapter aims to synthesize empirical insights and theoretical frameworks that explain and forecast the evolution of OBM in an increasingly complex and digitally interconnected world. Drawing from over three decades of research on industrial upgrading, innovation systems, global value chains, and latecomer strategies, we examine how OBM firms emerge, evolve, and potentially lead their respective sectors. In particular, the chapter focuses on Asia—where economies like South Korea, Taiwan, China, and Vietnam have showcased diverse and dynamic OBM trajectories—and explores the ways in which firms are engaging in strategic transformation, leveraging institutional ecosystems, adopting digital technologies, and repositioning themselves in global markets.

The OBM transition is often framed within the OEM–ODM–OBM continuum. However, this linear model increasingly gives way to more iterative, hybrid, and path-creating strategies. Lee et al. (2015) argue that East Asian firms often create their own development trajectories through recombinative innovation, blending global learning with indigenous strengths. Similarly, Gereffi (1999) emphasizes that global value chain dynamics create both constraints and opportunities for functional upgrading, while Hobday (2003) highlights the role of technological learning and capability building in breaking out of low-margin manufacturing. These insights converge in

Y. W. Park et al., *Original Brand Manufacturing Business Model*,
https://doi.org/10.1007/978-981-95-0253-0_9

the notion of path-creating OBM transitions—where firms move beyond imitation or linear progression and instead forge distinctive trajectories that reflect their internal competencies and external ecosystems.

The Asian experience offers especially rich lessons. For example, Taiwan's journey from a subcontractor economy to a hub for design and innovation underscores the importance of industrial policy and institutional support. South Korean chaebols have demonstrated the significance of brand power and vertical integration, while Chinese OBMs leverage state-driven innovation ecosystems and digital platforms to capture domestic and global markets. Vietnam, as a rising textile and garment exporter, reveals how supplier upgrading and CSR-oriented sourcing can underpin OBM ambitions.

We argue that successful OBM firms will increasingly need to integrate manufacturing excellence with design-led innovation, customer-centric branding, digital agility, and sustainability consciousness—thus becoming holistic value creators in the global economy.

Ultimately, this chapter offers not only an analytical framework for understanding OBM development but also strategic guidance for firms, policymakers, and scholars seeking to navigate the unfolding landscape of global manufacturing and branding in the twenty-first century.

Table 1 shows the core strategic pillars and evolutionary trajectories that define the transformation of Original Brand Manufacturing (OBM). The model highlights the interplay between key enablers such as strategic leadership, innovation systems, digital transformation, consumer insight, branding, and governance. It also maps how firms move from OEM and ODM toward OBM through iterative, hybrid, and path-creating strategies, ultimately aiming for sustainable, inclusive, and differentiated brand leadership.

2 Strategic Transformation and the OEM–ODM–OBM Trajectory

2.1 Patterns of Industrial Upgrading in Asia

The transformation from OEM to OBM has unfolded in distinct patterns across Asia. Following Gerschenkronian principles, late-industrializing countries often substitute for missing prerequisites through institutional and organizational innovations (Hobday, 1998, 2003). In Taiwan, firms leveraged OEM relationships with global brands to accumulate production capabilities before launching their own brands. Korea's SMEs, as shown by Lee et al. (2015), carved unique trajectories by combining existing production models with entrepreneurial agility.

In China, OBM transitions have been marked by scale and state support. The electronics and textile sectors, for instance, demonstrate how firms leverage domestic markets to cushion early branding attempts before venturing globally (Tsai-Lin et al.,

Table 1 Strategic pillars and trajectories of OBM evolution

Title	Main focus	Key themes and strategic insights
Capability development and strategic leadership	Examines how firms build organizational and leadership capabilities to drive OBM transition	– Dynamic capabilities – Leadership for long-term vision – Strategic alignment across functions
Innovation systems and knowledge flows	Investigates how internal R&D and external knowledge networks support OBM advancement	– Open innovation – University–industry collaboration – Ecosystem partnerships
Consumer insight and direct research capabilities	(Inserted between 9.3 and 9.4) Highlights the importance of OBM firms conducting direct consumer research and leveraging data for product development	– Consumer segmentation – Data-driven R&D – Personalized product strategies
The digital turn: technology and smart manufacturing	Analyzes the role of digital technologies in enhancing OBM capabilities and global responsiveness	– Industry 4.0/5.0 integration – IoT, AI, and big data – Smart production and agile systems
Design and brand differentiation	Focuses on how firms develop unique design and branding strategies to stand out in competitive markets	– Brand identity creation – Emotional branding – Global vs. local branding balance
Global supply chain governance and upgrading	Explores how OBM firms gain more control and value by upgrading within global value chains	– Capturing higher value-added activities – Supplier partnerships and coordination – Traceability and resilience
Sustainability and circular economy approaches	Discusses how circular economy models and sustainability initiatives support OBM's long-term competitiveness	– CE frameworks (e.g., 3Rs, 9Rs) – Eco-innovation – Stakeholder-driven sustainability

2021). Vietnam's more recent emergence follows a hybrid model, blending export-oriented OEM with rising domestic consumerism. Sri Lanka and Hong Kong, as Ranathunga Arachchilage et al. (2016) illustrate, highlight the centrality of design education and creative talent in apparel upgrading. In the case of Vietnam, Dinh et al. (2024) demonstrate that OBM success hinges on the ability to self-source raw materials from suppliers who meet criteria of cost-efficiency and corporate social responsibility (CSR). This supplier selection, increasingly based on data mining and association rule methods, aligns with broader OBM aspirations.

Industrial upgrading often follows a sequential yet non-linear progression, where firms experiment with multiple models before solidifying an OBM strategy. In some cases, hybrid business models involving OEM, ODM, and OBM co-exist, particularly during transitional periods. This flexibility allows firms to balance short-term revenue generation with long-term brand development. Case studies from Taiwan's PC industry and Korea's cosmetics sector reveal that such hybridization is often a deliberate strategy to manage financial risk while acquiring brand competencies.

State policies have also played a pivotal role in shaping these trajectories. South Korea's national champion approach provided targeted support to globalizing chaebols, whereas Taiwan relied on broader innovation infrastructure and SME-focused initiatives. In China, aggressive industrial policy and digital infrastructure investments have accelerated OBM capacity, particularly in tech-driven sectors.

2.2 Critical Capabilities for Upgrading

Transitioning to OBM requires a specific set of capabilities that go beyond manufacturing excellence. Tacit knowledge, often gained through trial-and-error learning in the OEM phase, provides a foundational base. Lee et al. (2015) emphasize that SMEs in East Asia have successfully transformed by integrating tacit production skills with formal knowledge systems and market insights.

The integration of R&D, design, and branding is a critical inflection point. OBM firms must invest in product innovation and establish unique brand identities to differentiate themselves in competitive markets. Yang et al. (2019) and Ng et al. (2014) highlight how design-led innovation contributes not only to functional differentiation but also to emotional brand value. Firms that prioritize consumer experience and cultural resonance tend to perform better in OBM transitions.

Branding itself becomes a strategic choice—one that entails trade-offs between scale, control, and long-term equity. Yang and Tsou (2017) and Chen et al. (2016) provide empirical evidence that firms pursuing OBM tend to outperform OEM peers in profitability, provided they successfully navigate the challenges of market entry, marketing costs, and brand management. Moreover, organizational culture, leadership, and the ability to manage cross-functional teams become crucial for sustaining OBM trajectories.

As the next sections will illustrate, these capabilities are further enabled or constrained by broader innovation ecosystems, digital infrastructure, and governance mechanisms that shape how firms create and capture value in the global economy.

3 Innovation Systems and Knowledge Flows

The role of innovation systems and knowledge flows is foundational in supporting OBM transitions. National Innovation Systems (NIS) theory suggests that firm-level innovation performance is strongly shaped by the broader institutional environment—such as universities, research institutes, financial systems, and government policy (Berger & Revilla Diez, 2006). For OBM firms, this means that the ability to innovate, design, and brand products is not simply an internal function but also a function of external linkages and systemic support.

In Taiwan, for instance, the alignment of educational infrastructure with industrial needs has created a talent pipeline for OBM development. Lin et al. (2015) highlight how vocational education, industry-university collaboration, and public R&D programs have collectively nurtured a mindset of innovation and entrepreneurship. Similarly, Sheng (2011) emphasizes how regional innovation clusters and localized policy support in Hsinchu and Tainan have helped SMEs move from OEM production to proprietary branding.

Institutional frameworks that promote open innovation and learning-by-doing are particularly relevant for latecomer firms. The diffusion of design knowledge, branding practices, and consumer insight through trade associations, export consortia, and design institutes creates cumulative learning effects. These channels are crucial for smaller firms seeking to engage in OBM but lacking the scale of multinational competitors.

Design and creativity represent another central pillar in knowledge-intensive OBM transitions. As Manzakoğlu and Er (2018) argue, design management functions as a bridge between technological capabilities and consumer preferences. Firms that effectively integrate design thinking into their business models often outperform those that treat design as a post-production afterthought. Recent studies show how Taiwanese and South Korean firms have incorporated cultural motifs and consumer co-creation into their design strategies, fostering brand loyalty and market distinction (Hsu et al., 2008, 2014; Huang & Intarakumnerd, 2019).

Cultural product design also plays a strategic role in OBM, especially in sectors like fashion, furniture, and cosmetics. Fritz et al. (2017) and Lin et al. (2007) provide evidence that embedding cultural semantics into product design enhances consumer identification and perceived authenticity—both of which are critical in building brand equity. This trend is particularly salient in East and Southeast Asia, where design aesthetics rooted in local traditions are being reinterpreted for global markets.

Knowledge flows in OBM are not limited to top-down transfers from lead firms or governments; they are increasingly networked and bidirectional. Firms collaborate with universities, design studios, and even customers to co-develop new products. These collaborations facilitate mutual learning and reduce the risk of market misalignment. Moreover, they enable OBM firms to develop "cultural agility"—the ability to adapt and localize products without diluting brand identity.

In sum, OBM evolution depends on vibrant innovation systems and dynamic knowledge ecosystems that extend beyond firm boundaries. Countries that cultivate such environments—through investment in design education, promotion of cross-sectoral collaboration, and support for creative industries—are better positioned to foster the rise of globally competitive OBM firms.

4 Consumer Insight and Data-Driven Brand Innovation

As firms transition from OEM or ODM to OBM, gaining a deep understanding of end users becomes not only advantageous but essential. Unlike traditional manufacturers who produce according to client specifications, OBM firms engage directly with consumers, allowing them to gather rich, firsthand data on behavior, preferences, and needs. This consumer-centric orientation enables firms to align product development, branding, and marketing with evolving social values and lifestyle trends, thereby creating a foundation for sustainable competitive advantage.

Consumer research provides the strategic compass for this transformation. It enables OBM firms to move beyond product features and embrace emotional, cultural, and ethical dimensions of value creation. Across industries—particularly in cosmetics, fashion, and lifestyle-oriented electronics—consumer insights inform decisions regarding color palettes, product functionality, packaging aesthetics, marketing tone, and digital engagement strategies.

A foundational study by Guthrie and Kim (2009) underscores the diversity of consumer involvement in cosmetics purchasing behavior. Using the Consumer Involvement Profile (CIP) model, they segmented female consumers into five types and revealed how brand personality attributes—especially "competence"—consistently predicted favorable brand attitudes. These findings emphasize the importance of psychological profiling and targeted brand positioning in OBM strategy. When OBM firms integrate such nuanced consumer segmentation into their marketing logic, they increase the precision and effectiveness of their branding efforts, particularly among younger demographics.

This psychological engagement aligns with rising trends in health consciousness and environmental awareness. Amberg and Fogarassy (2019) found that consumers are increasingly drawn to natural and eco-friendly cosmetic products. Through a cluster analysis of Hungarian consumers, they identified distinct groups based on consumption of organic food and preference for natural cosmetics. Their results showed that a large proportion of consumers now prioritize health and environmental factors over price or brand name—indicating a shift in purchasing drivers. This evolution compels OBM firms to integrate sustainability into both product development and brand narrative. For example, using biodegradable packaging, transparently sourced ingredients, and cruelty-free testing processes are no longer niche marketing points but fundamental expectations for a growing consumer base.

Furthermore, localized studies continue to reveal important socio-cultural dynamics. In India, Kajapriya and Surya (2015) examined cosmetic purchasing patterns among 120 women in Aruppukottai and found that media exposure, peer influence, and satisfaction levels strongly shaped preferences. Importantly, the study highlighted that exposure to diverse product information through media significantly influences consumer attitudes and buying decisions. For OBM firms expanding into emerging markets, this points to the critical role of culturally resonant storytelling, influencer marketing, and localized media strategies in cultivating brand loyalty.

Adding a future-oriented perspective, Chakraborty et al. (2024) identify five emerging trends reshaping the global cosmetics market: ingredient transparency, AI-driven personalization, gender-inclusive product lines, multifunctional formulations, and sustainability-based brand loyalty. These shifts reflect broader social transformations—such as the demand for inclusivity, the influence of digital platforms, and consumer expectations for ethical corporate behavior. Particularly notable is the rise of AI and big data analytics in enabling personalized marketing and predictive product recommendations. OBM firms that adopt these technologies are better positioned to anticipate demand trends, reduce time-to-market, and foster closer emotional connections with their customers.

A compelling real-world case of consumer insight integration can be seen in the strategy of COSMAX, the South Korean OBM manufacturer. In late 2023, it partnered with indie brand TIRTIR to develop a cushion foundation tailored for multi-ethnic skin tones—launching 30 shades within two months and expanding to 40 shades shortly after. This product became the top-selling cosmetic item on Amazon's US beauty category, exemplifying how OBM firms can convert consumer insights into rapid, inclusive, and commercially successful innovation. COSMAX's approach combined ethnographic data, AI-enabled skin tone analysis, and trend monitoring to tailor its offering for diverse consumer segments—a hallmark of mature OBM practices.

More broadly, the ability to generate, interpret, and act upon consumer data fosters organizational learning. Feedback loops—where consumer insights are continuously fed into R&D, design, and marketing functions—enable agile product iteration and responsive innovation (Ustymenko, 2023). This requires firms to build interdisciplinary teams that combine marketing intelligence, data analytics, and design capabilities. Consumer insights thus become not only a marketing tool but a core input for strategic decision-making across the firm.

The implications for OBM development are far-reaching. First, consumer research enables firms to identify underserved niches and develop tailored offerings that traditional mass producers overlook. Second, it enhances the credibility and authenticity of the brand by aligning with user values and expectations. Third, it provides the basis for innovation by revealing latent needs and emergent preferences before they become mainstream.

In sum, OBM firms that embed consumer insight into their value creation processes—from R&D and design to brand storytelling and digital engagement—are better equipped to build emotional, ethical, and functional resonance with global customers. As digital platforms democratize access to consumer voices and as sustainability imperatives reshape purchasing behavior, the strategic ability to listen, analyze, and act upon consumer data will define the next generation of globally competitive OBM firms.

5 The Digital Turn: Technology and Smart Manufacturing

The fourth industrial revolution is transforming the manufacturing landscape, and OBM firms are increasingly at the forefront of this digital transformation. Smart manufacturing technologies—including AI, big data analytics, Internet of Things (IoT), digital twins, and cloud computing—are enabling firms to enhance operational efficiency, customize production, and respond rapidly to market trends. These technologies are not only supporting functional upgrading but also allowing OBM firms to differentiate themselves through enhanced agility and customer-centricity.

One of the most compelling examples of digital transformation in OBM comes from the South Korean cosmetics manufacturer COSMAX. Park et al. (2023) document how COSMAX has implemented a fusion design lab integrating AI, big data, and IoT to capture customer preferences and rapidly translate them into new product designs. This data-driven approach has shortened product development cycles and enabled high responsiveness to consumer trends across different markets. The integration of digital technologies throughout its value chain—from R&D to logistics—has become a cornerstone of COSMAX's competitive strategy.

Digital twins and meta-inventory systems also exemplify the evolving capabilities of OBM firms. As Xiao et al. (2024) note, these systems enable real-time simulation and predictive maintenance, allowing manufacturers to preempt disruptions and enhance product quality. In contrast to traditional OEM models focused on cost and efficiency, OBM firms using digital twins can build customer trust through consistent quality and transparent operations. Furthermore, digitalization facilitates sustainability initiatives by enabling traceability and optimizing resource use.

Cloud-based platforms are another transformative element in the OBM landscape. Zhang et al. (2010) illustrate how home textile firms in China have leveraged cloud computing to transition toward service-oriented production. These platforms allow for real-time collaboration with clients and suppliers, fostering innovation ecosystems where design ideas can be co-developed and refined virtually. Such digital integration enhances the capacity for design-led innovation, particularly in fast-moving consumer sectors like apparel and home goods.

In East Asia, broader ICT infrastructure has supported the rise of virtual innovation systems. Yam et al. (2003) highlight how digital connectivity has facilitated knowledge sharing across firms, research institutes, and universities, creating fertile ground for OBM development. For example, Taiwanese and Japanese SMEs have utilized digital platforms to access global design trends, manage international collaborations, and crowdsource ideas from users.

Crucially, digitalization does not only improve internal efficiencies—it also reshapes market engagement. AI-driven recommendation systems, social media analytics, and direct-to-consumer e-commerce platforms empower OBM firms to build stronger relationships with end users. Firms can tailor marketing messages, personalize products, and gather feedback in real time, all of which strengthen brand equity and customer loyalty.

However, the transition to digital OBM models is not without challenges. Digital transformation requires significant investment in infrastructure, skills, and organizational change. Many SMEs face barriers related to digital literacy, cybersecurity, and integration with legacy systems. Moreover, as OBM firms digitalize, they must navigate issues of data governance, platform dependency, and algorithmic bias.

Despite these challenges, the digital turn represents a decisive shift in the OBM paradigm. Firms that embrace digital manufacturing and data-driven innovation are better positioned to compete globally—not only on price or quality but on speed, customization, and user experience. The integration of digital technologies with brand and design strategies offers a holistic path toward sustained OBM competitiveness in the twenty-first century.

6 Branding and Market Differentiation in Global Value Chains

As OBM firms mature, branding and market differentiation become crucial for establishing identity, building loyalty, and commanding higher value in global value chains (GVCs). In the early stages of industrial development, firms typically focus on contract manufacturing to gain production experience and scale. However, as they accumulate capabilities, OBM becomes the vehicle through which firms assert their distinctiveness in global markets. Branding is not merely a marketing exercise—it is a strategic tool for capturing and creating value.

One key dimension is the country-of-origin (COO) and its influence on brand equity. Chen and Su (2011) demonstrate how the perceived quality of products is affected by both the country of design and the country of manufacture. While firms from developed economies often benefit from positive COO associations, latecomer firms must invest more heavily in branding to overcome stereotypes associated with low-cost production. Liu et al. (2008) emphasize that strategic management of brand image can help firms mitigate negative COO effects by promoting unique value propositions tied to innovation, quality, or cultural authenticity.

In cross-border business-to-business (B2B) contexts, OBM branding plays a distinct role. Chen (2011), Tian et al. (2022), and Wang and Tzeng (2012) find that brand equity can facilitate trust in international transactions, reduce information asymmetries, and strengthen long-term buyer–seller relationships. OBM firms that develop credible and differentiated brands can better control their market positioning and pricing, reducing reliance on volatile OEM contracts. For example, Taiwanese IT firms have used branding to transition from anonymous suppliers to recognized innovators in global markets.

The dual role of OBM in supply chains also presents strategic tensions. On the one hand, OBM empowers firms to capture greater value through direct consumer relationships. On the other hand, it may conflict with OEM obligations or existing client relationships. Zhang (2011) and Li et al. (2020) explore how firms manage this duality by segmenting brands across markets, creating subsidiary labels, or adopting a mixed production strategy that balances OEM and OBM. This balancing act requires strategic clarity and often a shift in organizational priorities from short-term volume to long-term brand equity.

Institutional challenges further complicate branding efforts. Hollows and Clegg (2006) and Han et al. (2009) note that regulatory environments, intellectual property protections, and cultural barriers can hinder OBM growth. Moreover, firms operating in transitional economies may lack access to branding expertise or suffer from weak domestic support for creative industries. This is where strategic leadership becomes vital: leaders must not only champion the OBM vision but also orchestrate resources across marketing, design, and production functions to build a coherent brand strategy.

The Hong Kong experience offers instructive insights. Tam et al. (2005) analyze how Hong Kong's fashion and textile industries leveraged SWOT-based strategic planning to position themselves as Asia's fashion hub. A key recommendation was to develop OBM capabilities as a response to regional competition and market saturation. This case shows how a city-region can align its industry policies, education systems, and trade infrastructure to support OBM growth.

Furthermore, consumer insights, cultural fluency, and design integration play critical roles in OBM brand building. Firms that align branding with consumer values—such as sustainability, authenticity, and personalization—tend to perform better. The Vietnamese textile sector, for instance, is moving from CMT (cut-make-trim) to FOB (free-on-board), ODM, and OBM models. As Dinh et al. (2024) reveal, supplier selection based on CSR and ethical sourcing criteria is becoming essential for OBM firms seeking to meet global branding standards.

Finally, the digital economy has radically transformed the branding landscape. Social media, influencer marketing, and e-commerce platforms allow OBM firms to engage directly with global consumers, bypassing traditional intermediaries. Digital channels lower entry barriers for brand building and create opportunities for real-time feedback and co-creation. Firms like COSMAX use digital tools not only for manufacturing optimization but also for understanding and shaping consumer trends.

In conclusion, branding is both the outcome and driver of OBM success. It requires long-term investment, cross-functional integration, and strategic alignment with market positioning. By mastering branding and market differentiation, OBM firms can escape the commodity trap of OEM and carve out resilient, high-value niches in global value chains.

7 Governance, Interfirm Relations, and Strategic Leadership

The governance of interfirm relationships and the role of strategic leadership are central to the successful evolution of OBM firms. As firms move from OEM to OBM, they must not only develop internal capabilities but also manage complex external networks that involve suppliers, customers, investors, and policy stakeholders. Effective governance in this context entails fostering trust-based interfirm relationships, navigating institutional environments, and leveraging leadership vision to integrate and align diverse organizational elements toward long-term strategic goals.

A key factor in OBM development is the ability to build and sustain collaborative partnerships across the value chain. Eng (2009) and Eng and & Spickett-Jones (2009) emphasize that interfirm trust and knowledge exchange are foundational for firms transitioning in regions like the Pearl River Delta. These trust-based relationships enable the sharing of tacit knowledge, facilitate joint problem-solving, and reduce transaction costs, all of which are vital for the iterative processes of design, innovation, and branding inherent in OBM. Similarly, Luo and Chang (2011) highlight that resource-seeking behavior—such as seeking marketing knowledge or retail access from global partners—can accelerate OBM capability formation when underpinned by strong relational capital.

Strategic leadership is another critical determinant of successful OBM transformation. Yan et al. (2011) and Yan (2012) argue that visionary leaders are essential for overcoming internal resistance, reallocating resources, and driving cultural change necessary for OBM success. These leaders not only articulate a compelling vision of brand development and market positioning but also implement the necessary organizational changes to support it—such as investing in branding teams, aligning incentives, and shifting performance metrics from volume-based outputs to value-based outcomes. In many Asian contexts, family-owned firms or SME founders often play this transformative leadership role, providing the entrepreneurial momentum to leap from manufacturing anonymity to brand visibility.

In addition to firm-level governance, institutional and political contexts significantly influence OBM trajectories. One major consideration is the availability and distribution of state subsidies, as well as the mechanisms for technology transfer and spillover effects. Studies by Li et al. (2020) and Xie et al. (2023) explore how technology spillovers from multinational enterprises (MNEs) and strategic sourcing relationships can act as catalysts for OBM capability development. However, the benefits of such spillovers often depend on the absorptive capacity of the recipient firm and the strategic intent of leadership to channel those gains into proprietary brand development rather than reinforcing OEM dependency.

Government policies and institutional patronage further shape the OBM landscape. In China, Tang (2011) and Hollows and Clegg (2006) show how OBM development has been facilitated by targeted subsidies, tax incentives, and branding support programs. While such interventions can provide a necessary boost, they may also generate dependency or rent-seeking behavior if not coupled with performance accountability. The design of policy frameworks must therefore balance support with incentives for capability upgrading, innovation, and sustainable growth.

The interplay of politics and global competition also influences OBM governance. For example, trade regulations, intellectual property rights, and geopolitical dynamics can affect market access and brand viability. OBM firms must develop capabilities in regulatory navigation, compliance, and risk management, especially when entering high-value markets with stringent legal and ethical standards. This requires not only legal and logistical preparedness but also strategic communication to stakeholders about the firm's values, commitments, and market propositions.

Leadership, both at the firm and policy level, plays a unifying role in navigating these complexities. Adaptive leaders understand that OBM is not just about creating products under a proprietary label but about orchestrating a whole ecosystem of innovation, trust, and reputation. They invest in talent development, foster organizational learning, and build resilience through strategic alliances. Moreover, they shape internal cultures that value creativity, agility, and long-term value creation over short-term cost minimization.

In sum, governance and strategic leadership form the backbone of successful OBM transitions. While capabilities, branding, and technology are vital, their effectiveness is contingent upon the governance structures that coordinate them and the leaders who champion them. Firms that can master these relational and institutional dynamics are more likely to thrive as global OBM players in an increasingly volatile and competitive environment.

8 Global Trends and Sectoral Futures

The evolution of OBM is intricately linked to sector-specific dynamics and broader global shifts. As industries adapt to changing consumer preferences, digital transformation, environmental imperatives, and geopolitical uncertainties, OBM firms must navigate both challenges and emerging opportunities. Sectoral variation shapes the path and pace of OBM upgrading, while broader macroeconomic and technological trends redefine the nature of competition and innovation across industries.

8.1 Sector-Specific Pathways

Different industrial sectors demonstrate unique OBM trajectories due to the nature of production processes, customer engagement, innovation cycles, and regulatory environments. In the textile and garment industry, for instance, Vietnam's OBM ambitions have been fueled by its gradual transition from Cut-Make-Trim (CMT) to Free-On-Board (FOB), then to ODM and OBM, as noted by Dinh et al. (2024). The ability to source raw materials independently and emphasize CSR (corporate social responsibility) has become central to supplier selection and brand positioning. This trajectory reflects how upstream sourcing capabilities and ethical considerations are now vital to OBM development in labor-intensive sectors.

In the electronics and IT sectors, Taiwanese firms such as Acer and Asus exemplify latecomer innovation and OBM upgrading through innovation ambidexterity—balancing exploration and exploitation of technology and market opportunities (Kuo et al., 2018). The integration of R&D and marketing functions, coupled with forward-looking business models, has enabled firms to establish strong global brands. Similarly, in the cosmetics sector, Korean firms like COSMAX leverage digital platforms, design labs, and data-driven personalization to lead as OBM exporters, illustrating how cross-functional integration, digital adoption, and rapid design-to-market capabilities define success in fast-paced consumer industries.

Meanwhile, the furniture industry showcases how cultural product design and semantic design techniques are leveraged for niche OBM differentiation (Yodwangjai & Pimapunsri, 2011). Here, emotional resonance, localized cultural references, and customer co-creation are emphasized over pure functional utility, suggesting that design strategy and consumer perception are central to OBM success in home-oriented or aesthetic industries.

8.2 Future of OBM in Emerging Markets

Looking forward, OBM in emerging markets will be shaped by distributed innovation, leapfrogging strategies, and the development of new business models. Teece (2014) and Li et al. (2022) suggest that technological decentralization and dynamic capability allow firms in emerging markets to innovate without full vertical integration. As such, emerging market OBMs can capitalize on ecosystem partnerships, cloud-based platforms, and open innovation networks to reduce costs and increase agility.

In Vietnam and Bangladesh, the path from OEM to OBM increasingly emphasizes the role of supplier upgrading and the creation of indigenous brands. Studies by Le et al. (2019) and Fouji and Hoque (2021) highlight how investment in design, marketing, and leadership capacity enables garment suppliers to shift from low-margin subcontracting to high-value branding. Institutional support, improved public administration, and infrastructure development—often catalyzed by initiatives like China's Belt and Road—are critical to this transition.

Sustainability and social upgrading are becoming integral to OBM competitiveness. Barrientos et al. (2010) argue that economic and social upgrading must be linked for firms to thrive under new consumer expectations and regulatory frameworks. Circular design, ethical sourcing, low-carbon manufacturing, and community engagement are no longer optional but essential for long-term viability. In this context, the integration of ESG (Environmental, Social, and Governance) metrics into brand identity and operations will define competitive differentiation.

Additionally, OBM evolution will increasingly depend on talent development and the digital readiness of firms. Knowledge-intensive activities—such as product design, customer analytics, and digital marketing—require a skilled workforce and flexible organizational cultures. Countries that invest in education, vocational training, and digital infrastructure are more likely to foster globally competitive OBM firms. This aligns with studies showing that national innovation systems, institutional quality, and regional industrial clusters provide fertile ground for OBM transitions (Lin et al., 2015; Sheng, 2011; Zhu et al., 2017).

Finally, geopolitical shifts and regional integration (e.g., RCEP, CPTPP, AfCFTA) will shape the strategic environment for OBM. Firms must navigate protectionism, trade fragmentation, and shifting consumer geographies. Those that can build regional brand equity, customize offerings for multiple markets, and manage multi-local operations will outperform those that rely on single-market dependency.

In sum, OBM futures will be sectorally differentiated and globally interconnected. Firms must harness sector-specific strengths while adapting to systemic shifts in technology, sustainability, and geopolitics. Strategic agility, institutional support, design innovation, and social responsibility will be the cornerstones of OBM leadership in the decades to come.

9 Conclusion: Toward a Vision of the Future OBM

This chapter has explored the multifaceted journey of Original Brand Manufacturing as a strategic and evolutionary pathway for firms in emerging and established markets alike. As the global industrial landscape becomes increasingly dynamic and competitive, OBM presents a model of value creation that transcends the confines of low-margin production and emphasizes innovation, design, branding, and customer intimacy. Through the preceding sections, we have examined how OBM trajectories are shaped by strategic transformation, capability development, institutional ecosystems, digital technologies, branding strategies, and sector-specific dynamics. We have also seen how governance, global value chains, and sustainability concerns play a growing role in defining the contours of OBM competitiveness.

The future of OBM hinges on a holistic integration of internal capabilities and external partnerships, anchored by a forward-looking and adaptive mindset. Unlike the linear OEM–ODM–OBM model of the past, the emerging paradigm emphasizes iterative, non-linear development where hybrid strategies, leapfrogging, and ecosystem-based innovation are increasingly the norm. The firms that succeed will be those that move beyond narrow functional upgrading and pursue a multi-dimensional approach to value creation, embedding design, customer insight, and sustainability into their core operating models.

Strategic leadership and entrepreneurial agility are essential for OBM firms to thrive in the future. These firms must be led by visionary and adaptive leaders who can navigate technological, market, and geopolitical uncertainties. Entrepreneurial agility enables firms to sense emerging opportunities, pivot quickly, and engage in calculated risk-taking. Strategic leadership involves not only internal governance but also the cultivation of external relationships with suppliers, distributors, and institutional actors. It demands a culture of innovation, resilience, and continuous learning across the organization.

Institutional and innovation system support plays a pivotal role in enabling OBM transitions. The presence of national innovation systems, industrial policies, and public–private partnerships provides the foundational support that allows firms to upgrade and differentiate. Institutional support in areas such as research and development funding, vocational education, intellectual property protection, and export promotion creates an enabling environment for growth. Regional innovation clusters, sectoral associations, and global trade frameworks further provide the necessary scaffolding for OBM firms to scale and internationalize their operations.

Customer-centric innovation and digital transformation will define the next frontier for OBM. Firms must understand and respond to customer needs in real time, integrating customer insights into the design, development, and marketing processes. The adoption of digital tools such as big data analytics, artificial intelligence, cloud platforms, and smart manufacturing enables mass customization, predictive design, and agile supply chains. Customer-centric innovation is not only about fulfilling existing needs but also about anticipating future desires, creating emotional connections through brand storytelling, and engaging customers as co-creators of value.

Sustainability and social responsibility must be viewed as essential and integrated dimensions of OBM strategy. As consumer expectations shift and regulatory landscapes evolve, OBM firms must embed environmental, social, and governance principles into their business models. This includes ethical sourcing practices, eco-friendly design, circular production systems, and fair and inclusive labor standards. Aligning profitability with purpose allows OBM firms to differentiate themselves, build trust, and contribute to a more sustainable and equitable global economy.

The evolution of OBM is not merely a process of moving up the value chain or achieving brand recognition. It represents a fundamental rethinking of how value is created in a globalized, digitized, and sustainability-focused world. Firms that succeed in this transformation will be those that combine strategic vision, institutional engagement, and customer-driven innovation. They will not only capture market share but also redefine industry norms and drive inclusive and sustainable development across regions.

Looking forward, OBM offers a powerful and forward-thinking vision for manufacturing in the twenty-first century. It envisions a convergence of design excellence, technological advancement, and purposeful leadership. This vision demands deliberate and sustained action, cross-sector collaboration, and an unwavering commitment to innovation and adaptation.

References

Amberg, N., & Fogarassy, C. (2019). Green consumer behavior in the cosmetics market. *Resources, 8*(3), 137.

Barrientos, S., Gereffi, G., & Rossi, A. (2010). Economic and social upgrading in global production networks: Developing a framework for analysis. *International Labor Review, 150*(3–4), 319–340.

Berger, M., & Revilla Diez, J. (2006). Do firms require an efficient innovation system to develop innovative technological capabilities? Empirical evidence from Singapore, Malaysia and Thailand. *International Journal of Technology Management, 36*(1–3), 267–285.

Chakraborty, D., Polisetty, A., Rana, N. P., & Khorana, S. (2024). Unlocking the potential of AI: Enhancing consumer engagement in the beauty and cosmetic product purchases. *Journal of Retailing and Consumer Services, 79*, Article 103842.

Chen, D., Wei, W., Hu, D., & Muralidharan, E. (2016). Survival strategy of OEM companies: A case study of the Chinese toy industry. *International Journal of operations & Production Management, 36*(9), 1065–1088.

Chen, Y. H. H. (2011). Trade, industrial structure, and brand. *Industrial and Corporate Change, 20*(1), 133–174.

Chen, Y. M., & Su, Y. F. (2011). Do country-of-manufacture and country-of-design matter to industrial brand equity? *Journal of Business & Industrial Marketing, 27*(1), 57–68.

Dinh, T. H., Nguyen, T. T. T., Do, T. T. T., Nguyen, T. V. T., & Nguyen, H. L. (2024). Selection supplier for textile and garment enterprises in Vietnam using association rules. *The Asian Journal of Shipping and Logistics, 40*(4), 206–212.

Eng, T. Y. (2009). Manufacture upgrade and interfirm relationship development: The case of electronics firms in the Pearl River Delta. *Asia Pacific Business Review, 15*(4), 507–525.

Eng, T. Y., & Spickett-Jones, J. G. (2009). An investigation of marketing capabilities and upgrading performance of manufacturers in mainland China and Hong Kong. *Journal of World Business, 44*(4), 463–475.

Fouji, M. H., & Hoque, I. (2021). Supplier internationalization through upgrading in global supply chain: Evidence from the garments industry of Bangladesh. *International Journal of Global Business and Competitiveness, 16*(2), 116–129.

Fritz, K., Schoenmueller, V., & Bruhn, M. (2017). Authenticity in branding–exploring antecedents and consequences of brand authenticity. *European Journal of Marketing, 51*(2), 324–348.

Gereffi, G. (1999). International trade and industrial upgrading in the apparel commodity chain. *Journal of International Economics, 48*(1), 37–70.

Guthrie, M. F., & Kim, H. S. (2009). The relationship between consumer involvement and brand perceptions of female cosmetic consumers. *Journal of Brand Management, 17*(2), 114–133.

Han, X., Wen, Y., & Kant, S. (2009). The global competitiveness of the Chinese wooden furniture industry. *Forest Policy and Economics, 11*(8), 561–569.

Hobday, M. (1998). Latecomer catch-up strategies in electronics: Samsung of Korea and ACER of Taiwan. *Asia Pacific Business Review, 4*(2–3), 48–83.

Hobday, M. (2003). Innovation in Asian industrialization: A Gerschenkronian perspective. *Oxford Development Studies, 31*(3), 293–314.

Hollows, J., & Clegg, S. R. (2006). Brand development: Institutional constraints on Chinese businesses. *Management Research News, 29*(7), 386–401.

Hsu, C. H., Fan, C. H., Lin, J. Y., & Lin, R. (2014). An investigation on consumer cognition of cultural design products. *Bulletin of Japanese Society for the Science of Design, 60*(5), 5_39–5_48.

Hsu, C. W., Chen, H., & Jen, L. (2008). Resource linkages and capability development. *Industrial Marketing Management, 37*(6), 677–685.

Huang, Y. L., & Intarakumnerd, P. (2019). Alternative technological learning paths of Taiwanese firms. *Asian Journal of Technology Innovation, 27*(3), 301–314.

Kajapriya, R., & Surya, R. (2015). An analysis on insight of women consumer's towards cosmetic products. *International Journal of Management Research and Reviews, 5*(4), 246.

Kuo, T. K., Lim, S. S., & Sonko, L. K. (2018). Catch-up strategy of latecomer firms in Asia: A case study of innovation ambidexterity in PC industry. *Technology Analysis & Strategic Management, 30*(12), 1483–1497.

Le, Q. A., Tran, V. A., & Duc, B. L. N. (2019). The belt and road initiative and its perceived impacts on the textile and garment industry of Vietnam. *Journal of Open Innovation: Technology, Market, and Complexity, 5*(3), 59. https://doi.org/10.3390/joitmc5030059

Lee, K., Song, J., & Kwak, J. (2015). An exploratory study on the transition from OEM to OBM: Case studies of SMEs in Korea. *Industry and Innovation, 22*(5), 423–442.

Li, G., Wu, H., & Dai, J. (2020). Production sourcing strategy for an apparel original brand manufacturer in the presence of technology spillover. *IEEE Transactions on Engineering Management, 70*(4), 1283–1294.

Li, L., Tong, Y., Wei, L., & Yang, S. (2022). Digital technology-enabled dynamic capabilities and their impacts on firm performance: Evidence from the COVID-19 pandemic. *Information & Management, 59*(8), Article 103689.

Lin, R., Kreifeldt, J., Hung, P. H., & Chen, J. L. (2015). From dechnology to humart–a case study of Taiwan design development. In *Cross-Cultural Design Applications in Mobile Interaction, Education, Health, Transport and Cultural Heritage: 7th International Conference, CCD 2015*, Held as Part of HCI International 2015, Los Angeles, CA, USA, August 2–7, 2015, Proceedings, Part II 7 (pp. 263–273). Springer International Publishing.

Lin, R., Sun, M. X., Chang, Y. P., Chan, Y. C., Hsieh, Y. C., & Huang, Y. C. (2007). Designing "culture" into modern product: A case study of cultural product design. In Usability and Internationalization. In *HCI and Culture: Second International Conference on Usability and Internationalization, UI-HCII 2007*, Held as Part of HCI International 2007, Beijing, China, July 22–27, 2007, Proceedings, Part I 2 (pp. 146–153). Springer Berlin Heidelberg.

Liu, F. H., Liu, H. Y., & Lin, T. L. (2008). The competence and constraints of brand building for contract manufacturers. *Journal of Brand Management, 15*(6), 412–432.

Luo, C. M., & Chang, H. F. (2011). SME competitive strategy: Learning from Taiwan's ODM industry. *Business Strategy Series, 12*(3), 107–114.

Manzakoğlu, B. T., & Er, Ö. (2018). Design management capability framework in global value chains: Integrating the functional upgrading theory from OEM to ODM and OBM. *The Design Journal, 21*(1), 139–161.

Ng, S. C. H., Zhao, X., Fan, X., & Rungtusanatham, J. M. (2014). TQM and brand-building by Chinese original brand manufacturers: Impact on business performance. *International Journal of Production Research, 52*, 825–846.

Park, H., Hong, S., & Shin, H. (2023). Rising and thriving in the post COVID-19 era: A case study of COSMAX, a leader of the Korean cosmetic industry. *Asia Pacific Business Review, 29*(4), 1105–1124.

Ranathunga Arachchilage, S. C. G., Payne, A., & Buys, L. (2016). Industrial upgrading in the apparel value chain and the role of designer in the transition: Comparative analysis of Sri Lanka and Hong Kong. *Asia Pacific Journal of Multidisciplinary Research, 4*(4), 103–112.

Sheng, P. L. (2011). Diversity of design education in china. *Iridescent, 1*(1), 130–136.

Tam, F. Y., Chan, T. S., Chu, P. W., Lai, T. C., & Wang, L. L. (2005). Opportunities and challenges: Hong Kong as Asia's fashion hub. *Journal of Fashion Marketing and Management: An International Journal, 9*(2), 221–231.

Tang, H. (2011). The route choice of the brand creation of Chinese textile original equipment manufacturers in the post-financial crisis era. In *2011 International Conference on Management and Service Science.*

Teece, D. J. (2014). The foundations of enterprise performance: Dynamic and ordinary capabilities in an (economic) theory of firms. *Academy of Management Perspectives, 28*(4), 328–352.

Tian, C., Xiao, T., & Shang, J. (2022). Channel differentiation strategy in a dual-channel supply chain considering free riding behavior. *European Journal of Operational Research, 301*(2), 473–485.

Tsai-Lin, T. F., Chi, H. R., & Chang, Y. C. (2021). The business model and innovation mix in the transition of contract manufacturers in the greater China region. *Asia Pacific Business Review, 27*(3), 444–469.

Ustymenko, R. (2023). Trends and innovations in cosmetic marketing. *Economics & Education, 8*(3), 12–17.

Wang, Y. L., & Tzeng, G. H. (2012). Brand marketing for creating brand value based on a MCDM model combining DEMATEL with ANP and VIKOR methods. *Expert Systems with Applications, 39*(5), 5600–5615.

Xiao, J., Ma, S., Wang, S., & Huang, G. Q. (2024). Meta-inventory management decisions: A theoretical model. *International Journal of Production Economics, 275*, Article 109339.

Xie, L., Liu, Y., Han, H., & Qiu, C. M. (2023). Outsourcing or reshoring? A manufacturer's sourcing strategy in the presence of government subsidy. *European Journal of Operational Research, 308*(1), 131–149.

Yam, R. C., Lo, W., Sun, H. Y., & Tang, P. Y. (2003). Enhancement of global competitiveness for Hong Kong/China manufacturing industries through i-agile virtual enterprising. *International Journal of Technology Management, 26*(1), 88–102.

Yan, H. D. (2012). Entrepreneurship, competitive strategies, and transforming firms from OEM to OBM in Taiwan. *Journal of Asia-Pacific Business, 13*(1), 16–36.

Yan, H. D., Chiang, C., & Chien, C. S. (2011). From original equipment manufacturing to branding: Entrepreneurship, strategic leadership, and Taiwan's firm transformation. *International Entrepreneurship and Management Journal, 10*, 81–102.

Yang, C. H., & Tsou, M. W. (2017). Does an own-brand produce higher profitability? Evidence from Taiwan's manufacturing firms. *Journal of Business & Industrial Marketing, 32*(7), 925–936.

Yang, T. Y., Yang, Y. T., Chen, J. R., & Lu, C. C. (2019). Correlation between owner brand and firm value–Case study on a private brand in Taiwan. *Asia Pacific Management Review, 24*(3), 232–237.

Yodwangjai, S., & Pimapunsri, K. (2011). Application of semantic differential technique and statistical approach to evaluate designer's and consumer's perception in furniture design. *Applied Science and Engineering Progress, 4*(1), 23–30.

Zhang, B. (2011). Optimal policy for a mixed production system with multiple OEM and OBM products. *International Journal of Production Economics, 130*(1), 27–32.

Zhang, K., Ma, B., Dong, P., Tang, B., & Cai, H. (2010). Research on producer service innovation in home-textile industrial cluster based on cloud computing platform. In *Proceedings of 2010 IEEE International Conference on Service Operations and Logistics, and Informatics* (pp. 155–160)(July). IEEE.

Zhu, S., Pickles, J., He, C., Zhu, S., Pickles, J., & He, C. (2017). Geographical dynamics and firm spatial strategy in China. In *Geographical Dynamics and Industrial Relocation: Spatial Strategies of Apparel Firms in Ningbo* (pp. 51–72). China.

The manufacturer's authorised representative in the EU is Springer Nature Customer Service Centre GmbH, Europaplatz 3, 69115 Heidelberg, Germany. If you have any concerns regarding our products, please contact ProductSafety@springernature.com

Printed and bound by CPI Group (UK) Ltd, Croydon, CR0 4YY

30/09/2026

02225300-0020